IN PURSUIT OF PERFECTION

Kennikat Press
National University Publications
Series in Literary Criticism

IN PURSUIT OF PERFECTION

Courtly Love in Medieval Literature

A Collaborative Study by

The Editors

Joan M. Ferrante & George D. Economou

and

Frederick Goldin
Esther C. Quinn

Renata Karlin
Saul N. Brody

National University Publications
KENNIKAT PRESS • 1975
Port Washington, N.Y. • London

For W. T. H. Jackson

Library of Congress Catalog Card No. 74-80596
ISBN: 0-8046-9092-8

Manufactured in the United States of America

Published by
Kennikat Press Corp.
Port Washington, N.Y./London

Library of Congress Cataloging in Publication Data

Ferrante, Joan M 1936–
In pursuit of perfection.

(National University Publications: Series in literary criticism)
Includes bibliographies and index.
1. Literature, Medieval--History and criticism.
2. Courtly love. I. Economou, George, joint author.
II. Title.
PN682.C6F47 809.1'4 74-80596
ISBN 0-8046-9092-8

Contents

LIST OF ABBREVIATIONS

Archiv	Archiv für das Studium der Neueren Sprachen und Literaturen
BBSIA	Bulletin Bibliographique de la Société Internationale Arthurienne
CCM	Cahiers de Civilisation Médiévales
CDU	Centre de Documentation Universitaire
CFMA	Classiques Français du Moyen Âge
ChauR	The Chaucer Review
CL	Comparative Literature
ELH	Journal of English Literary History
FR	The French Review
GL&L	German Life and Letters
GR	Germanic Review
JEGP	Journal of English and Germanic Philology
MGH	Monumenta Germaniae Historica
MLR	Modern Language Review
MS	Mediaeval Studies
PL	Patrologia Latina
PMLA	Publications of the Modern Language Association
PQ	Philological Quarterly
QFSK	Quellen und Forschungen zur Sprach und Kulturgeschichte der Germanischen Völker, N.F.
RomN	Romance Notes
RPh	Romance Philology
RR	Romanic Review
SATF	Société des Anciens Textes Français
SMed	Studi Medievali
SMV	Studi Mediolatini e Volgari
SP	Studies in Philology
SPCK	Society for the Propagation of Christian Knowledge
WW	Wirkendes Wort
ZDP	Zeitschrift für Deutsche Philologie
ZFSL	Zeitschrift für Französische Sprache und Literatur
ZRP	Zeitschrift für Romanische Philologie

Preface

Each chapter of this work, conceived and written by an individual, has passed through several readings and discussions by the contributors. The introductory chapter is a collaboration of ideas and language that reflects not only the unanimity of our effort but also the fundamental agreement on the subject that made this book possible.

There are many fine works about courtly love and various aspects of medieval literature and culture without which this book could never have been written. Although we indicate our specific indebtednesses to them in our footnotes, we wish to acknowledge them here generally, for what scholar's thinking has not been broadly influenced by the standard works in his field? Our purpose, however, has not been to discuss them at length in the text or the notes.

Neither do we pretend to have dealt with every literary text that reflects the conventions of courtly love, but we do believe our approach can be applied to any medieval poem that treats the theme of love. Indeed, we eagerly invite our readers to extend our views to works omitted here. We have tried to avoid overlapping in the division of our labors, but some works inevitably come up in various chapters in different contexts.

Finally, we wish to state that our book does not attempt to treat the literature of courtly love from every possible point of view. We want neither to cover ground that has already received authoritative treatment nor to engage in disputation for its own sake. We wish simply to proceed from our mutual conviction that the presence of courtly love in medieval literature warrants close study of the effects of that presence in the various genres and poets involved. It is noteworthy that several prominent medievalists have recently commented upon the desirability of just such an approach to the subject.[1]

1. See Theodore Silverstein, "Guenevere, or the Uses of Courtly Love," in *The Meaning of Courtly Love,* ed. F. X. Newman (Albany: State University of New York Press, 1968), pp. 87–88; Charles Muscatine's review of the same volume in *Speculum* 46 (1971): 747–50; and Francis L. Utley, "Must We Abandon the Concept of Courtly Love?" *Medievalia et Humanistica,* N.S. 3 (1972): 299–324.

Introduction

Courtly love has been the focus of much critical attention in recent years. Its very existence as a medieval concept has been seriously questioned, mainly in reaction against the attempts to present it as a formal system.[1] Certainly the flurry of scholarly activity which followed Gaston Paris's introduction of the term *amour courtois* into critical language in 1883 led to a distorted or exaggerated sense of the phenomenon, but the counter–reaction has also been extreme. It is one thing to point out that Andreas's *De arte honeste amandi* is a satire on, rather than a bible of, courtly love, but quite another to conclude that if Andreas is not to be taken seriously, neither is courtly love.[2] A distinction must be made between an established doctrine, a rigid system of rules of behavior, which did not exist, and a mode of thought, expressed in literary conventions, which can be traced through so much medieval literature from the twelfth century onwards. The concept is not a simple one, but rather a cluster of personal feelings and social values, all of which can be found in the early troubadour and *Minnesang* lyrics. In other genres, poets treat certain aspects of courtly love in connection with moral and religious problems. The poet's response to courtly love varies, depending on his point of view as well as on the genre in which he chooses to work, but whatever his attitude, whatever the genre—lyric, romance, allegory, fabliau—he does deal with it. For medieval writers, courtly love is real.

The term courtly love is modern, but the concept is not. Although *amor cortes* occurs rarely in medieval literature, it has its medieval equivalents which occur frequently: *fin' amors* in Provençal, *fin' amore* in Italian, *hohe minne* in German. We continue to use Paris's phrase because it evokes to the modern mind the general subject we are discussing. And the choice has some merit, for the essence of courtly love is the courtliness it nourishes.[3] It does not exist apart from an aristocratic milieu or a courtly audience. When the values of the audience shift from aristocratic to bourgeois, the literary tradition of courtly love declines.

Courtly love is the expression of the ideals and values of an aristocratic class, which has its own pattern of behavior and derives its sense of superiority by thinking and acting in ways others cannot.[4] The courtly code of conduct, of which love is an essential part, evolved in the late eleventh century to fill the needs of a relatively new and still fluid class, the knights. Young men from noble families but without lands of their own went into the service of more powerful men in order to make their fortunes or to engage in their favorite occupation, fighting: some simply wandered in search of combat and booty.[5] They took their identity from the community of fellow knights; to counterbalance the violence, crudity and instability of their lives they needed an ideal or secular code. In a period of increasing culture, of heightened self–awareness, of literate rulers and ladies who patronized the arts,[6] it is not surprising that this code found literary expression in all forms of vernacular literature.

As the class of knights became more stable by law and custom,[7] the divisions between the classes became more sharply defined; sumptuary laws regulated dress by class and marriage between classes was discouraged. As the wealthy bourgeois became more powerful and sought to rise to knighthood, the nobles felt themselves threatened and entry into the class was severely restricted. At the same time in the thirteenth century, the nobles' glory and to some extent their prerogative, fighting, decreased in importance.[8] The conventions of the class now became stylized and were retained less as an ideal to aspire to, than an artificial means of preserving differences between them and the wealthy bourgeois, who copied what they could of noble conventions in order to appear noble themselves.[9] Literature reflects this stage by satirizing and ridiculing the emptiness of the forms and the lack of nobility of those who adhered to them, or by denouncing the forms as hypocritical and immoral. In the twelfth century, men were able to maintain a balance between opposing ideas and authorities, but by the next century, thought, like class structure, had become more rigid.[10] When they fail in the attempts to resolve the conflicts, men are left to choose between alternatives. It is no accident that the courtly ideal which is founded on paradoxes worked best in the twelfth century and, although it never altogether disappeared, began to fall apart in the thirteenth.

Courtly love first appears as a literary convention in the lyric where the poet, playing the role of the lover, gives voice to aspirations of the courtly class. It is his love which defines the poet as a member of that class. Love makes him noble, for if he were not noble, he could not love. The language and forms of his devotion are drawn from feudal and religious contexts. The essence of his love is the worship of an ideal, incarnated in or transposed to a woman. The continual striving to be worthy of, to attain that ideal, is what ennobles the lover and provides an example for those who can understand and follow him. The worship is carried out through the songs that celebrate the love and praise the lady. These songs in her praise constitute the lover's service, which may or may not be rewarded. The lover does not insist on reward; he performs the service for its own sake, to exalt his love and to share it with his friends. Although he may not reveal the identity of his lady, he must declare his love because his own courtly identity depends on it. And the spiritual benefits to be derived from the love depend on the lover's willingness to serve without any assurance of reward. These are the essential assumptions of courtly love: the nobility of the lover, the sometimes insuperable distance between him and the lady, the exalting nature of his devotion, and the social context of the love.

These elements are present in the earliest courtly lyrics, but not as part of a rigid system. They can be varied at will by the poets. Later, when courtly love ceases to be the expression of a class and becomes the empty convention of a poetic school, rules are formulated for the writing of love poetry—thirteenth century Provençal *Leys* and the German *Meistersingschule*—but not for the practice of love. The rules proclaimed by the God of Love in Andreas's *De arte* and Guillaume's *Roman de la Rose* are meant to reveal the foolishness or hypocrisy of the traditional lover, not to offer others a model to follow. These "rules" are derived from courtly literature, but the poets who wrote the early lyrics followed no set pattern; they only shared the idea of ennobling love. Where that idea came from is not under consideration here—what does concern us is that it exists and that it gives form and meaning to a vast body of medieval literature.

To trace the chronological development in anything so elusive as the history of an idea is difficult—expressions of what are put forth as "earlier" stages will too often be found contemporary with "later" examples. Still, in the history of this particular idea, a certain pattern of responses does emerge. The earliest extant literary expressions of courtly love in the troubadour lyric and in the *Minnesang* affirm the beneficial effects of faithful devotion to an ideal. The poems succeed, literarily and psychologically, because they also acknowledge the physical needs that cry out for satisfaction and that must occasionally be met. The love they expound is possible only for a select few—most men are limited either by an overwhelming desire for physical satisfaction, or by the inability to accept a paradoxical existence. The same is, unfortunately, true of most poets. There are those who take the spiritual nature of the love too solemnly; others reject the posture of self-denial as unnatural and seek instead a mutual physical satisfaction. But there are some few poets, most notably Walther von der Vogelweide and Neidhart von Reuental, who, recognizing the need for spiritual striving, turn back from mutual love to an affirmation of courtly love.

It is only in the lyric that courtly love can exist in its purest form and even then not for long, because only in a lyric mode can the opposing tendencies of physical desire and spiritual yearning be alternated and counterbalanced. The strength of the early lyric treatment of love is that it allows for the human need to attribute a higher purpose to sensual impulses, to attempt to refine them through constant and self–consciously imposed or accepted suffering. The lyric focuses on the conflict between these impulses in the realm of romantic love, but this conflict reflects a larger one between harmony and discord in a moral and religious sphere. The physical need for sexual satisfaction can be a selfish and potentially destructive impulse or, if properly directed, it can be turned to the service of God within the natural order. These two impulses are represented in philosophical poetry by the concept of two Venuses, one who inspires passion and lust, the other, universal harmony through love. Man is caught in a continual struggle between the two. That man's two needs should be mutually exclusive is a basic paradox of postlapsarian existence, because it is only since the Fall that man's sexuality became potentially destructive. From the doctrinal point of view, the only solution to the paradox is grace. The emotional aspect of this struggle is presented in the lyric; the moral side is dealt with in philosophical and theological works, or in poetry with philosophical overtones.

The early courtly lyric explores the possibility that in his love for a woman, a man might search for an ideal which could refine his being. The lover proclaims in his lyric that there is a side of him which is not carnal; he knows well enough that he has the ordinary physical desires of men, but he asserts that he is more complex than ordinary men. Even among courtly persons he has the potential for a special courtliness—and he asks his courtly audience to recognize the validity of the ideal he seeks, to endorse the idea of perfection which he sees in a woman and pursues in himself. The audience is not asked to see him as the ideal incarnate—they know him too well for that—but to acknowledge that the courtliness he seeks could give their world a special perfection. The lyric poet does not say that the courtly ideal *will* make men perfect; he only speaks about what might be. Yet men are prompted to ask whether ideals have practical possibilities, whether the courtly ideal can retain its ideality in the real world. As men of this world, they need satisfaction of their desires, but in this world the rewards for service must inevitably compromise their courtliness.

In courtly literature, the problem is not resolved. The lyric poet can maintain a tension between the two impulses, spiritual and sexual; he can preserve the former by honestly, even humorously, acknowledging the latter. But the lyric poet need only describe his feelings and the reactions of others to them; he does not have to find a solution in his poetry. The narrative poet, on the other hand, has to bring his story to a conclusion; he cannot leave the opposing tendencies suspended in a tenuous balance but must opt for one or the other. If he emphasizes the physical nature of the love, then the love becomes destructive; if he avoids that aspect and stresses the formal conventions of love, the love appears as no more than abstract theorizing or empty ritual and loses all its beneficial powers. Although the early romance poets seek to preserve the ennobling force of courtly love, and put it to the service of society, they are hampered by the demands of their genre. What is only suggested in a lyric, must be given visible form in a narrative. The service the lyric lover performs by composing and singing his poetry, praising the lady and giving expression to his feelings, is transformed into physical service, chivalric activity, which must of necessity involve other people and therefore a more clearly defined code of social responsibilty. The lover must consider not only his lady, but friends to whom he owes loyalty and enemies who threaten his safety and interfere with his pursuits. All of these characters are alluded to in lyric poetry, but in a narrative they become real presences.

Because the romance poet must translate abstractions into realities, because he must face the consequences of real actions and real relationships, he cannot maintain the lyric balance of opposing tendencies. As a result, he is forced either to play down the power of love, reducing it to a set of unrealistic conventions, or to condemn it as an impulse harmful to society and incompatible with the love of God. Again and again, romance writers show that in the world of men and women, courtly love brings little glory to the knight, few benefits to society, and no grace to Christian souls.

The grounds for the rejection of courtly love were present from the very beginning, and consequently the literature of courtly love can be read as the struggle to preserve the ideal from destruction. The lyric poets, and Gottfried von Strassburg after them, try to save the courtly ideal by removing it from the world of the court and locating it in the hearts of perfect, noble lovers. The problem is rooted in the inadequacy of the world, which regularly proves itself to be complacent, sensual, and vulgar. A different solution is to reject the world by substituting perfect love for God for imperfect courtly love. But whether a poet reaffirms the validity of the courtly ideal in spite of the world's carnality, or whether he rejects that ideal precisely because of that carnality, he does take the dual nature of man into account. The poets who can find no alternative simply follow the old conventions with little understanding of what they meant and of what has been lost; those who can see how empty these ideals are, ridicule them and finally help destroy them.

This study will consider works of various genres from the twelfth to the fourteenth century which are concerned with courtly love in some significant way. The first chapter sets the contradictory tendencies inherent in the concept of courtly love within the larger context of the philosophical and mythographic tradition of the two Venuses. This classical tradition persisted through the Middle Ages, sometimes in the company of courtly love. Chapter II investigates courtly love in the poetry which shaped its literary form, the early Provençal and German lyrics. It shows how a poet could preserve the idealized aspect of his love without denying his physical nature: by seeing himself through the eyes of his less sympathetic fellows, ridiculing himself, as they might have done, he was able both to answer their objections and to reaffirm the value of his own position. In the German lyric, the courtly tradition hung on after the height of the *Minnesang*. The most interesting of the later poets preserved what they could of the tradition, even though the only setting in which it could flourish had disappeared. Chapter III looks at the work of two of these early thirteenth century poets, Walther von der Vogelweide and Neidhart von Reuental. The conventions had a different fate in the romance. Chapter IV traces courtly love from its earliest appearance in the French classical romances, where it was little more than an embellishment, to Arthurian romances, in which it was an essential element meant to inspire the knight to chivalric action for the good of society, but often interfering with his duty. By the late prose romances, courtly love is condemned as antisocial and antireligious. Chapter V investigates in detail two romances that move away from courtly love in opposite directions, one, Gottfried's *Tristan,* towards a mutual love, a physical and spiritual union of highly attuned spirits; the other, the *Queste del Saint Graal,* deals with the religious renunciation of the flesh and affirmation of charity and sacrifice. Both works use the same imagery, the highly sensual language of Bernardine mysticism, to express the love they propose. A rejection of courtly love in favor of Christian love is one direction writers could take; the other was to continue to work with the courtly conventions, but to make fun of them. Chapter VI takes up a group of poems which view the courtly ideal as laughable, given the carnal setting of this world. The ridicule of courtly love poetry may well have been generated by two interrelated phenomena: the failure of those poets who lack the saving perspective of the earlier period to see that perfect courtliness may be pursued but not overtaken; and the foolishness of advocating courtly conventions in a society without courtliness.

Although the six chapters cover what the writers feel to be the most important or most interesting works in the courtly love tradition, readers will inevitably think of others that might have been included. That they are not discussed here does not mean they do not have a place in the courtly tradition. Marie de France and Andreas Capellanus, for example, may seem odd omissions, both of them writing at the height of the tradition in the late twelfth century, and both concerned with courtly love in some way. Marie's lais, taken together, present the basic elements and problems of courtly love: the loyalty and devotion of true lovers, the suffering and long separations, the dangers of enemies—jealous husbands, or envious courtiers who cannot understand the love or properly value the lover, the misuse of courtly language by false lovers to disguise their lust. In her last lai, *Eliduc,* Marie turns away from courtly love, not by condemning it, but by transcending it, moving its adherents towards the only love which can resolve the inevitable conflicts of earthly loyalties, the love of God.[11] Andreas, on the other hand, does condemn courtly love, because it endangers the soul. Although his work was nowhere near as important an influence on medieval literature as it has been on modern criticism, it presents the problems of courtly love in an interesting light. He shows that courtly love is a very dangerous game to play, unless one is aware of the inherent paradoxes and of one's own nature. Very few men, indeed very few poets, can safely play it. If the naive lover fails to see its inherent contradictions and rationalizations, and attempts to put the conventions of the system into practice by confusing literature with life, he runs a severe moral risk. Better for him to eschew it altogether and to concentrate on the one love that cannot fail him and that will ensure the salvation of his soul, the love of God.

Although they finally reject courtly love, both Andreas and Marie wrote about it in the setting in which it had developed and flourished. The basic elements of the courtly tradition are the same for them as for the poets of the early lyric and romance. But as courtly literature moved out of the small court of Southern France, Bavaria and Champagne, it necessarily changed. It might retain many of the formal conventions but not its essence. This was possible only in a court in which the poet gave voice to the aspirations and values he shared with his audience, and the audience derived its ideal identity from the poet's words. It would be possible to trace the appearance and use of those conventions through later lyric, to Petrarca and beyond, as we have to some extent traced the persistence of "courtly" forms in narrative, as late as Chaucer and even Malory. But in narrative, the social setting of the love, however modified, persists so that the public and private aspects of the love can still be treated together, even if only to be burlesqued. However, in lyric, the immediate audience is smaller, less formally identifiable—a friend, a sympathetic lady—the poetry more personal or more abstract, but without social overtones. All of the works dealt with here are concerned primarily with the definition and valuation of courtliness. For this reason, we have not devoted any lengthy discussion to the lyrics of the trouvères and the stilnovists, for these poets had quite different concerns.[12]

The trouvères, whose songs were set in a court, were primarily interested in exploring and developing the possibilities of figurative language; courtly life was not the subject of their lyrics, but rather the context which determined their figures of speech and their diction, and in this respect its function was no different from the context of any utterance. But the troubadours and the *Minnesänger* conceived of their songs as a service that they performed for the court: a celebration of the values of courtly life and an idealizing portrait of the courtly class. The Northern French lyrics were not composed for any such utilitarian purpose. They sought to elaborate and to arrange figures of speech in such a way that their meaning and effectiveness would be independent of the conditions in which they were performed.

The stilnovists, though they inherited much from the troubadours, completely rejected the courtly setting and every theme associated with it. They sought to create a new lyrical rhetoric and a new setting for their songs: they substituted for the real courts of the troubadours and the Sicilians an even more exclusive fellowship of poets, and the language they developed was not intended for the celebration of the ethical effect of love. They sought, by their difficult vocabulary, to make their language the unifying force of their intimate and exclusive circle. Here again, their poetic ambitions were quite different from those of the troubadours and the *Minnesänger.*

The stilnovist cannot do what the Provençal poet does: he cannot save himself by occasionally changing his perspective, looking at his image, his lady, from a different point of view and seeing her as an imperfect being, for the lady in the Italian lyrics is not a figment of the poet's imagination, which remains perfect only so long as he believes in it. Instead, she is God's creation, perfect by virtue of His endowments; she has a reality of her own and, potentially, a real power over the poet which he cannot control. Dante's early lyrics were written in the tradition of a noble-sounding but basically self-centered love. At the beginning of the *Vita Nuova,* his desire for Beatrice's greeting is a selfish one, to alleviate his suffering and to affirm his own worth. When he finally recognizes that her greeting cannot be counted on because it depends on his worth, he turns his attention to praising her for what she is; that remains constant, because God, not the poet, invested her with her goodness. Once he has shifted his perspective to her, which he can do fully only when she is dead, Dante can integrate his love with the religious sphere, that is, he can achieve what the courtly poets could not. The tension between spiritual and physical desires is eliminated; the problems courtly love poses in this world are evaded by moving the object of love into another world. Thus, in the *Divine Comedy,* Dante carries this tradition to its limit. He has Beatrice, his poetic inspiration, lead him finally back to the God who had sent her. Along the way, he divests himself of attachments to the courtly tradition. In the Francesca episode (Inf. v), he shows up the hypocrisy of the "courtly" lover. Francesca condemns herself out of her own mouth; she utters the conventional high-sounding clichés (11. 100, 103), but follows them with words that reveal the selfish and sensual nature of her attachment to Paolo (11. 101, 104). She makes the Lancelot story the external agent of her love affair but distorts it to suit her own purposes, having the hero, rather than the heroine, take the first step in love. The contrast between the poetic ideal of the unattainable lady and the reality of the passionate woman, between the noble pretense and the indulgent action, reiterates the problem inherent in courtly literature from the beginning.[13]

That Dante has moved far beyond older conventions is acknowledged by the poet Bonagiunta in Purgatory; he recognizes Dante as the major exponent of the "sweet new style," the one who untied the knots that bound Guittone and Jacopo and himself (Purg. xxiv, 55–57). Dante has come so far that he can describe Matelda, and his desire to join her in the Earthly Paradise, in the language of classical and courtly love (Purg. xxviii), without a trace of sin or sexual desire. And when he sees Beatrice and feels *i segni dell'antica fiamma* (Purg. xxx, 48), we recognize through the words of Dido, that Dante has overcome the obstacles of classical and courtly love and is ready to accompany his lady to heaven. There in the planet of Venus (Par. ix), Dante will meet Cunizza, a lady who not only inspired love poetry, but was known for her love affairs, and Folco, a poet who began in the courtly lyric tradition and ended a religious poet and bishop. Dante, in other words, has so purified his own love, that he can now see courtly lovers saved.

Dante gives the concept of woman as heavenly inspiration its most perfect expression. Although one can go no further, the idealized love of woman continues as a literary tradition long after the fourteenth century. Filtered through the poetry of Petrarca and the Petrarchisti, it is given serious expression in the poetry of Spenser and the sentimental romance of Tasso, burlesqued by Ariosto, Shakespeare, and Cervantes. Indeed, it has never really ended. This kind of love—in which the lover glorifies the beloved and aspires to the transcendent experience he believes it is in her power to grant him—is a familiar theme in romantic literature and in many works of our own century.

Notes

1. E. T. Donaldson, "The Myth of Courtly Love," *Speaking of Chaucer* (New York: W. W. Norton, 1970) reprinted from *Ventures* 5 (1965) and *The Meaning of Courtly Love,* ed. F. X. Newman (Albany: State University of New York Press, 1968), particularly the chapters by R. Benton and D. W. Robertson. In *A Preface to Chaucer* (Princeton: Princeton University Press, 1962), however, Robertson cautiously accepts the use of the term "courtly love," saying that such a love presupposes a Christian feudal society and is a peculiarly medieval phenomenon, p. 457. P. Dronke, *Medieval Latin and the Rise of European Love-Lyric,* 2 vols. (Oxford: Clarendon Press, 1968), accepts the concept of *amour courtois,* but denies that it is a medieval, French or aristocratic phenomenon, ch. I.
2. Robertson (*Preface,* ch. V), Donaldson, and W. T. H. Jackson ("The *De amore* of Andreas Capellanus and the Practice of Love at Court," *RR* 49 (1958): 243–251), are in agreement, albeit for different reasons, that the first two books of Andreas are not to be taken as a serious expression of a system of love. One might add that the third book would lose much of its force if Andreas's audience were not well acquainted with the conventions he mocks in the first two books. Douglas Kelly offers an attractive solution to the question of Andreas's attitude. He suggests that courtly love is an intermediate degree of love, neither so low as the purely physical nor so high as religious love; it may serve a limited purpose but ultimately is to be rejected in favor of the love of God ("Courtly Love in Perspective: the Hierarchy of Love in Andreas Capellanus," *Traditio* 24 (1968): 119–141).
3. A. J. Denomy, "Courtly Love and Courtliness," *Speculum* 28 (1953): 44–63, for the connections between *cortezia* and love in Provençal poetry. M. Lazar, *Amour courtois et "fin' amors" dans la littérature du XIIe siècle* (Paris: C. Klincksieck, 1964), distinguishes between *fin' amors,* love in the lyric, which is sensual as well as idealist, and *amor courtois* in the romance, which combines courtliness and conjugal love. Courtliness, however, is an essential element of the lyric tradition as well.
4. E. Gilson, *La théologie mystique de saint Bernard, Études de philosophie médiévale,* 20 (Paris: J. Vrin, 1934), published in English as *The Mystical Theology of St. Bernard* (New York: Sheed & Ward, 1940), Appendix IV, "St. Bernard and Courtly Love." Gilson suggests that courtly love is the attempt by a society, polished and refined by centuries of Christianity, to elaborate a code of love that is neither mystical nor Christian, but more refined than the "broad license of Ovid," in which sentiment takes precedence over sensuality. Cf. M. Bloch, *Feudal Society,* trans. L. A. Manyon, 2 vols. (London: Routledge and Kegan Paul, 1961, reprint University of Chicago Press, 1968, 7th ed.): ". . . the fact that these precepts of courtly love were subsequently so easily propagated shows how well they served the

new requirements of a class. They helped it to become aware of itself. To love in a different way from the generality of men must inevitably make one feel different from them" (p. 310). Much of the historical material in this and the succeeding paragraph is drawn from Bloch's study.

5. G. Duby, "Au XIIe siècle: les 'jeunes' dans la société aristocratique," *Annales* 19 (1964): 835–46.
6. On the high level of literacy among rulers and in their courts, see J. F. Benton, "The Court of Champagne as a Literary Center," *Speculum* 36 (1961): 551–591, and Rita Lejeune, "Rôle littéraire de la famille d'Aliénor d'Aquitaine," *CCM* 1 (1958): 319–337.
7. The right to be made a knight became a hereditary principle between 1130 and 1250, Bloch, *Feudal Society,* p. 320.
8. By the late thirteenth century, the ritual of initiation into knighthood was avoided in many parts of Europe because it involved great expense, Bloch, *Feudal Society,* p. 326. Cf. M. R. Powicke, "Distraint of Knighthood and Military Obligation under Henry III," *Speculum* 25 (1950): 457–470, and "The General Obligation to Cavalry Service under Edward I," *Speculum* 28 (1953): 814–833. Powicke discusses the shift in England from military obligation based on rank alone to military service based on wealth.
9. J. Huizinga, *The Waning of the Middle Ages* (New York: Doubleday Anchor Books, 1954, orig. publ. in Dutch, 1919), p. 128.
10. See Norman Cantor, *Medieval History, The Life and Death of a Civilization* (New York: Macmillan, 1963), p. 548.
11. For a study of love in Marie's *Lais,* see E. J. Mickel, "A Reconsideration of the *Lais* of Marie de France," *Speculum* 46 (1971): 39–65.
12. For a discussion of the lyrics of the trouvères and the stilnovists, see F. Goldin, *Lyrics of the Troubadours and Trouvères* (New York: Doubleday, 1973) and *German and Italian Lyrics of the Middle Ages* (New York: Doubleday, 1973).
13. For Francesca's use of the Lancelot story, see A. Hatcher and M. Musa, "The Kiss: *Inferno V* and the Old French Prose *Lancelot,*" *CL* 20 (1968): 97–109; for her use of the lyric clichés, see J. Ferrante, "The Relation of Speech to Sin in the *Inferno,*" *Dante Studies* 87 (1969): 42.

CHAPTER I

The Two Venuses and Courtly Love

George D. Economou

It has been a commonplace in modern criticism of medieval literature to distinguish between two profoundly different kinds of love: Christian charity, *caritas,* or divine love and earthly love, *amor.*[1] This point of view has undoubtedly led to a greater understanding of medieval poetry, for the distinction between earthly and divine love was one that medieval men made with great conviction and, at times, eloquence. The scriptures and their commentaries, the writings of theologians and philosophers, of preachers and poets, all attest to the reality of this distinction. And yet, despite its authenticity—indeed, perhaps because of its unarguable definitiveness—it is possible that we observe it with less care than did those who originally made it and that we sometimes write misleadingly about it. This is especially true in criticism which interprets representations of earthly love in medieval poetry as sinful. Medieval man believed that man's sexuality—like all his qualities—was seriously affected by the Fall. The originally innocent and divinely ordained instinct for procreation became degraded and shameful through the perversion of the will; it became, from this point of view, lust. But it was also possible to love virtuously and positively. The conflict in man's will concerning his sexual conduct was not simply whether to love or not to love—a choice between earthly and divine loves—it was also a choice between two kinds of earthly love.

Pope Innocent III explains the effects of lust in his *De miseria humane conditionis.*

O extrema libidinis turpitudo, que non solum mentem effeminat, sed corpus enervat, non solum maculat animam, sed fedat personam. . . . Semper illam precedunt ardor et petulantia, semper comitantur fetor et immunditia, semper secuntur dolor et penitentia. "Favus enim distillans labia meretricis et nitidius oleo guttur eius; novissima autem illius amare sicut absinthium et lingua eius acuta quasi gladius biceps."
[Prov. 5: 3–4]

O extreme shame of lust, which not only makes the mind effeminate but weakens the body; not only stains the soul but fouls the person. . . . Always, hot desire and wantonness precede lust, stench and filth accompany it, sorrow and repentance follow it. "The lips of the harlot are like a dripping honeycomb and her throat smoother than oil; but her end is as bitter as wormwood and her tongue is as sharp as a two-edged sword."[2]

This explanation is quite traditional, although we ought to remark that the quotation from Proverbs suggests that medieval writers were not confined to Ovid for figures that conveyed the contradictions of erotic love. Pope Innocent did not write about the positive side of human existence, *de dignitate humane nature,* as he promised to do in his prologue to the *De miseria.* Fortunately, we need not rely on any such single document for proof that the medieval conception of man was not limited to an emphasis on his degeneracy and misery. Sexual love had its justification and its place. Basically following Saint Augustine's *De bono conjugali,* a twelfth-century mystical theologian like Hugh of St. Victor could write of sex in marriage as generally beneficial because it provides mankind with a legitimate avenue of expression for a powerful and ultimately natural urge: "as blessed Augustine says, the good of marriage in some manner limits and modifies the evil of the disobeying members, so that carnal concupiscence becomes at least conjugal chastity."[3] One of the most important points that Hugh is making in this part of his work is that marriage and procreation existed before the Fall and that this, the first of all the sacraments, supports man in his weakened moral condition after the Fall.

Although all the sacraments took their beginning after sin and on account of sin, we read that the sacrament of marriage alone was established even before sin, yet not as a remedy but as an office. . . . The author of marriage is God. For He himself decreed that there be marriage, when He made woman as an assistance to man in the propagation of the race. . . . The institution of marriage is twofold: one before sin for office, the other after sin for remedy; the first, that nature might be multiplied; the second, that nature might be supported and vice checked.[4]

The dominant tradition in the Middle Ages was that even during their prelapsarian perfection Adam and Eve were meant to reproduce sexually. Saint Augustine refers explicitly in his *De civitate Dei* to the act which was to have been performed in response to God's commandment, "Increase and multiply, and fill the earth," Gen. 1:28.

Let us be far from suspecting that with things so easily acquired and with man so happy, offspring could not have been begotten without the disturbance of lust. On the contrary, those parts were moved by that act of will which moves the other members, and without the ensnaring stimulus of hot desire, in tranquility of soul and no loss of corporeal integrity did the husband pour out his seed into the womb of his wife.[5]

Like all of his endowments, man's sexuality enjoyed a period of innocent perfection in which it was totally controlled by his reason. This was an important idea in the natural philosophy of Chartres. Poets like Alanus de Insulis and Bernardus Silvestris depicted original man as a perfect microcosm; the restoration to this state—it was itself a sign of grace in prelapsarian man—was possible only through divine grace. Earthly love was understood in its cosmic context, and even after the Fall it was man's moral duty to try to love in accordance with Nature's laws for the continuation of the fallen, but not forsaken species. Sexual or earthly love was not simply sinful, *luxuria* or *cupiditas;* no matter how far it might have departed from its original dignity and nobility, this love—like every aspect of man's nature—had its purpose under providence and credentials from Eden.

Since earthly love was not simply and exclusively lust, its possibilities were frequently represented by the double Venus figure of medieval mythography. There was a good Venus who fostered an earthly love that was in harmony with the natural and therefore divinely established laws of the universe. And there was an evil Venus who promoted lasciviousness and lust. An excellent example is provided by Boccaccio's own gloss on his

Teseida in which he analyzes Venus *in bono* and *in malo*. In the former aspect, she represents honorable and legitimate desire; in the latter, she represents lasciviousness and vulgar love.[6] Boccaccio's understanding of this two-sided Venus, like that of medieval poets before him, indicates that for him she fundamentally represented two kinds of earthly love, despite her extraordinarily rich and complex background in pagan philosophy and astrology. One of the most powerful and attractive conceptions in that background was that of twin Venuses, heavenly and earthly, found in Plato's *Symposium* and Plotinus's *Enneads*. But there is no definitive evidence that medieval mythographers and poets were well-versed in this platonic tradition or that they identified their good Venus with *caritas* as Ficino later did with the platonic heavenly Venus.[7] It is dangerous to regard the two Venuses of medieval mythography and poetry as being aligned within an opposition of *caritas* and *cupiditas* when the mythograpic moralizations and poetic uses concentrate upon a single context. That context is earthly love and the two Venuses represent two different dispositions within it: the one, legitimate, sacramental, natural, and in harmony with cosmic law; the other, illegitimate, perverted, selfish, and sinful.

This tradition is generally pertinent to all medieval love poetry. The basic opposition of constructive, natural love and destructive, sinful love that the double Venus tradition conveys is as fundamental to the courtly lyric and romance as it is to allegory or didactic literature. It cannot work, of course, in exactly the same way in all of these genres, but it is just as viable in works of a secular orientation as it is in works with a religious or doctrinal orientation. Perhaps even more so, for it is ultimately the source of the contradictions and paradoxes that appear in any medieval poem—no matter what its formal or historical exigencies or point of view—that deals with the theme of *amor*. It is, in a word, a representation of the paradox of human existence since the Fall: a single instinct or impulse, which before the Fall enjoyed both moral and psychological integrity, may lead to opposite and mutually exclusive ends because it has become fragmented and confused in human consciousness.

The idea of two Venuses, or of two kinds of love that are her sons, is not exclusively a medieval one. It can be found, for example, in Ovid's *Fasti* and in Pythagorean writings of late antiquity. The Pythagorean division of divinities into celestial and infernal pairs and the view of two kinds of love—Ovid's *Geminorum mater amorum*—became a cultural commonplace in the hands of medieval mythographers and commentators. The double definition of the goddess of love as chaste and legitimate on the one hand, and as lecherous and illegitimate, on the other, was repeatedly used by such writers as Fulgentius, Remigius, John Scotus, the third Vatican Mythographer, and Bernardus Silvestris. This tradition of two Venuses during the medieval period contributed to the development of the theme of two kinds of love that culminates in the neoplatonic sacred and profane loves of the Renaissance. Throughout the Middle Ages, the basic view remains the same, though statements of the concept may vary in minor details in connection with the roles of either type of Venus. John Scotus, one of the first medieval authors to write on the subject, puts it quite succinctly:

> Due Veneres sunt, una Voluptaria, id est libidinosa, cuius filius est Ermafroditus, altera casta quae erat uxor Vulcani. Est etiam amor castus et amor impudicus.[8]

> There are two Venuses, one the goddess of pleasure, i.e., a lustful one, whose son is Hermaphroditus, and another chaste one who was Vulcan's wife. Thus there is a love that is chaste and one that is shameful.

In the same work, the commentary *in Marcianum,* he identifies the wicked Venus as the symbol of original sin, an early indication of the readiness and ability of Christian writers to assimilate pagan mythology to Christian morality.[9] Writing on the *Fasti,* Remigius of Auxerre makes virtually the same observations. Remigius provided the basis for the comments on this aspect of Venus by Mythographer III (Albericus), a man whose work may well be thought of as the *summa* of medieval mythography.

> Duae autem secundum eundum Remigium sunt Veneres; una casta et pudica, quam honestis praeesse amoribus, quamque Vulcani dicit uxorem; dicitur altera voluptaria, libidinum dea, cujus Hermaphroditum dicit filium fuisse. Itidemque Amores duo; alter bonus et pudicus, quo sapientia et virtutes amantur; alter impudicus et malus, quo ad vitia inclinamur.[10]

> Moreover, according to this same Remigius, there are two Venuses: a chaste and modest one who, he says, presides over honorable loves and is Vulcan's wife; the other is called Pleasure, the goddess of

lechery, whose son, he says, is Hermaphroditus. And likewise there are two Loves: a good and modest one through whom wisdom and the virtues are loved; the other is shameful and evil, through whom we are inclined towards the vices.

In his commentary on the *Aeneid,* Bernardus Silvestris repeats the basic distinction but gives it a cosmological context and implications.

Veneres vero legimus duas esse, legitimam et petulantiae deam. Legitimam Venerem dicimus esse mundanam musicam, i.e., aequalem mundanorum proportionem, quam alii Astream, alii naturalem iustitiam vocant. Haec enim est in elementis, in sideribus, in temporibus, in animantibus. Impudicam autem venerem, petulantiae deam, dicimus esse carnis concupiscentiam quia omnium fornicationum mater est.[11]

We read that there are two Venuses, a legitimate goddess and a goddess of lechery. We say the legitimate Venus is worldly music, that is, the equal proportion of worldly things, which some call Astrea, and others call natural justice. For she is in the elements, in the stars, in living things. But the shameful Venus, the goddess of sensuality, we call concupiscence of the flesh because she is the mother of all fornication.

Later in the work Bernardus identifies the good Venus as *mundi concordiam* and contradicts the earlier identification of the wife of Vulcan as the chaste Venus by explaining that Venus with Vulcan symbolizes the voluptuousness of the flesh, a view which is also presented in the *Ovide moralisé*: "Venus, c'est a dire luxure,/ Feme de Vulcan."[12] This is typical of the minor differences in the face of the tradition as it was known by the end of the twelfth century. The wicked goddess, mother of lust and sensuality, was associated with sin and fornication, and the legitimate goddess was associated, as in the passage from Bernardus, with Boethian, cosmic love, with the way the universe naturally operates. The setting of the good Venus in a cosmological context made it easier for Christians to accept her divine credentials—after they had been modified. For she exists in the universe God created and she has her divinely appointed purpose. Frequently, this Venus was identified with the planet, as she was by Mythographer III in some of his comments on the *Aeneid.* He chose to interpret the Venus of the *Aeneid* and her actions as those of a beneficent star and thereby avoided any connection with the goddess who symbolized the destructive power of lust.[13] Generally speaking, it is safe to assume that the planetary goddess was closely associated with the moralized good Venus of medieval mythography. This identification of the planet with the kind of love the good Venus sponsors was an especially Christian view and clearly illustrated by Dante's opening lines of *Paradiso viii:* "Solea creder lo mondo in suo periclo/che la bella Ciprigna il folle amore/raggiasse, volta nel terzo epiciclo." ("The world once believed, to its peril, that the fair Cyprian, wheeling in the third epicycle, rayed forth mad love.") If Dante understood the planet Venus to represent the love associated with the *Venus legitima* in the tradition, it is easy to understand why he claimed the ancients' cult of her "mad love" put them in peril.

The mythographic tradition provides a meaningful background to the study of medieval literature. It can be particularly useful in our interpretations of the courtly lyric and romance in which a figure like Venus rarely appears but is apostrophized, referred and alluded to, and invoked. The influence of the mythographic two Venuses on medieval poetry is more obvious in the genre of allegory however, for in this mode either goddess may, and often does, appear as a personification. These appearances provide the strong thematic bond among works like the *De planctu naturae,* the *Roman de la Rose,* the *Parlement of Foules,* and the *Confessio Amantis,* works which share strong formal and generic elements. They all deal with questions that pertain to man's sexual conduct, including individual poets' conceptions of courtly love. If these works are regarded as a class with its own tradition and development, they can then be considered profitably in light of parallel developments in the traditions of the lyric and the romance. Each genre, of course, had to develop and treat courtly and other conceptions of love in its own way, but there was undoubtedly a great deal of cross-pollination and influence from genre to genre just as there was from poet to poet. This is especially the case in a subject matter that was as pervasive as courtly love.

The *De planctu naturae* of Alanus de Insulis (c. 1128–1202) is a brilliant and extremely important work. Alanus was a man of literary intelligence and imagination as well as a first-rate theologian, whose work had an enormous influence on subsequent literature. It would not be rash or irresponsible to assume that some of medieval Europe's greatest poets read him and read him carefully. The *De planctu naturae* is an allegorical vision in which the Goddess Natura appears to the narrator and complains about mankind's failure to heed her laws, her natural justice and virtue. Rather, he has willfuly chosen a life of excess and vice, a perversion of the rules the goddess has given him. Man, Natura says, has betrayed his original nature and has chosen the life of sensuality over the life of reason. The Fall and man's condition ever since is basically Alanus's concern in the poem. His allegory is not mere poetic elaboration but a serious accounting, under the veil of a fable, of the cause of the tear—mankind's unnatural and vicious behavior—in Natura's tunic.

Alanus's original use of the mythography of the two Venuses informs the entire work. Its basic meaning is explained by the *vicaria Dei* herself. Entrusted by God with the duty of replenishing the sublunary mutable world with living creatures—a war against the Fates—Natura worked hard and faithfully with her hammer and anvil to keep up the continuity of that which God had created *ex nihilo.* To aid her in her work she enlisted Venus, wife of Hymen and mother of Cupid. But, Natura explains, Venus became childish and wanton and, growing weary of her daily duties, committed fornication with Antigamus. The issue of this union was Jocus, as much like his father as Cupid was like his. Immediately after this rebellious act of Venus there followed the birth of all the vices known to man.

It is not difficult to see how thoroughly acquainted Alanus was with the tradition of the two Venuses; it is also obvious that he altered the tradition to suit his needs, for he combines both kinds of Venus as two dispositions within a single figure. These two dispositions of the same goddess—*Venus caelestis* and *Venus scelestis*—correspond quite closely to their counterparts in the tradition. *Venus scelestis* is the *Venus impudica, libidinum dea,* John Scotus's "generalis et specialis libido," the mother of all sin and vice, sexual and otherwise. *Venus legitima,* particularly as she is described by Bernardus Silvestris, is the *Venus caelestis,* whose cosmic function is represented by her appointment as Natura's subvicar in procreation. Physical passion under Natura serves God, is holy, natural, and responsible to God's law through its submission to Natura's law. It does not come as a surprise to find the wronged Hymen in Natura's company of virtues in the final scene of the work. Most important are the implications in this innovative treatment that the fusion of the two Venuses represents the confused state of human psychology because of mankind's abuse of his passionate nature. The love man was originally meant to obey has been perverted by weakness and immoderate sensuality, and, once corrupted, human nature's apprehension of love becomes blurred and confused, a pattern which informs the entire poem, but especially in the opposition of Cupid and Jocus. The two sons of Venus are indeed twin Loves, for they are the sources of the sweetness and bitterness of love, and Alanus suggests, are frequently confused with one another—Jocus is "Cupid perverted" and to be identified with the fallen Cupid which Alanus refers to in several passages. The mythography of Venus and her sons provided Alanus with the material for his fable's primary myth: the conflict within man—the *psychomachia*—is represented by the opposition between the two aspects of Venus, between Cupid and Jocus; the macrocosmic aspect of this conflict is represented by the warring daughters of Genius, Veritas and Falsitas.

The mythographic tradition of the two Venuses became part of the literary tradition once it began to play a significant and integral role in the creation of a poem. Alanus's use of Venus in the *De planctu* helped open a way for other poets of every genre to follow. For poets who were opposed to courtly love or felt ambiguously towards it, the wicked Venus became a convenient representative symbol. The good Venus, though less popular than her competitor (*in rerum natura*), has moments of prominence, even exaltation, in later poetry in which she often represents or motivates *amor naturalis*. This natural love could be anticourtly or it could be courtly love at its best. The tradition of courtly love was extremely complex, and the Venus figures provided poets with a means of communicating their moral judgments. With a few significant exceptions, European poets from the middle of the twelfth century on associated courtly love with *Venus impudica, luxuria, scelestis*. Just when this became "conventional" would be very difficult to say. The *Roman de la Rose* of Guillaume de Lorris and Jean de Meun is clearly anticourtly, and the poem's use of the *De planctu naturae* as a major source is well known. Indeed, Alanus's awareness of the courtly love tradition and his use of it certainly needs further study; for there are hints that the seeds of an anticourtly position may already exist in his poem.

In the opening lines of the work's first *metrum*, the statement of the theme and the major myth through which it will be conveyed is clear, as are the antithetical terms which make up the central contradiction or paradox of most of the literature of courtly love.

> In lacrimas risus, in luctus gaudia verto,
> In planctum plausus, in lacrimosa jocos,
> Cum sua Naturae video decreta silere,
> Cum Veneris monstro naufraga turba perit;
> Cum Venus in Venerem pugnans illos facit illas;
> Cumque suos magica devirat arte viros.[14]

> I turn laughter into tears, joys to lamentation,
> Applause to complaint, merriment to weeping,
> When I see Nature's decrees stilled,
> When the shipwrecked mob is destroyed by the monstrousness of Venus;
> When Venus fighting Venus makes he's into she's;
> And when she unmans men through her magic arts.

The *Roman* and Chaucer's *Parlement* exhibit this opposition of earthly love; it seems the sides have been picked as early as the *De planctu naturae.* The poem deals not just with love but with man's choice of a way of life that denies his essential and original humanity: "Se negat esse virum, Naturae factus in arte, / Barbarus" (p. 430). In this denial, male sexuality has been rejected, for, as the narrator says, Venus has turned men into hermaphrodites, a fitting transformation under the influence of the evil Venus of mythographic tradition.

The narrator's concerns at the beginning of the poem and throughout should not, however, be too closely identified with those of the poet. Like the narrators of many medieval allegories, the narrator of the *De planctu naturae,* who suffers from limitations, biases, blind spots, undergoes a certain amount of education and alteration in the course of the poem, a device which medieval poets learned from Boethius's *Consolation of Philosophy.* Alanus the poet is concerned with man's lapsed condition and the disintegration of his original moral stature and with the possibility of his restoration. The narrator sees only a corner of the entire picture, being concerned primarily with the most extreme and perverse offense against *Natura procreatrix;* but even he himself is part of the problem Alanus is exploring. In the second half of the opening *metrum* and elsewhere in the work, the narrator betrays himself as holding some notions of love that hardly measure up to Natura's revelations of love's cosmic meaning and purpose. Although he mentions adultery as a form of disobedience, the major conflict for him seems to be between two Venuses who sponsor heterosexual and homosexual love. He laments the fact that the beauty of woman, before which man has ever humbled himself, is now scorned. After Natura, whom he has failed to recognize, identifies herself and begins to explain her procreative function in the sublunary world and mentions how she appointed Venus and Cupid as helpers, he interrupts her and demands an account of the god of love. The narrator's behavior illustrates what has gone wrong with the sublunary world; he would prefer a lesson on Cupid to one on divinely ordained procreative law. This interruption prompts Natura to accuse him—sympathetically but accurately—of being a soldier in Cupid's army, "Credo te in Cupidinis castris stipendiarie militantem" (p. 471), a status which the Amans of the *Roman* shares and which Gower's Amans and Chaucer's narrator aspire to.

Realizing that the narrator suffers from the shortcomings common to all men since the Fall, Natura consents to give him a description of love and its lord. Yet before she provides what in some manuscripts is introduced by the rubric *Descriptio Cupidinis,* she announces that the subject is one that is full of contradictions; to define it is to try to demonstrate the undemonstrable, to untangle the inextricable. Alanus's myth of the two Venuses helps explain and illustrate how human passion became tainted with lust, how the original purpose of Eros and man's understanding of his sexuality fell into confusion and abuse. Thus, what happened to Venus has happened to her son, which is the condition of love in the world, and Cupid and Jocus stand opposed as the two polarities that yield the series of contradictions that must be used to define love. Oxymoron becomes the appropriate figure of speech for a human nature which has lost its harmony and integrity and become contradictory and conflicted. The well-known Ovidian stance, which is the literary source, becomes in a Christian context a symbol of the tragic condition of fallen man.

> Pax odio, fraudique fides, spes juncta timori,
> Est amor, et mixtus cum ratione furor.
>
> [p. 472]

Peace joined to hate, faith to fraud, and hope to fear,
Is love, a madness mixed with reason.

After twenty lines devoted to this point, Natura gives the narrator various examples from classical mythology of men and women that Cupid has transformed, and closes the poem with a portrait of Cupid that many subsequent poets, certainly Guillaume de Lorris, Jean de Meun, and Chaucer, made very good use of.

Cupidinis ire sub hasta
Cogitur omnis amans, juraque solvit ei.
Militat in cunctis, ullum vix excipit hujus
Regula, cuncta ferit fulminis ira sui
In quem non poterit probitas, prudentia, formae
Gratia, fluctus opum, nobilitatis apex.

[p. 473]

Under Cupid's spear
All lovers march and pay him his dues.
He wars on everyone, excepts hardly anyone
From his rule, he offers everyone the anger of his thunderbolt
Against which uprightness is no help, nor prudence,
Nor beauty, a stream of wealth, nor the height of nobility.

In his kingdom, honesty, reason, moderation, and faith are replaced by their opposites which nevertheless claim their names, and the god of love poisons, harms, and corrupts under the name of sweetness and joy. There is only one remedy—flight.

Ipse tamen poteris istum frenare furorem,
Si fugias, potior potio nulla datur.
Si vitare velis Venerem, loca, tempora vita;
Et locus et tempus pabula donat ei.
Prosequitur, si tu sequeris; fugiendo fugatur;
Si cedis, cedit; si fugis, illa fugit.

[p. 474]

Yet you can check that madness,
If you flee, no better medicine is given.
If you wish to shun Venus, shun her places and occasions;
Place and occasion give her nourishment.
She attends if you follow, she is put to flight by fleeing;
If you retreat, she retreats; if you flee, she flees.

How well mother and son work together is emphasized in the last lines of the passage: they are, in their degeneracy, the predominating form of love in the world. They can be overcome by avoidance, also the advice of Jean's Raison and the black inscription in Chaucer's *Parlement,* "Th'eschewing is only the remedye!"

This kind of reaction to Venus and Cupid eventually works out as a case against courtly love. Cupid demands and usually gets the dues originally meant for Genius in a cause that is sterile and artificial, not to mention sinful. But this is by no means a case against love itself. For as God's vicegerent the Goddess Natura herself explains, righteous and legitimate love can be attained through modesty and moderation, through the effort to restore balance between reason and appetite. It is not perfect love but love as it has devolved in the world's history with which Natura must work as *procreatrix et pronuba.* She, however, is powerless to effect that which may come about only through a conscious act of the human will. Jean de Meun understood this very well and takes Alanus as his starting point in his explorations of earthly love.

Jean de Meun (c. 1260–1315) adapted most of Alanus's *Descriptio Cupidinis* and assigned it to the character Raison (4291 ff.),[15] the most formidable opponent of Venus and Amor in the poem. Guillaume had introduced Raison briefly (2971–3098) to warn the Amans against the god of love—but the attempt was a dismal failure. The reintroduction of Raison shortly after Jean picked up the narrative thread suggests that Jean had something important to add to what had already been said. The return of Raison, in fact, shows Jean's profound understanding of Alanus and his awareness of the double Venus tradition. From the outset, the *Roman de la Rose* is a poem about adulterous love, which means that only one Venus will play an active role, a fact which Guillaume makes clear by his making Jocus and Amor the lords of the Garden of Deduit. They both had been identified as the sons of the evil Venus by Bernardus Silvestris. In retaining all of Guillaume's characters, Jean reveals that he understands Guillaume's point of view, but he brings back Raison in order to clarify the issues of his continuation. *Venus scelestis* belongs to the world of the poem's action; *Venus caelestis* belongs to the world of Raison's argument, which is heavily indebted to the lectures of Alanus's Natura as well as to Boethius. To find that kind of love, *amor naturalis,* the Amans would have to leave the garden in which he has been made prisoner and servant of Amor. Raison explains to Amans the madness that has possessed him and offers exactly the same advice Alanus's Natura did.

Se tu le suiz, il te suira,
Se tu t'en fuiz, il s'en fuira.

[4357–58]

If you follow him, he'll follow you,
If you flee him, he'll flee away from you.

Raison's arguments for "natural love" and attacks upon what no medieval reader or listener had to be told was courtly love are made in vain because the Amans is already thoroughly in love and thoroughly imbued with Amor's doctrine. It is only a matter of time.

Venus herself enters the action of the poem relatively late, after the psychomachic struggle within the beloved has reached a stalemate and Amor begs her to come to his assistance (15659 ff.). She comes, in Jean's words and in her own, to wage war against Chastity. From the moment she enters the battle, she dominates the action. That Jean suspends the action when she regroups Amor's barons in order to introduce Natura and Genius is extremely significant. For all the differences between the goddesses and priests of Alanus and Jean, one thing is very clear: Venus, as Alanus's Natura explained, was assigned by her to help fulfill her procreative duties: Venus's power over lovers stems originally from her stewardship to the *vicaria Dei.* It is difficult to define the first stirring of passion and desire to possess the rose as lechery or as courtly love; but it is obvious that it takes only a moment for the natural urge to be taken over. In the *Roman,* as in the *De planctu naturae,* the tithes that were meant for Genius are usurped by Venus, her son and a very willing lover. Thus, when Genius is sent by Natura to the camp of Amor and his barons to urge them to further the cause of procreation, Amor decks him out as his own bishop with chasuble, miter, ring, and cross, and Venus laughingly puts one of her candles, which were not made of virgin wax, in his hand (19477–90). After Genius finishes his sermon on fecundity and flings down the torch of Venus, she fans the fire until it intoxicates every woman's heart and body. The Amans is now assured of victory and, as all readers of the poem know, takes the rose with the help of Venus and Amor.

The victory of the Amans through Venus and Amor is a perversion of the cosmic power that gave them their being. Amans's desire might have been channeled into the legitimate, natural love had Raison's advice been heeded. But as Jean shows, Amans is captivated and captured by Amor and his mother, the Venus known as *luxuria* and *voluptaria.* They have convinced the lover to replace the rules of procreation with the rules of a sophisticated game; they have convinced him to make his end sexual pleasure, which was Natura's means to a holy end. The *Roman* is a magnificent and fully explored instance of the very condition that gave Alanus's Natura cause for complaint. The outcome of the poem seems to suggest what Jean is saying, somewhat pessimistically, that given the choice between the kinds of love offered by Raison and by Venus and Amor, man will invariably opt for the latter. The conclusion of the poem shows no trace of the optimism, however slight, in the final scene of the *De planctu naturae.* There the condemnation by Genius, which had been requested by Natura, summons up a picture of the ideal from which human nature has fallen and to which it can be restored. It may be that Alanus's narrator represents mankind more generally than does the Amans of Guillaume and Jean, as Amans may be readily seen as a figure for the courtly lover. Whether he represents the courtly lover in particular or mankind in general, the Amans by the end of the poem shows no sign of redeeming virtue within himself and seems to have learned nothing.

Like the Amans of the *Roman,* Chaucer's narrator of the *Parlement of Foules* is exposed to the full spectrum of love's possibilities. Although he is incapable of participating in love, he is still eager to learn about it, and faithfully reports everything he sees in his vision. The Goddess Natura is the central figure in the *Parlement* (see Chapter VI), but Chaucer's use of the double Venus tradition in the poem plays a significant role in preparing for the climactic scene in Natura's grove. The good Venus is actually outside the vision, for the poet invokes her assistance in the stanza just before he begins to narrate his dream, "Cytherea! thow blysful lady swete" (113–119).[16] It is to the planet Venus that the poet turns for support, "So yif me myght to ryme and ek t'endyte!" because she, the beneficent goddess of legitimate love, stands opposed to the sterile, destructive love represented by the evil Venus in the temple and stands behind the love that Natura sponsors. Represented in the allegory are the two antagonistic kinds of love, but the entire poem, with its triumph of Natura at the end, is written under the inspiration of the planetary goddess. It is the same Venus whom John Gower's Genius serves in the *Confessio Amantis.*[17] It is the good Venus, associated with Natura (VIII. 2337–44) and identified as the planet (VIII 2942–

44), that brings the old Amans to his senses. She leads him to self-recognition and reason and urges his return to studies. The edifying effect this instance of the good Venus has on the life of a deluded, well-intentioned old man contrasts sharply and tellingly with the effect the wicked Venus, who laughs triumphantly at his wedding (IV. 1723–24), has on the life of January. The one is released from care and is granted insight and moral rectitude, while the other is hopelessly enmeshed in a life of lechery only to be rewarded by spiritual and moral blindness.

If the mythographic tradition of the two Venuses and the twin Loves provided poets of allegory with a frame of reference in which they could define and evaluate the meaning and role of erotic love in terms of the cosmos and divine providence, it also provided the poets of romance with a figure of reference which they could use to support the view of love that character, plot, and setting revealed. In the allegories, Venus not only defines earthly love as legitimate or illegitimate, as natural or lustful, she also personifies it, for in these works she is usually an actual character. In the romance she recedes into the background and becomes a force behind and a power that motivates the actions of the knight. This shift of Venus's role from within the scene to behind the scene is only one—and a rather obvious one—of a number of significant differences in the handling of the elements of courtly love between the romance and other genres. The unrelieved tension inherent in the lover's situation in the lyric begins to dissolve. The magic circle within which his love is free to pursue its virtually unattainable end—unaffected by and protected from the conditions of the ordinary life beyond its circumference—tends to break down once that love becomes the subject of a narrative. In the world of romance the conventions of courtly love are put to a severe test, for the very emotion which may sustain the lyric poet for song after song can only be treated as a temporary state in the protagonist of the romance. And the resolution, which the lyric poet may effect in so many ways within his own consciousness, does not enjoy such a closed context for the narrative poet, because he must resolve problems which pertain to society and morality as well as to the individual. The lyric poet may write about his love in a way that gives the illusion of a perpetual balancing of the opposition of the two Venuses. The romance poet cannot afford to suspend the clarification of the difference between them, which is admirably illustrated by an episode from the *Yvain* of Chrétien de Troyes (fl. 1155–85).

After Yvain mortally wounds the Knight of the Fountain he pursues him to his castle where he becomes trapped between two portcullises. Eventually discovered and hidden by the Queen's handmaiden, Yvain sees Laudine, the grieving widow of his victim, and immediately falls in love with her. Forgetting Kay and his reputation at Arthur's court, he falls hopelessly in love with an enemy, with one who must obviously feel only hatred for him. And this, Chrétien observes, is ample revenge for her lord's death, for Amors has taken complete possession of Yvain's heart. Although he does not hesitate to acknowledge the basic nobility of his protagonist's character, the poet does not hesitate to reveal that his feelings about Amors are ambivalent at best: "It is a great shame that Love is such, / And that she proves herself so evil, / That she finds lodging in a base place / Just as readily as in the very best in the world" (1386–90).[18] Love, which generally lacks discrimination in selecting her lodgings, has this time shown that she is capable of selecting a noble heart, though, he reiterates, she betrays her nobility by often descending to low places. Chrétien clearly insists that Love herself is blind to the kind of distinction he makes here—a confusion of her function that resembles Alanus's ingenious adaptation of the mythography of Venus in the *De planctu naturae* in which the original cosmic function of Venus becomes confused with lechery. For love, Chrétien continues, invoking a commonplace of the poetry of Venus and courtly love, is like one who applies her balm to ashes and dust, and mixes sugar with gall, and honey with suet (1398–1402). The language of paradox here, unlike its purpose in the *Descriptio Cupidinis* of Alanus's Natura and Jean de Meun's Raison, is suggestive as well as definitive. It relates to the poet's desire to foreshadow action as much as it does to his desire to supply a moral characterization of the goddess Love as she enters the career of the hero. For, as his story unfolds, Yvain loses his lady's love and must endure grief and pain—even the loss of his sanity—before he achieves the sense of balance that eventually leads to his being reaccepted. His fault is not simply that he loves adventure to excess but that there is in his nature a general tendency to excessiveness that manifests itself in other matters. That the poet intended to explore this problem in his hero and to prepare the reader for the overt disturbance of balance when Yvain sets out with Gawan on the road to adventure, is suggested by the concluding lines of this part of the poem. As soon as Yvain admits to himself that he is completely possessed by his passion for Laudine, he praises her beauty by asserting that Nature has exceeded herself in the creation of his beloved; in fact, he continues, it must have been God himself that made her. Nature could never hope to equal such an achievement, and God, were He to try, could never duplicate this success (1491–1506). The power of Venus has made the lover question, indeed upset, the hierarchy of the *opus Dei* and the *opus Naturae*.[19] On one hand, such an excessive and confused view is to be expected, perhaps even excused, in a man in his condition. On the other hand, the passage exposes an important quality of Yvain's character. The way in which Amors, the goddess of Love, takes possession of Yvain is unique to him and in harmony with his character throughout the poem.

A more unusual treatment of the goddess appears in the *Parzival* of Wolfram von Eschenbach (c. 1170–1220). It is unusual because while Wolfram's digression on Venus (X. 532–33)[20] reflects her tradition with considerable learning and subtle manipulation it is, at the same time, an utter if oblique rejection of it as an emotion of any value to his hero. Venus is introduced, quite appropriately, during the adventures of Gawan in the second half of the poem. While Parzival is following his destiny to the Grail castle, Gawan is travelling the lower road of Arthurian adventure on which he becomes ensnared by his love for the lady Orgeluse. Though he is cruelly treated by her, the situation still bears all the earmarks of the conventional situation of lover and lady in the Arthurian romance. Wolfram sums up the situation succinctly through the essential paradox of courtly love: she was both a joy and a sorrow to him, sweetness to his eyes and sourness to his heart ("ougen süeze unt sûr dem herzen bî"), loss and gain, sickness and health, captor and liberator (X. 531.24–29). It is against this background, ironically enriched later by the knowledge that it was Anfortas's love for Orgeluse that caused his fall and infirmity, that Wolfram suspends his narration to comment upon Venus and her sons Amor and Cupid.

Throughout the digression, which is itself interrupted by ironic comments on Gawan's plight and statements on the only love that is really true (*triuwe*), Wolfram reveals his easy familiarity with the tradition of Venus as he simultaneously rejects it totally. The opening lines unmistakably establish his learning and position.

> Manec mîn meister sprichet sô,
> daz Amor unt Cupîdô
> unt der zweier muoter Vênus
> den liuten minne gebn alsus,
> mit geschôze unt mit fiure.
> diu minne ist ungehiure.
>
> [X. 532.1–6]

> Many a master of mine says
> that Amor and Cupid
> and Venus, the mother of them both,
> give love to people
> with darts and torches.
> This love is unwholesome.

In spite of the fact that he acknowledges twin loves by name, Wolfram refuses to concede any difference between them. They are condemned along with their mother as fostering love that is unhealthy. The basis for this rejection is fundamentally Wolfram's own view of true love, which is characterized by faithful, unwavering devotion, a love which neither alters nor admits impediments and stands high above all others: "diu minne ist ob den andern hôch" (X. 533.30). It is, of course, the love which Parzival and Condwiramurs share and which reaches its perfection when they attain their thrones in Munsalvaesche. Wolfram, having eluded the weapons of Venus and her sons, claims to know this loyal love very well. His rejection of mother and sons humorously foreshadows the triumph of the love of the hero and his wife, which produces two sons of its own. Nevertheless, Wolfram does not fail to admit a kind of distinction between two aspects of Venus. He accomplishes this through a superb device—he abandons the mythological names of mother and sons and speaks of the love they cause under the more common personification *Minne*. He translates the mythology and mythography of his masters, perhaps even Alanus was one, into the language of his medium. Does *Minne* cause so much grief because she enjoys mischief? She is too old for that. Or is it her childishness which causes such sorrow to the heart.

unfuoge gan ich paz ir jugent,
dan daz si ir alter braeche tugent.
vil dinges ist von ir geschehn:
wederhalp sol ich des jehen?
wil si mit jungen raeten
ir alten site unstaeten,
so wirt si schiere an prîse laz.
man sol sis underscheiden baz.

[X. 533. 13–20]

I would sooner put it to her youthfulness,
than have her do mischief to her old age.
Many things have happened because of her:
from which of these two shall I say they come?
If she with childish notions
wants to abuse her old age,
then she will earn less praise.
One must discriminate better in this.

Wolfram implies a nobler side of *Minne* which comes from her old age but which seems to have been debased by her youth. This resembles the situation Alanus explained in the *De planctu naturae:* the earlier, older aspect of Venus served Natura faithfully until the later aspect confused her purpose by succumbing to her youthful and childishly wanton impulses and betrayed Hymen with Antigamus.

Illa igitur magis appetens otiis effeminari sterilibus quam fructuosis exerceri laboribus, ferialis operationis exercitatione negociali praeposita nimiae otiositatis enumerata desideriis coepit infantibiliter juvenisci.

[Wright, p. 479]

Then she, craving to be womanized in unfruitful idleness more than to be kept busy with fruitful labors, though set in command, as related, over the exercise of festal activity, became childishly wanton over the longings of excessive idleness.

The state of love in Alanus's sublunary world and Wolfram's Arthurian world is one of hopeless confusion. Alanus offers a ray of hope by asserting that man's original goodness is capable of cooperating in his restoration. Wolfram suggests that one ought to be more discriminating in the matter of the old and young *Minne* but quickly moves on to his own solution. He reminds us once again of that pure love (*luter minne*) which his hero pursues and which is one of the great themes of his poem.

Thus Wolfram concludes his digression on Love by offering his vision of high love as the only alternative to the welter of confusion and contradiction that Gawan's situation represents. Returning to his story of Gawan's painful joy (X. 534), Wolfram admits he can do nothing to help him and makes his only concession to love as it is understood in the Arthurian world. A man must not resist it, since it is the only thing that can help him. Gawan must suffer this pain, and accepts it gladly, in order to receive a reward which he, like those he represents, will overestimate in value. But Parzival endures a suffering and achieves a joy which is reserved for the few who are destined to transcend the ordinary life of the courtly world.

While Wolfram solved the problem of courtly love by exposing it and substituting for it his own religiously oriented vision of love, his contemporary Gottfried von Strassburg (fl. c. 1210) in his great poem *Tristan* embraced the love sung by the lyric poets as no poet before or after him had done and transformed it into a love which reached perfection through the physical and spiritual union of his lovers. The love of Tristan and Isolde is very special and cannot be identified, as Gottfried insists throughout his work, with the kind of love practiced by heroes and heroines of other romances. He wrote of another world for the select few, the *edele herzen,* who understand what noble and perfect love really is.[21] Both poets abandon courtly love as too worldly and place their trust in a higher love, which they, in their own way, invest with a spiritual value which sets it above its courtly counterpart. Yet, the differences between their loves and their worlds of romance are very great.

Not long before his poem ends and Tristan departs for Arundel, having been discovered by Mark in Isolde's arms somewhat more definitively than in the past, Gottfried pauses from his narrative to discuss the subject of woman's nature and her love (17933–18114).[22] He condemns surveillance (*huote*) not only because it is unworthy and ignoble but also because women tend to respond to prohibition and close control by doing things they would probably refrain from doing were they free to do them. Eve is the mother of this perversity and all women follow her in its practice. It is not unreasonable for Gottfried to introduce this topic, for as he later points out, Tristan responds to Isolde's invitation that he ignore great peril and visit her in the orchard at noon just as Adam responded to Eve's invitation that he partake of the fruit she offered him. But the pressure from Mark prompted Isolde to take such a chance: the spying has whetted her appetite and caused her attempt to elude the watch, an attempt which is a fatal turning point in the poem. She has ignored her understanding with Tristan that when occasion and place are dangerous the will to love may be considered equal to the act. It is not so much a condemnation of Isolde as it is an indication of the impossibility of the lovers' situation in their world. If Isolde is a daughter of Eve, it is Mark's jealousy and surveillance that has brought out the worst in her. Gottfried suggests throughout his poem that the world—the immediate social environment in which the action is set—is not only hostile to the lovers but also unworthy of the love that secretly thrives, despite all of the obstacles, for as long as it does in its midst. Isolde, then, is not really at fault. It is as if Gottfried is saying that given the circumstances she responds naturally or normally because she is a woman and a daughter of Eve. It is too much to expect of her to be absolutely perfect in this place, to transcend her nature under these conditions (17971–75). To be a woman, and Tristan's equal, as she was in the Love Grotto, Gottfried's figure for the prelapsarian Eden of his lovers' career, Isolde needs an environment that will support her better nature, not the Cornwall that has brought her to play the fatal role in the love affair. Moderation, the poet continues, enables a woman to sustain her body and her honor through joy and sorrow. It is moderation which ultimately saves a woman from self-destructive acts, from acts which demean her and the quality of her love (18037–40).

Like so many poets before and after him, Gottfried uses the tradition of two opposite kinds of love to show how *Minne,* the term for his perfect love, can be brought down by loss of control over its source—passion. But since he has posited a special love that cannot survive in the world, a love that is destined to achieve its perfection beyond this world, Isolde is not to blame. The immoderate act in her has been provoked by a world in which base immoderation is the rule. She and Tristan are exemplars of the noblest love and their story is "bread" to the *edele herzen* who understand and emulate their love. The lovers' story is their nourishment; it is a model that should be imitated but cannot be duplicated, any more than the Bernardine love that provides Gottfried with a terminology and modality can be duplicated. The poet, therefore, can say that the virtuous woman—and Isolde is clearly her prototype—can bring a man into paradise (18045–114); that for others, *after* Tristan and Isolde, there is a possibility of achieving happiness and freedom in this world. Although it is doomed to extinction, the love of Tristan and Isolde has left behind an ideal for other lovers. In a sense, it has made it possible for others to attain the happiness that the world refused them, not as a love that can actually be matched but as one that shows the way. As an ideal love to be followed by generations of noble hearts, it is analogous to the ideal marriage that is sketched in the concluding episode of the *De planctu naturae.* The Latin work's climax is the excommunication by Genius of all who break Natura's laws, for the disintegration of man from cosmos and God is a very real condition of the world. Yet present in the scene are the moderate Hymen, who wears garments on which there are somewhat faded ideal pictures revealing the events of marriage and Natura's virtues, Chastity, Temperance, Generosity, and Humility. Natura addresses them as lonely lamps in human darkness and morning stars of a setting world, "O sola humanae tenebrositatis luminaria, occidentis mundi sidera matutina" (Wright, pp. 509–10), because they represent the beauty of a humanity which, paradoxically, wishes to drive them out of the world. This ideal, not quite completely lost and capable of being regained, is paralleled by the ideal of Tristan and Isolde as lovers. For Gottfried and the *edele herzen,* their lives, like Adam's and Eve's, embodied the ideal, failed to hold it, but left enough of its image for others to aspire to.

Like Gottfried's *Tristan,* Chaucer's *Troilus and Criseyde* records the career of a great love. In each of these poems the nature of society influences the course of the love affair and contributes finally to its undoing. Courtly poets had long recognized and developed this relationship between society and the individual, and Chaucer continued the tradition. But he links them even further through the concept of the good Venus, the goddess who gives the "lawe of kynde" to the lover and city alike. So closely related are the two spheres in Chaucer's poem that the city benefits directly from Troilus's love service, and the lovers suffer fatal consequences at the hands of the city. For the medieval myth of the two Venuses informs the entire poem, providing the central context in which positive and negative actions of individuals and nations can be understood. The presence of the good Venus is more prominent, because of Troilus's devotion to her and the narrator's respect for her, but the wicked Venus has her moments, particularly in the Trojan parliament and with Criseyde in the Greek camp. In the last analysis, each Venus is a metaphor for a moral choice and commitment.

That the history of Troilus and Criseyde is closely related to the history of Troy has been widely recognized for some time. The poem opens at a time when the city's defenses are enjoying unqualified success in holding the Greek threat in check—even though the seeds of Troy's destruction have already been sown by the defection of Criseyde's father, Calkas the priest. Throughout the first three books, which record the love affair from its inception to consummation, the characters show no indication that they doubt Troy's ability to withstand the Greek attack. The narrator's historical perspective of the events—presented chiefly in the invocations—is quite different, but it does not dominate our awareness of the situation until the fourth book. During this period, Troilus emerges as one of Troy's most formidable champions. His effectiveness as a warrior increases as he takes on "Loves heigh servise" and reaches its highest point with his fulfillment as a lover, a development fully in keeping with the courtly tradition of the lover's private and public lives coming together. At the start of his love affair, the courageous young prince can manage no more than trepidation and self-pity until he ties his hopes to the skills of his friend Pandarus. Nevertheless, he becomes a leading protector of the city, "next his brother, holder up of Troye" (II. 644). After consummating the love he becomes an example of moral virtue as well.

> Thus wolde Love, yheried be his grace,
> That Pride, Envye, and Ire, and Avarice
> He gan to fle, and everich other vice.
>
> [III. 1804–06]

Love has transformed him into the best young man he can become, and his love prospers as long as the city is safe. But a single event undoes the love and eventually the city. The decision of the Trojan parliament to exchange Criseyde for Antenor destroys both the security of lovers and city. This decision overrides the advice of Troy's greatest champion and noblest man, Hector, who rejects the proposed exchange completely: "We usen here no wommen for to selle" (IV. 182). The parliament, however, decides in favor of "selling" her; in ignoring Hector's argument the city relinquishes the kind of conviction and integrity that gave it its civilization, and the weakening of character shows in its individuals. Criseyde, with every intention of returning, goes to her father and never comes back, losing love, reputation, and self-respect. Antenor returns to his city, only to betray its sacred trust and protection. Troilus, in despair over what his beloved has done to herself, as well as to him, loses the will to live and begins to fight with dangerous abandon; eventually, he is killed by Achilles, the arch-slayer of Trojan protectors. The dissolution of the bond between Troilus and Criseyde presages the fall of the city. Both are inevitable, and the realization of one reminds us of the imminence of the other; exchanging Criseyde for Antenor is a critical error in a series of lethal mistakes through which Troy brings about its own doom.

At the same time, it is important that to Chaucer the story of Troy was part of a great historical movement which culminated in the establishment of Rome and his own city of London.[23] The decay and fall of Troy could certainly serve as a warning to the New Troy of which it is the exemplar: for London had its share of political and social turbulence in the last quarter of the fourteenth century. In the poem much of what was good and noble in Troy dies with the city, but that goodness and nobility was vindicated in time through Aeneas. Venus, through her son Aeneas, insures that the world of the future will share in the best that the world of Troy could offer. It is, in part, that surviving goodness and nobility that Chaucer sees threatened by the kind of turmoil that helped bring down Troy. Most important, this historical movement was directed by divine providence. Troilus had no way of understanding that and so accepted his circumstances as predestined, but the poem's audience could see that providence gives even to pagans the freedom to choose their destiny: Troy will fall, but its people make it deserving of its fate; the Trojan parliament ratifies the plan to exchange the prisoners.

The parallelism between the careers of the city and lovers is most meaningful when it is understood as a statement of the total breakdown of the pagan world of Troy. The order and harmony of that world proceeded from the "law of kynde," the Boethian cosmic love associated with the mythological and philosophical meaning of Venus, planet and goddess of love. Troy falls apart when the Trojans fail to live up to the precepts of that love. Human and political integrity fail together, just as they survive together, at the end of the Knight's Tale where political stability and personal virtue become attuned to the Boethian "faire cheyne of love." History cannot be changed, however sorrowful its tale, but an effort can be made to understand it. The world of Troilus and Criseyde crumbles because it is an instance of a pagan society that does not avail itself of the greatest wisdom its culture has attained. Furthermore, Chaucer makes it clear that this world of his lovers is separated from him and us by "the great barrier of God's revelation at Sinai and in Christ."[24] The consolation of Christian revelation was unavailable to them. This point is especially crucial in the last few stanzas of the poem which provide the final perspective from which the whole must be viewed. Up to that point Chaucer has deliberately confined himself to informing the poem with patterns of meaning from the *Consolation of Philosophy*.

It is well known that the Boethian themes Chaucer introduced to his version of the story helped distinguish it profoundly from Boccaccio's *Filostrato*. Through the characters and the voice of the narrator, Chaucer has made the world of the lovers one in which the concepts of fate, destiny, fortune, and natural law are of the utmost importance. It is particularly illuminating to consider the "law of kynde" and its cosmological and moral ramifications in the poem. This natural law, the binding force of harmony in the universe, is represented by the God Love and especially his mother, Venus. It is no coincidence that almost every passage that deals with Venus and cosmic law and love has been introduced by Chaucer. The one major exception is the invocation to the third book; but even that is not strictly a matter of following a source, for in Boccaccio, it is part of a speech by Troilo. Perhaps this is a subtle and early instance of that process of lessening of distance between the hero and narrator until the final, definitive shift that comes at the end. The *Filostrato* does not contain: the narrator's introduction of "law of kynde" (I. 236–38); Pandarus's confidence that Criseyde is subject to "love of kynde" (I. 974 ff.); Troilus's appeals to "blisful Venus" for help (I. 1014–15, III. 705 ff.); the narrator's explanation that Venus was well disposed towards Troilus in his nativity (II. 680 ff.); and finally Troilus's hymns to Venus and Love in the middle and at the end of the third book (III. 1254–74, 1744–71). These additions, like the identification of Antenor as a traitor (II. 204), which Boccaccio had dropped, are deliberate and purposeful. They emphasize the relationship between the lovers and the city by showing they are both subject to the same law. Thus, Troilus may finally hold Criseyde in his arms and praise Venus as the power which has beneficently disposed itself towards him as individual lover.

> O Love, O Charite!
> Thi moder ek, Citherea the swete,
> After thiself next heried be she,
> Venus mene I, the wel-willy planete!
>
> [III. 1254–57]

and then identify it further, as "Benigne Love, thow holy bond of thynges" (III. 1261). And again at the end of the third book he sings praises to this love and identifies it with the love that rules the universe for God, "that auctor is of kynde" (III. 1765), by adapting the *Quod mundus stabili fide* of Boethius (II. m. viii).

> Love that of erthe and se hath governaunce,
> Love, that his hestes hath in hevenes hye,
> Love, that with an holsom alliaunce
> Halt peples joyned, as hym lest hem gye,
> Love, that knetteth lawe of compaignie,
> And couples doth in vertu for to dwelle,
> Bynd this accord, that I have told and telle.
>
> [III. 1744–50]

To this must be added the beautiful invocation to Venus that opens book three, "O blisful light, of which the bemes clere/ Adorneth al the thridde heven faire!" for a complete picture of the meaning and function of this "love and lawe of kynde" in the poem's world.

Chaucer took a story of two pagan lovers—the strong historicity of his material proved a great advantage in the long run—and showed what heights could be attained by the earthly love represented and promoted by the good Venus. The love which sustains Troilus and Troy is none other than that which Bernardus Silvestris called *Venus legitima* and *mundana musica.* In a historical setting that is sharply separated from the world of the poet and his audience, the young pagan Troilus is touched by this love and responds by eventually attaining a rare state of personal and social excellence. He follows the good Venus to his exaltation, and even his vision from the eighth sphere after his death may be understood as a reward for his "trouthe" to the highest principle of his world.

Chaucer, like Boethius, did not mistake this principle for Christian love. If there is one medieval love poem which offers positive proof that the two Venuses were not just one more pattern of the opposition of earthly and Christian love, it is the *Troilus.* The meaning of the good Venus receives the highest respect from the poet; the love that drives and binds together the universe uplifts and distinguishes the hero for a brief moment. When he transcends earthly joy and woe after death, he attains a new perspective, the closest one to the new dispensation that is possible for him. From this new vantage point he can even reject that which guided him through his earthly existence with nobility and honor, because he has left it forever. Christian love has meaning only for Chaucer and his audience. There is yet one more point of view from which things can be examined, but it is a point of view which can be achieved only if one is on the right side of providential history's great divide. It is eminently natural for Chaucer to end his poem with his message of Christian mystery and love. But this message does not reduce the rest of the poem to the status of an illustration of lust; and it no more nullifies the human truth and value of Troilus's love, than Genesis was considered to nullify the intellectual truth and value of *Timaeus.*

The triumph of Troilus's love, as has been indicated already, is brief. That is as it had to be. For Chaucer understood that whether pagan or Christian, the nature of the world since the Fall has known no serious change. Although "In sondry londes, sondry ben usages," and although things like language change—a condition of which the poet shows a keen and apprehensive awareness—for a Christian like Chaucer, the nature of the world was essentially the same in the time of Troilus as it was in his own. It has been in a fallen condition all along—the defects have always been the same but the remedies have not. Troilus's world—the best of which Chaucer thought was summed up in Boethius—sought to overcome disorder, to find meaning and fulfillment through its great discovery of the "law of kynde," a discovery which few, if any, Christian thinkers believed was negligible simply because it was made by pagans. Again, the correct reading of the poem's last few stanzas is crucial to understanding the entire work. Since the incarnation and passion of Christ, mankind has been granted the means to overcome the defects in its nature. Chaucer presents this simply and directly and even shows some bluntness in the way he asserts his complete faith in the only possible restoration. The "law of kynde" ennobles Troilus, but the "law of kynde" still exists in the world and because of it Troilus's blissful joy must be short-lived. It is part of the nature of the world, and there is nothing permanent and immutable in it. The characters in the poem are part of a world with a closed end: it is a world at Fortune's mercy, which it knows it must transcend, but with no way of perceiving the providence whose agent Fortune is. It is a world which has discovered the operation of the universe and even recognized that that operation has a divine source, but it has no way of seeing the ultimate end and justice it is moving towards. These are definitive, not mitigating circumstances. It is a perfect world for illustrating what good end earthly love is capable of, and how that good is confounded and finally, undone by the nature of earthly love itself. Paradoxically, the story of Troilus's "wele and wo" advocates that recognition and tribute be paid to its human greatness and frailty, so that we might believe with deeper faith in the mystery of our only redemption.

In his myth of Venus, Alanus had allegorically described the source of love's confusion. With the Fall, Venus's identity and role became fragmented into two dispositions, a positive and a negative. In Chaucer's romance, these two separate but inseparable dispositions, ultimately account for the major actions. The transformation of Troilus has already been mentioned. Ironically, the love that ennobles him also benefits those who seem at first to be much better versed in the ways of love. For practical and humorous reasons, Chaucer clearly gives the advantage to Pandarus as far as worldly wisdom and know-how go. Even Criseyde enjoys the advantage of him when it comes to dealing with the opposite sex. Yet, the greatest happiness for all three of them springs not from the knowledgeability and manipulative talents of Pandarus, nor from the excellent sense of timing and womanliness of Criseyde; it springs from the noble nature—the depth and sincerity of Troilus's love. No matter how foolish and inept he appears at times, no matter how much help he needs, it is his love and character that most profoundly affect his friend and lady. Chaucer has set the positive aspect of Venus in Troilus. Once circumstances turn against the lovers, it is Criseyde who succumbs to the negative aspect. Ironically, the only time she mentions Venus is at the end of the fourth book (1661) when she swears by "blisful Venus" to return. This speech, which is not in Boccaccio, anticipates Henryson's *Testament of Cresseid.* The false oath by Venus looks ahead to the later blasphemous attack on the goddess. With troubled times, truth and honor take firmer root in Troilus, but falseness and dishonor take possession of Criseyde. Chaucer is frank about his unhappiness with a situation in which his heroine is utterly culpable. Yet, as narrator, he cannot avoid reporting what she said and did. Linking the lovers' story to that of the city does not remove the blame from Criseyde but it does serve to mitigate it somewhat. Chaucer cannot go as far as Gottfried did when he insisted on placing the blame on the spying world of Cornwall rather than on Isolde's lack of self-control and moderation. But each poet unmistakably concedes that if he must give frailty a human name it must be a woman's. Isolde does demand that Tristan love her in the garden at noon and Criseyde does give herself to Diomede.

Of all the vernacular poems that show the influence of the two Venus tradition, *Troilus and Criseyde* is the one in which it is used with the greatest completeness. The *Roman de la Rose,* particularly the continuation of Jean de Meun, provides a thoroughly explored instance of the amorous behavior of fallen human nature. It comes as no great surprise that the wicked Venus triumphs, for that is the way of the world. She triumphs also in Chaucer's poem, only it is not so apparent in a romance as in an allegory. Jean took Alanus's myth of Venus and showed her doing what the Goddess Natura complained of; he made an allegorical narrative out of Natura's fabulous account of the Fall. But in the world of Chaucer's romance, the old conflic exists as the very life of its characters. Jean personifies and Chaucer incarnates the meaning of Alanus's myth of human confusion and yearning. Chaucer found a way to pursue the highest limits of earthy love, and concentrated on the good Venus rather than on the wicked one. Then, more explicitly than in the *De planctu naturae* or the *Roman de la Rose,* the poet nullifies the wicked Venus's victory: he defines the only love that fully answers man's need, after he has shown that virtuous love does exist in the world—if only to be failed by a passion or weakness that cannot answer such love.

Notes

1. The distinction eventually reaches back to the Greek *agape* and *eros*. It should be understood that the use of the medieval terms *caritas* and *amor* for divine and earthly love, respectively, reflects a common but not exclusive tradition. *Amor,* especially, was used ambiguously by some writers. The subject is thoroughly treated by Irving Singer, *The Nature of Love, Plato to Luther* (New York: Random House, 1966).
2. Lotharii Cardinalis (Innocenti III) *De miseria humane conditionis,* ed. Michele Maccarrone (Lugano: Thesaurus Mundi, 1955), 2. 21, p. 55. The translation is from Donald R. Howard, ed. *On the Misery of the Human Condition,* trans. Margaret Mary Dietz (New York: The Bobbs-Merrill Co., Library of Liberal Arts, 1969), pp. 48–49.
3. Hugh of Saint Victor, *On the Sacraments of the Christian Faith* [*De Sacramentis*], trans. Roy J. Deferrari (Cambridge, Mass.: The Mediaeval Academy of America, 1951), Book 2, Part 11. 7, p. 339.
4. *Ibid.,* 1–3, pp. 324–25.
5. Saint Augustine, *De civitate Dei,* 14. 26. The translation is from George Boas, *Essays on Primitivism and Related Ideas in the Middle Ages* (The John Hopkins Press, 1948; reprint ed., New York: Octagon Books, 1966), p. 49.
6. Giovanni Boccaccio, *Teseida,* ed. Aurelio Roncaglia (Bari: G. Laterza, 1941), *Chiose,* p. 417. I am indebted for this passage to Chauncey Wood, *Chaucer and the Country of the Stars* (Princeton: University Press, 1970), p. 68.
7. Erwin Panofsky, *Studies in Iconology* (1939, Oxford University Press; reprint ed., New York: Harper & Row, Harper Torchbook, 1962), p. 142. The works of Panofsky and Wood (cited

above) along with those of Jean Pépin, *Mythe et Allégorie* (Paris: Aubier, 1958) and Jean Seznec, *The Survival of the Pagan Gods,* trans. Barbara F. Sessions (1953, Pantheon Books; reprint, New York: Harper & Row, Harper Torchbook, 1961) supply valuable background to the subject. Specific discussions of the two Venuses may be found also in D. W. Robertson, Jr., *A Preface to Chaucer* (Princeton: Princeton University Press, 1962), pp. 124–27; Richard L. Hoffman, *Ovid and the Canterbury Tales* (Philadelphia: University of Pennsylvania Press, 1966), pp. 13–17, and "*The Canterbury Tales,*" in *Critical Approaches to Six Major English Works,* ed. R. M. Lumiansky and Herschel Baker (Philadelphia: University of Pennsylvania Press, 1968), pp. 54–59.

8. Iohannis Scotti, *Annotationes in Marcianum,* ed. Cora E. Lutz (1939, The Mediaeval Academy of America; reprint ed., New York: Kraus Reprint Co., 1970), 62. 12, p. 67.
9. *Ibid.,* 8. 8, p. 13: "Hinc est generalis et specialis libido"; and 12. 15, p. 21.
10. *Scriptores Rerum Mythicarum Latini Tres Romae Nuper Reperti,* ed. G. H. Bode (1834, Celle; reprint ed., Hildesheim: Georg Olms, 1968), Mythogr. III. 11. 18, p. 239. For Remigius, see E. H. Alton, "The Mediaeval Commentators on Ovid's *Fasti,*" *Hermathena* 20 (1930): 136.
11. Bernardus Silvestris, *Commentum super sex libros Eneidos Virgilii,* ed. W. Riedel (Greifswald, 1923), p. 9.
12. *Ovide moralisé,* ed. C. de Boer, *Verhandlingen der Koninklijke Akademie van Wetenschappen,* Afdeeling Letterkunde, 15, 21, 30, 37, 43 (Amsterdam, 1915–1938), Book 4, 21: 1634–35.
13. *Scriptores Rerum Mythicarum,* ed. Bode, pp. 230–32.
14. *The Anglo-Latin Satirical Poets and Epigrammatists of the Twelfth Century,* ed. Thomas Wright, *Rerum Britannicarum Medii Aevi,* Rolls Series, 59 (1872; reprint ed., Wiesbaden: Kraus Reprint Ltd., 1964), vol. 2, 429. All quotations and references are to this edition. See the excellent studies by Richard Hamilton Green, "Alan of Lillie's *De Planctu Naturae,*" *Speculum* 31 (1956): 649–74; and Winthrop Wetherbee, "The Function of Poetry in the *De Planctu Naturae* of Alain de Lille," *Traditio* 25 (1969): 87–125.
15. Ernest Langlois, ed., *Le Roman de la Rose,* 5 vols., SATF 71 (Paris, 1920–1924). All quotations and references are to this edition. A useful recent study of the poem is that by John V. Fleming, *The Roman de la Rose: A Study in Allegory and Iconography* (Princeton: Princeton University Press, 1969).
16. F. N. Robinson, ed., *The Works of Geoffrey Chaucer,* 2d ed. (Boston: Houghton Mifflin Company, 1957), p. 312. All quotations and references to the works of Chaucer are to this edition.
17. All references are to the edition by G. C. Macauley, *The Complete Works of John Gower* (Oxford: Oxford University Press, 1901), vols. 2 and 3. See George D. Economou, "The Character Genius in Alan de Lille, Jean de Meun, and John Gower," *ChauR* 4 (1970): 203–10. For a full treatment of the Natura allegories and their background, see Economou, *The Goddess*

Natura in Medieval Literature (Cambridge, Mass.: Harvard University Press, 1972).

18. All references are to the edition by T. B. W. Reid, *Yvain* (Manchester: Manchester University Press, 1967).
19. It is interesting to note that in *Erec et Enide* (411 ff.) Chrétien invokes this commonplace without disturbing the hierarchy in the description of Enide.
20. All quotations and references are to the edition by Karl Lachmann, *Wolfram von Eschenbach* (Berlin: Walter de Gruyter & Co., 1926, reprint ed. 1965).
21. See W. T. H. Jackson, "The Literary Views of Gottfried von Strassburg," *PMLA* 85 (1970): 992–1001.
22. All references are to the edition by Friedrich Ranke, *Tristan und Isold* (Dublin/Zurich: Weidmann, 1968).
23. For a succinct account, see D. W. Robertson, Jr., "The Concept of Courtly Love," in *The Meaning of Courtly Love*, ed. F. X. Newman (Albany: State University of New York Press, 1968), pp. 9–12.
24. Morton W. Bloomfield, "Distance and Predestination in *Troilus and Criseyde*," in *Essays and Explorations: Studies in Ideas, Language and Literature* (Cambridge, Mass.: Harvard University Press, 1970), p. 207. This influential essay first appeared in *PMLA* 72 (1957): 14–26, and has been reprinted in *Chaucer Criticism*, vol. 2, ed. Richard J. Schoeck and Jerome Taylor (Notre Dame: University of Notre Dame Press, 1961), pp. 196–210.

Bibliographic Note

In addition to the works cited in the footnotes, the following studies are pertinent to some of the authors and poems discussed in Chapter I. C. S. Lewis, *The Allegory of Love* (London: Oxford University Press, 1953) is a necessary starting point for the student of allegory. F. J. E. Raby, *A History of Christian Latin Poetry*, 2d ed. (Oxford: The Clarendon Press, 1953) and *A History of Secular Latin Poetry in the Middle Ages*, 2 vols. (Oxford: The Clarendon Press, 1934), along with Ernst Robert Curtius, *European Literature and the Latin Middle Ages*, trans. Willard R. Trask (New York: Pantheon, 1953) are standard works in their subjects. Peter Dronke, *Medieval Latin and the Rise of European Love-Lyric*, 2 vols. (Oxford: The Clarendon Press, 1965) offers a fairly comprehensive view of the relationships between Latin poetry and that of the vernaculars. The best single volume available on the intellectual backgrounds of Alanus de Insulis and the School of Chartres is M.-D. Chenu, *La théologie au douzième siècle* (Paris: Librairie Philosophique J. Vrin, 1957); many of this work's chapters have been collected and translated into English under the title *Nature, Man, and Society in the Twelfth Century* by Jerome Taylor and Lester K. Little (Chicago: University of Chicago Press, 1968). The recently published work of Winthrop Wetherbee, *Platonism and Poetry in the Twelfth Century: The Literary Influence of the School of Chartres* (Princeton: Princeton University Press, 1972) is also an important study. J. A. W. Bennett, *The Parlement of Foules: An Interpretation* (Oxford: The Clarendon Press, 1957) deals with several subjects that are relevant to this chapter; the same author's essay "Gower's 'Honeste Love'," in *Patterns of Love and Courtesy,* ed. John Lawlor (Evanston: Northwestern University Press, 1966) is also useful. The bibliography of *Troilus and Criseyde* is too great to cite at any length; Charles Muscatine's chapter on the poem in *Chaucer and the French Tradition* (Berkeley and Los Angeles: University of California Press, 1957) has been highly influential. Alfred David, "The Hero of the *Troilus,*" *Speculum* 37 (1962): 566–81, presents a reading of the poem that agrees in some ways with the one presented here.

CHAPTER II

The Array of Perspectives in the Early Courtly Love Lyric

Frederick Goldin

The tradition of the two Venuses offered a way of representing one of the basic and most intriguing subjects of medieval literature: the opposed tendencies of earthly love. Oriented upward, love is in harmony with a divine intention and with the true welfare of a community; sinking down to lust, love is blind to everything but itself and thus destructive. The integrative and disintegrative power of love is revealed through its effect in a community, whether a court or a city.

Encircling the central love-relation in the romance is a broad array of characters who are ruled in varying degrees by *Venus legitima* and *Venus scelestis,* and who therefore react in different ways to the lovers in their midst. Some are deeply sympathetic, others intent on destroying and discrediting them; at times, there is something defective in this love-relation, and the external view of it has the effect of correcting and enhancing it.

This romance pattern of a central love-relation defined by the various perspectives on it has a precise parallel in the courtly lyric. The courtly community is represented in the lyric by the audience; the directions that love may take, by the different kinds of persons in that audience and the conflicting impulses of the "I," the courtly lover, in the lyric. In close correspondence to the characters of the romance, the lyric audience consists of friends and enemies who are so designated by the singer as he responds to them in the course of his song. Thus both the courtly romance and the courtly lyric set out a pattern of friends and enemies radiating from a central love-relation upon which they are all intent. The romance being narrative, the lovers and those who witness their relation are in continual movement; the lyric is expressive, the pattern static.

This pattern of perspectives is already present in some of the lyrics of "the first troubadour," Guillem IX (1071–1126).[1] In these same lyrics the essential themes of courtly love appear fully developed, and this repertory of themes hardly changes throughout the entire period with which we are concerned in this chapter, neither among the troubadours nor among the *Minnesänger*. Because of this, it is difficult, if not impossible, to prove a "development" in the history of the early courtly lyric, or even in the work of a single poet. It does often happen that a poet who writes courtly love lyrics on conventional themes will also take up the theme of "low love," ridiculing that posture of service and longing in which courtly lovers stand so still, or repudiating all earthly love in the light of heavenly love. But it is not always demonstrable that the songs celebrating one kind of love came before or after the others, or even that there was any kind of thematic sequence at all.

It is clear, however, that the poets who seem most committed to courtly love are among the most eager to make fun of it. This is one of the most striking characteristics of the courtly love lyric, and the idea of "development" hardly accounts for it, especially when courtly love is affirmed and repudiated in the same lyric—a regular occurrence, as we shall see. It is clear that the repudiation of courtly love was also a part of the repertory of essential themes that remained constant throughout the classic or best period. These conflicting attitudes toward courtly love express the same tendencies toward the order of community and toward the chaos of self-regard represented by the figure of the two Venuses.

The basic fiction which provides the subject matter of these lyrics is everywhere the same, and it is every bit as stereotyped as all the other elements of courtly love poetry, both lyric and romance. In the lyric, this fiction is fragmented, analyzed into a fixed register of episodes, moods, and postures, from which the poet draws in order to arrange a certain nonnarrative pattern.[2] The main effort of this chapter will be to describe those various fragments and to define the principle by which the poets arranged them in a lyric form.

The courtly audience knew this fiction thoroughly, and once it heard the opening lines it would place each lyric at a specific point in the round of courtly love. At the beginning of every song there is a clear indication as to where the lover is, in the pattern of his amorous career. He may be in or out of harmony with the season; overcome with joy at what he believes is a promise of the lady's love, or beginning to wonder why she sends no sign; calling for the counsel of his friends, or singing of his loneliness in exile; bragging about the joys of "low love," or remembering the illusion of his joy. The opening lines, like the opening moves of a game, determine the possibilities that can follow. Every lyric finds its place in the fixed and universal fiction of courtly love. Once the audience located the lyric, it would know exactly what to expect, and the poet would go on to satisfy or astonish his listeners. The song we read today was first written as an arrangement of the audience's expectations. That is why it is necessary, for a moment, to abstract that fiction from the poetry that gives it life.

The courtly man loves a beautiful lady whose name he cannot publicly reveal for fear of the harm that would come to her reputation through the spies and slanderers who infest the court. Those who sympathize with him, however, those whom he calls his friends, understand that she is the most beautiful and virtuous lady in the "world," or the small circle of courtly society. He has served this lady long and faithfully—he was born to serve her—as a vassal serves his lord, and he has for too long been denied requital for his service. Sometimes—not so rarely as has been made out—the "reward" is given. Usually, however, the lover must be deprived of it for countless reasons: the ubiquitousness of those spies and slanderers; the great social and ethical distance, often represented as a spatial distance, that separate this aspiring lover from that exalted lady; or the murderous jealousy of the lady's husband, if she has one. There are dozens of reasons for the separation—each a pretext to preserve the distance of the lady and the illusion of her ideality.

Across that distance, if the lover is fortunate, a sign may come from the lady, in rare moments of extraordinary grace, a sign that the lover may regard as a recognition of his courtliness and devotion. That sign may be anything from a fleeting smile to the gift of her body: it hardly matters, so long as what is given is regarded as a signal gift, a marking of the lover's worth and, to a certain degree, his acceptance. As long as lover and lady are still felt to be related as aspirant and ideal, she may even grant the lover everything he prays for and still retain that imperious and anonymous dignity. But the singer—the performer who stands before the audience in the role of a courtly lover—must not hint of any passion on her side, because her passion would transform her into an ordinary woman, a mortal and faulty and desiring creature, like everyone else. Once blemished by concern and desire, she can still serve as the object of the lover's lust—as she does in other lyric genres—but not of his adoration, which alone gives dignity to his longing and subservience. Nor can she have much personality. If she is identified and localized, she again becomes a mere woman, impossible to idealize: the lover who worships a distant and unnameable lady knows perfectly well what to make of a mere woman, for as man he is full of lust, and as a literary man he is heir to a long tradition of antifeminism. This vagueness regarding the beloved lady—her namelessness, her abstract qualities, her continual absence—are all necessary to make her credible as the goal of the lover's service and the judge of his worth. Therefore, there is something positive about that vagueness, which expresses, in the language of ordinary things, her ideality and universal meaning.

The unattainability of the lady and the suffering of the lover are ethical necessities in the fiction of courtly love. Courtly love, *fin' amors,* is the love of courtliness, of the refinement that distinguishes a class, of an ideal fulfilled in a person whom everyone recognizes.[3] This love-relation enables the courtly man to declare his commitment to the ideals of his class, and to exemplify the behavior in which those ideals are realized: steadfastness, optimism, devoted service, formality, personal grace, self-esteem, self-sacrifice. The singer describes for his audience how, in his devotion to this mirror of courtliness, he has known such suffering and joy as only a man of inherent nobility can experience. He suffers loneliness because he must remain distant from his beloved; uncertainty, because she is capricious as grace itself; despair, because gazing on her beauty and her moral perfection he understands he must renounce every claim to requital. But the surprising thing is that this despair brings him great joy, for it proves beyond all doubt the steadfastness of his devotion. In renouncing his vassal's "right" to requital, he proves that the lady's virtues are more precious to him than any common pleasure: for these are the virtues that define the courtly class, and his devotion proves his courtliness. Somehow, miraculously, through love, he has been brought to a level of refinement where a greater joy awaits him than any he ever knew or hoped for. The signal of that joy is the lady's smile of pleasure, but its source is his awareness of his own worth and nobility. Only a truly courtly man can love without requital; only such a man can have as the real object of his love the perfect courtliness embodied in the lady. The very condition of loving and desiring her is the condition of being courtly—longing for her is more valuable than possessing her. The singer can boast of his loyalty in the absence of all recognition, even in the absence of his beloved: such restraint and constancy are the signs by which the courtly man is recognized. The lady may be remote and unresponsive, but the courtly audience recognizes him, and itself in him. They behold in him the ideal of the courtly man, and in his service the very activity of courtliness. The moral dignity of the whole class is expressed in this rare love, which transcends the desires of the body and defers requital for the sake of refinement. The song thus has a universal and an individual significance: the singer reveals to the audience its own idealized image and at the same time proves his right to belong to the courtly class. The singer represents the courtly class in its most glorious light through the figure of the courtly man in the service of love.

Courtly love is an integrative force, a legitimate love, uniting the members of the audience, and the courtly singer with his class. This public value has a parallel in the inner life of the lover, for the poet declares that love alone gives order to all his inner motions and stability to his character. Without love he would be nothing, he declares, speaking continually out of the sense of his own incompleteness; and so he makes demands upon himself, ethical demands that he represents as coming from the lady. In struggling to fulfill those demands, he fulfills himself.

All conscientious men, of whatever time or place, make demands upon themselves because they are aware of their own unfulfilled potentialities; they struggle to repair this incompleteness, each by cleaving to the image of his perfected self and laboring to realize it. The force with which each man strives to become one with that idealized image is the force that preserves his identity. This stabilizing effect of the self-image is a fact of human nature: what distinguishes the courtly man is that this image of his hoped-for self has merged with the image of the lady in his mind. To judge his present worth he looks to her, and if he is fortunate, she will give him some sign, and then he will know whether he is on the way toward becoming what he wants to be, what he knows he ought to be.

He therefore gives her a terrible power over him, the power to judge him and to formulate his identity. He derives great advantages from it: a single goal for all his endeavors, a meaning for all his experience and, most important, the present and immediate sense of courtly worth. The distance that separates him from the lady is impenetrable and precious, because it is a visual translation of the distance that separates every man from the guiding image of his completeness. The courtly man is localized in time and place and distinguished from aspiring men of other generations in these two ways: first, that image coincides with the self-image of his class, so that the more he pursues his own desires, the more he is at one with his equals, the more he is part of a community; second, that personal image of his own perfection, because it is embodied in the person of the lady, is now capable of responding to him, of loving him and making it possible for him to be at one with the image that guides him. This joy is worth the renunciation of every other joy, for it gives inner peace and certainty. Here now is the perfect dream of love: all the aspects of the courtly man become harmonious and one.

All these advantages have to be paid for, however, and at a steep price. Since distance is the necessary condition of his love, the lover usually has nothing of the lady but her image. Even if her body visits him from time to time, it is so glorified by those multifarious distances that he is, in effect, bereft of her presence.[4] This makes his life very hard, because even though he is a spiritually privileged nobleman, he also has the ordinary man's desires—he makes that very clear—and those desires cannot find much satisfaction in an image.

But there is worse yet in store for him. Since he spends so much time alone with that image in his heart, adoring its perfection, the moment must come when he must wonder about its validity: does that image in the heart coincide, morally, with the real living lady who is far away? If that image represents to his inward gaze a goodness that will not let him suffer vainly and that rejoices in his love of virtue, then how, considering the indifference of the real lady (as distinct from the image in his mind), can goodness be said to dwell in her? The courtly lover must eventually suspect that the image surpasses the fact. Once that happens—and it must, for it is part of the framing fiction of courtly love—he must suffer grave doubts about the moral reality of the real lady. Once his belief in her perfection falters, he is in danger of losing everything, all reason for action, all meaning to his life. His love for her identifies him as a courtly man: if this lady turns out to be merely ordinary, his public reality is obliterated. She is no paragon but a mere woman now, and service to her no longer corroborates his identity. Even her beauty seems to be diminished. Heinrich von Morungen, in a famous lyric (MF 145, 1–32), laments the *versertez mündelin,* "the damaged mouth," of the lady in his dream, a grave distress caused by his awakening.

This doubt and its disturbing consequences arise from the very nature of courtly love. As a literary theme it is an ameliorating and unifying influence, but as the basis of an actual relation between flesh-and-blood lovers it is simply ridiculous. The most obvious reason for this is the virtual dematerialization of the lady: she is far away, abstract, devoid of mortal qualities. As part of an ethical system, this vagueness may be understandable, but as part of a love affair, judged by common sense and common experience, it can easily make the poetry seem absurd. And, equally impossible to believe is the lover's servility. The courtly lyric sets forth a lonely man longing for an invisible and often insensate lady, a man proud of being deprived and content with ethereal rewards, convinced by the lady's cruelty of her beneficent effect. Who in his right mind could believe such things? And how can any literature extolling such love be anything but ridiculous?

And yet, surprisingly enough, the poets found a way to overcome the absurdity inherent in their subject matter, and they sang of this love in such a way that their songs inspired the most sophisticated audience in their time and still remain moving and admirable in ours. It was, in part, through their expression of doubt that they triumphed over the foolishness of their theme.

Courtly love could be esteemed, and the lover's loyalty applauded, as long as the fictional frame was visible—as long as those who heard the song did not believe what they heard in the same way that they believed the literal truth. Courtly love understood as fiction might be inspiring; understood as autobiography it would be contemptible. The poets found a simple and wonderful way of preventing their words from being mistaken for literal truth: they showed how ridiculous their love would be if it *were* the literal truth. A love full of nothing but promises—man's flesh could not stand it! When these poets deal with the carnal inadequacy of courtly love, they are very funny; indeed, no one could make fun of them as brilliantly as they make fun of themselves. But they gained a point by their self-mockery. For once they dissolved, by their laughter, all that was ridiculous in their love, they showed they still had something left, something precious and worthy of veneration—and undeniable.

But first they had to laugh at themselves. Often they signalled the absurdity of their love by representing themselves as their enemies saw them. These enemies, who can neither understand nor tolerate the singer's claim that he loves like an angel, are amply represented throughout the courtly love lyric.

Every reader knows them, for they are continually cited by the poets, and they form a kind of hierarchy of maliciousness and vulgarity. In the *Minnesang* they are called *die nideren, die lugenaere, die merkaere, die huoter, die valschen*—vulgarians, slanderers, spies, watchers, hypocrites. This does not by any means exhaust the list, and even the meanings of these terms vary from context to context. The troubadours call them *lauzengier, trichador, savai, fola gens, fals amador*—flatterers and slanderers, intriguers, vicious ones, mad ones, false lovers. The terms, and the types they designate, are numerous. The singer must know them and their habits, because unless he can defend himself against them, they will ruin all his hopes. For what they all have in common is a wish to discredit his love.

The false lovers, to begin with them, are masters of the art of praise, but in truth they have no feelings; nothing in them can ever be moved but their tongues. That is bad enough, however, for their tongues have great derivative power. Since the courtly love lyric is a literature of clichés, the false lovers say exactly the same things in their songs as the true lover says in his. Heinrich von Morungen calls them parrots: they can say "*Minne*" and never think of what it means (MF 131, 25 ff.). They are so numerous and their songs sound so convincing that the lady might not be able to distinguish these parrots from the man who speaks with brains and heart. After all, if a man says that he writes more than a hundred letters with his tears and sends them on to the lady (Bernart, *Erd•m cosselhatz*), how can one tell, from his words alone, whether he is expressing real grief and devotion, or like the false lovers only mouthing it? The great danger is that the lady might believe the true lover's words to be as empty as theirs, for it is very hard to distinguish intentions when everyone must speak in platitudes. Every poet wishes there were a way to recognize these flatterers and false lovers. If only they had horns on their foreheads, says Bernart (*Non es meravelha*).

Besides their power to cast a pall of hypocrisy over the most heartfelt words, these enemies present another danger: the lady might start believing them. If that ever happens, the true lover—the singer—will be out in the cold. For the false lovers' praise, though hypocritical, is maddeningly accurate; and once she takes it seriously, she will never take *him* seriously, she will misprize his sincerity and trust their flattery. Eloquent testimony, this fear of the poet's, that his glorious ideal of courtliness is lodged in a weak vessel. Bemused by flattery, she will disdain the only man whose praise begins in love. Bernart says more than once that he has lost his joy through the flattery of his enemies.[5]

These people who debase the language of devotion are not the only enemies the singer must overcome. However empty their hearts may be, they play along, they speak the formulas and make the gestures of courtly love. There are others still who want to wreck the game entirely, because they cannot understand it, or because they take it all too seriously. To them the singer is simply a liar. In Huizinga's terms, the false lovers are cheats because they play with nothing real at stake.[6] But these others—*diu liute,* the *gens vilana,* "the vulgar ones"—they are spoilsports who, in their pure carnality, cannot believe that anything is true unless it is literally true.

They listen to the singer's words and watch him closely. To them he appears like a man engaged in a conversation with a concealed interlocutor, and they want to know who this other person is, assuming that she even exists, and what the singer really means by the things he says about her. For he says that her "goodness" has inspired him to renounce every demand for requital. When they hear that, they know that such love cannot exist: no normal man would idolize a woman and wait endlessly for her favor; and he surely would not boast about it if he did. And so these "vulgar ones" hang on to his words, scrutinizing them for evidence of his insincerity, because they know in their bones that he could not mean what he says, at least not in the way people ordinarily mean things. "They twist the meaning of my words," says Heinrich. "There love is vulgar love (*amors communaus*)," says Bernart; "it does not love unless it gets something (*si non pren*)."[7] Their great hope is to prove that the singer's love is no different from their lust; or else that the singer's posture of humility is simply contemptible, the fawning of a fool.[8]

The false lovers, on the other hand, are eager to pay lip service to the loftiest Venus they can imagine, for they are hypocrites, and their praise costs them nothing. They are, it is clear, the other poets of the court, the singer's rivals.[9] Now he, being a poet and, whether he likes it or not, a colleague of theirs, can pick them out immediately and recognize their ignobility and disorder by their language:

Be conosc a lor parladura
qu'ilh renhon mal, contra natura.

Be·m cuidei de chantar sofrir

I can tell by their words
that they lead bad lives, unnatural lives.

This is a constant theme in Bernart's poetry: the song's worth depends on the depth of the singer's love (*Non es meravelha*). Hence the debased poetry of the "false lovers."

Will the lady be able to see this, or will anyone else? To the ear that is not correctly attuned—a sure sign of inner disorder —these songs sound much alike. The singer can never be sure about the lady's powers of discernment. Sometimes he despairs of her ability to see that the truth lies only in his songs and not in theirs; sometimes he thinks she will see it, after all. In *Can la freid' aura venta,* for example, he complains that true lovers are rarely loved in return; a deceitful man has better luck in love. If it were not for "the vulgar ones" and the slanderers, he would enjoy love in certainty. But he has one hope: she told him, that week when he parted from her land, that his songs pleased her, thus suggesting, perhaps, that she perceives the difference between his songs and theirs. Now he waits, in complete uncertainty, to find out whether this is true.

Thus the singer's enemies threaten him in two ways; they want to taint his love with their carnality; and by their very presence they obliterate his sincerity. They threaten to make his foolish words appear to rise, like their own, from a scheming head and an empty heart. How can he, composing in the vein of this formalistic and platitudinous poetry, somehow sound different from them? How can he do something in his song that they cannot do, even though they share a common station and a common repertory of themes and figures of speech?

He was, in fact, already distinguished from them in one telling way: he could understand their point of view, for he was, like them, a carnal man; but they could never understand his, for they were nothing but carnal. Therefore, he could represent his love as they saw it—servile and ridiculous—and he could praise its nobility and reveal its meaning, as they could not. Because they saw the courtly lover as a fool he would often mock himself. But that self-mockery would prepare the way for his triumph over them; he would defeat his enemies by incorporating them into his song.

This strategy of representing both the friendly and hostile viewpoints of the singer's audience is a definitive characteristic of the early courtly love lyric. Bernart de Ventadorn, whose songs we shall now consider, is unsurpassed in this regard.

Lancan vei la folha
jos dels albres chazer,
cui que pes ni dolha,
a me deu bo saber.
No crezatz qu'eu volha
flor ni folha vezer, [I.]
car vas me s'orgolha
so qu'eu plus volh aver.
Cor ai que m'en tolha,
mas no•n ai ges poder,
c'ades cuit m'acolha,
on plus m'en dezesper.

Estranha novela
podetz de me auzir,

que, can vei la bela
que•m soli' acolhir,
era no m'apela
ni•m fai vas se venir. [II.]
Lo cor sotz l'aissela
m'en vol de dol partir.
Deus, que•l mon chapdela,
si•lh platz, m'en lais jauzir,
que s'aissi•m revela,
no•i a mas del morir.

Non ai mais fiansa
en agur ni en sort,
que bon' esperansa
m'a confondut e mort,
que tan lonh me lansa
la bela cui am fort, [III.]
can li quer s'amansa,
com s'eu l'agues gran tort.
Tan n'ai de pezansa
que totz m'en desconort;
mas no•n fatz semblansa,
c'ades chant e deport.

Als non sai que dire
mas: mout fatz gran folor
car am ni dezire
del mon la belazor.
Be deur' aucire
qui anc fetz mirador! [IV.]
Can be m'o cossire,
no•n ai guerrer peyor.
Ja•l jorn qu'ela•s mire
ni pens de sa valor,
no serai jauzire
de leis ni de s'amor.

Ja per drudaria
no m'am, que no•s cove;
pero si•lh plazia
que•m fezes cal que be,
eu li juraria
per leis e per ma fe, [V.]
que•l bes que•m faria
no fos saubutz per me.
En son plazer sia,
qu'eu sui en sa merce.
Si•lh platz, que m'aucia,
qu'eu no m'en clam de re.

Ben es dreihz qu'eu planha,
s'eu pert per mon orgolh
la bona companha
e•l solatz c'aver solh.
Petit me gazanha

lo fols arditz qu'eu colh, [VI.]
car vas me s'estranha
so qu'eu plus am e volh.
Orgolhs, Deus vos franha,
c'ara•n ploron mei olh.
Dreihz es que•m sofranha
totz jois, qu'eu eis lo•m tolh.

Encontra•l damnatge
e la pena qu'eu trai,
ai mo bon uzatge:
c'ades consir de lai.
Orgolh e folatge
e vilania fai [VII.]
qui•n mou mo coratge
ni d'autra•m met en plai
car melhor messatge
en tot lo mon no•n ai,
e man lo•lh ostatge
entro qu'eu torn de sai.

Domna, mo coratge
•l melhor amic qu'eu ai, [VIII.]
vos man en ostatge
entro qu'eu torn de sai.

I. When I see the leaves
falling from the trees—
whomever that may grieve,
it gives me pleasure.
Do not think I want
to see flowers or leaves,
for the one I most desire to have
is haughty toward me.
I have the will to leave,
but not the power;
for I always think she may yet receive me,
even as I most despair of it.

II. There is this strange news
that you can hear about me:
when I see the beautiful lady
who used to receive me,
she does not call me now
or summon me to her.
The heart in my breast
wants to break with grief.
If it please God, who governs the world,
may He let me have some joy of her,
for if she keeps on resisting me,
there is nothing left but to die.

III. I have no more faith
in augury and divination,
for good hope

has destroyed and slain me,
because the beautiful lady I love so much
thrusts me so far away from her
when I seek her love
as though I had done some great wrong.
This grieves me so,
that I am in despair.
But I do not show it,
for I continue to sing and act joyful.

IV. There is nothing else I can say
but this: I commit a great folly
because I love and desire
the most beautiful lady in the world.
I would have gladly slain
the man who invented the mirror.
When I think about it,
I do not have a worse enemy.
From the moment she gazes on herself
and thinks of her great worth,
I shall never enjoy
her or her love.

V. Let her not love me with her body,
for that would not be fitting.
But if it should please her
to do me any kind of good,
I'd swear to her,
on my loyalty,
that the good she did me
would never be revealed by me.
Let it all be as she pleases,
for I am at her mercy.
Let her kill me, if she wants to;
I would not complain about a thing.

VI. But it would be right that I lament
if I, through my pride, should lose
her good company
and the pleasure I used to have.
My foolhardiness
has gained me little,
for she whom I most love and desire
is hostile to me.
O Pride, God shatter you,
for now my eyes must weep because of you.
It is right that I lack
all joy, for it is I who deprive myself of it.

VII. Against the loss
and the pain I bear
I have my own good way:
I always think of the place where she is.
Whoever tries to change my heart

or distract me with another woman
is guilty of pride and madness
and villainy,
for I have no better messenger
in all the world [than my heart],
and I send it to her as a hostage
till I return from here.

VIII. Lady, my heart,
the best friend that I have,
I send to you as hostage
till I return from here.

The first two strophes find the lover cultivating the mood of despair. In I, he is environed and in an odd way pleased, by the natural image of his desolation. In II, his present misery puts him in mind of a past time that was happier, and makes him look forward either to a happier future or no future at all. This love, therefore, has been of some duration, has gone through many vicissitudes and will go on to death. But through his expectations in the past and his disillusionment now, he has been freed from the tortures of hope. The proof that he no longer rises to the lure of the future (in III) is that he no longer puts any faith in augury and prophecy.

Then, rather suddenly, after thirty-four lines of specifying his misery, he turns this long complaint into a boast. No amount of suffering can eradicate his quality as a poet and courtly man: *c'ades chant e deport,* he continues to hold to that gay and graceful bearing which distinguishes his class. And then we know who that "you" is, whom he addresses in the first two strophes (*crezatz, podetz*): the courtly audience, before whom he is proving his right to take his place among them.

Before this audience, he exalts the lady beyond the reach of ordinary passion. His despair is the most nearly adequate way he has to praise her perfection. Just as he depicted himself encircled by desolation, now he depicts the lady involved in a circle of self-contemplation before her mirror, for her virtue is so great that only her own image is adequate to her. The lady and her lover are as far apart as can be, but somehow, in their very oppositeness, they are related, for she is the mirror of courtliness and he yearns to be an image of that perfection, to be her mirror. At the present time, only his despair can mirror her perfection, but being born of love and loyalty it exalts him in the eyes of the audience. It is a static, tense relation that the audience beholds and finds itself involved in: those who are truly courtly recognize their perfect image in him—his very despair perfects it. He stands before them as though his gaze were fixed on his lady; she is depicted as locked beyond all pity in her self-regard.

The lover and his lady are so enclosed within their separate and remote circles that there is no way to her; though he perpetually ascends some scale of worthiness, he will never reach the level of her mirror. Only if by some unexpectable grace she should turn her gaze from that mirror to look, if only for a moment, upon her aspiring lover, may he enjoy at least some sign from her. Let her not love me with her body, he says, for he has renounced all hope of that. But if she should do him "some kind of good," he would never tell about it.

With this promise to keep secret anything he might get from her, the singer can no longer be looking up toward her or mindful of his sympathetic friends. He casts a nervous glance through the audience, scanning it for the presence of those who hang on his words ready to smell out the least breath of scandal and spread slander. This sign of his awareness of the presence of his enemies is immediately followed by an example of their effect on him. They think that if he really means the things he is saying, he is a fool. That is what he promptly becomes, and the worst kind of fool, too, a woman's slave: Let her kill me if she wants to, I wouldn't complain about a thing.[16] The sequence that we see here we shall find again and again in Bernart's songs: some sign of the singer's awareness of his enemies is followed by a hyperbolic statement that sounds like self-mockery.

Confronting his enemies now, he is repelled by their carnality. For he, too, is a man full of lust, and now he suffers for it. The lady has thrust him away because of his *arditz* (66), his foolhardiness, his rashness, his physical demands: he has even just now asked for "some kind of good," the kind of good that has to be kept secret. That indirection was another example of his foolhardiness, when he forgets that he must assume a posture of despair and, like his enemies, wants to "get something."

He can, however, turn away from that viewpoint. In his loneliness he always thinks of where she is, and he will not let his heart be distracted. Whoever tries to entangle him with another woman is guilty of "vulgarity," "madness," and "presumption." He will stay faithful to her till he returns *de sai,* "from here," from this region of exile and desolation. Again, for the second time, he faces his enemies, only this time he defies them, whereas before he accommodated them. The lady is "there," the lover is "here," and in this state of separation, which is the essential state of the courtly-love relation, he defeats his enemies, who want to subvert his love by getting him to love another lady, someone close by. They think they can enter the poet's noble circle of despair, and so they are guilty of "presumption."

All the relations in this lyric fit into a pattern of concentric circles: in the very center, the perfect circle of self-reference defined by the lady and her mirror; around her, the orbiting circle of the lover's admiration; around him, the circle of the poet's friends, the true audience of his lament, witnessing his devotion; and outside all these circles of civility, the undemarcated, actual, raptureless world of those excluded enemies. These, then, are the substantive elements of the courtly love lyric: the lover, the beloved, and the audience of friends and enemies.

The strophic order of this song, and the order of the lines within each strophe, are determined by the singer's successive awareness of the various segments in his audience during the performance of the song. Although the song was not exactly ad-libbed, being obviously composed in advance of the performance, it was composed *as* a performance and was meant to sound like a patter of spontaneous references to a familiar, and live, audience.

The song begins with the singer's eye on the friends, whom he addresses directly. The opening gambit, the *Natureingang,* immediately identifies a courtly love lyric. The singer's despair, and his careful avoidance of hope as he considers the future, prepare the friends for words that will certify his courtliness and reaffirm his vow. In the fourth strophe, the idealizing image of the mirror follows naturally from the celebration of the lady as a model of courtliness. But the singer's eye has already begun to move toward his enemies. Their outlook already contaminates that sublime image of the lady rapt in contemplation before the mirror; for their eyes perceive in that image a vain, idle, trivial, and sensual woman, a heartless and mindless sexual creature, such as all women are to the singer's enemies.[11] And the following lines in which he expresses his fear of losing her forever once she sees in the mirror how much she is worth, signify either his respectful sense of unworthiness, or the stupor of her vanity (compare Oiseuse): it all depends on the point of view. By the next strophe (V) he speaks with the coy indirection of pure carnality; for now, beholding her with the eyes of his enemies, he no longer respects that inspiring distance around her: he wants to "get" something. In this same strophe, the singer regards the figure he impersonates, the "courtly lover," from the same point of view, and passes into self-mockery: in this posture of exaggerated vassalage, he becomes the fool his enemies see. But then this comic posture of submission recalls the serious commitment that it mocks. And now (VI) come forth the reaffirming words of humility and loyalty. Once he has returned to himself—or rather, once his eye returns to the regard of his friends, the singer repudiates his enemies and confirms his vow. He is "the man who invented the mirror." He continually adjusts it so that it reflects every segment of his audience and contains every image they see.[12]

This technique of playing through the perspectives of an audience, the technique of the performed song, is the most distinctive feature of the troubadour lyric and of the *Minnesang*. When one compares the two bodies of poetry, the troubadours seem far more playful, less committed to the point of view of the friends. The *Minnesänger* nearly always end their songs on an affirmative note. This is not the case with Bernart and the other troubadours, who are much more prone to acknowledge their sympathy with the enemies, especially when doing so makes for a good ending. For the reaffirmation of service to the rehabilitated lady is only one of two basic endings in Bernart's songs. The other is a precise contradiction: at the end of the song the singer boasts openly that he has abandoned the lady who never requited him and that he has found another who willingly grants him what he most desires, and he is not coy in specifying what that is. Or, if he has not changed ladies, he denounces, or grieves over, the carnality of the lady he has served. And when he boasts, he sounds exactly like those vulgar, mad, presumptuous fools who urged him to do what he is now doing.

Bernart's song, *Be m'an perdut lai enves Ventadorn,* is a

virtuoso performance in this regard. This song, too, begins with the singer in the exile of the lady's rejection, and with his eye on the friends, whom he assures three times over that there is not one bad thing he can say about his lady: he would gladly tell of her faults if he knew of any; but, as he does not know of any, he keeps still. Then he says in the fourth strophe:

> Totz tems volrai sa onor e sos bes
> e•lh serai om et amics e servire,
> e l'amarai, be li plass' o be•lh pes,
> c'om no pot cor destrenher ses aucire.
> No sai domna, volgues o no volgues,
> si•m volia, c'amar no la pogues.
> Mas totas res pot om en mal escrire.

> I shall always desire her honor and her good,
> and I shall be her man, and her lover, and her servant,
> and I shall love her whether it pleases her or grieves her,
> for no one can constrain a heart without killing it.
> I don't know one woman that I could not love,
> if I wanted to, whether she wanted it or not,
> But anything can be set down as something bad.

Now some kind of pivot takes place in this strophe, for the following one (V) begins: *A las autras sui aissi eschazutz,* "And so I have now become available to all other women / anyone who wants to can get me to come to her . . .", and it ends, *car traït m'a la bela de mal aire,* "for that beautiful lady, with her evil nature, has betrayed me." Thus the lady who had absolutely no faults a minute ago, has now, with her evil nature, committed treachery.

In the performance situation, however, this confusing strophe becomes clear enough: the singer's eye has passed into the sector of the enemies, and their look turns him into one of them. The pivot line is the one about the heart's refusing to be constrained, line 25. Heard as the conclusion of the two *pedes,* and therefore as a conclusion drawn from the three lines preceding, this line speaks to the friends: no matter how she receives his love, nothing can stop him from loving her, nothing can "constrain his heart" to withdraw its love because of her indifference.

This line, however, is closely bound to the *cauda,* because it contains the thought or the image, the verbal substance, that the *cauda* will develop. This transitional function of the fourth line is inevitable in any tripartite strophe beginning with *pedes,* such as this one. The structure makes the fourth line responsible for maintaining continuity when the melody and the meter turn. In this particular strophe, Bernart does something extra to ensure that the three lines of the *cauda* will sound consistent with the *pedes:* he repeats, in parallel grammatical form, the idea that the lover is determined to love no matter how the lady reacts: *be li plass' o be•lh pes/ volgues o no volgues.*

If we read line 25 according to its place in the strophic pattern—that is, as an introduction to the *cauda,* the three lines following—we suddenly find that it now speaks to the enemies: since "no one can constrain a heart," nothing can stop him from loving any lady in the world. And so he has become "available" to all women, as he says in the following strophe; any woman that wants him can have him, provided that she does not make him pay too dearly for the "good" she has it in her heart to do him. The meaning of that pivotal line, since by virtue of its position it participates in two contradictory contexts, is impossible to pin down. It all depends on the point of view, for instead of maintaining the coherence of the strophe, it breaks the strophe into two parts that can never fit together.

Thus the alternation of perspectives is played off against the fixed patterns of the song. The interest, the unity, and indeed the meaning of the song reside in this tension between its fixed and variable elements, between everything that is abstract and predetermined and everything that is immediate and spontaneous. The song fits into a fixed design, traced out by the syllable count in the lines, the rhyme pattern, the strophic structure, and a certain thematic program which the motifs, falling predictably into place, fulfill. Upon this grid, the poet plots a much freer movement through an array of perspectives, a movement that draws its energy from the responses of an audience and that overrides the fixed units, sometimes coinciding with them, sometimes almost obliterating them.

This song was severely criticized by Raimon Vidal in the *Razos de Trobar* (before 1240) because of its *razos mal continuadas,* its incoherent or inconsistent assertions.[13] It will be clear from many comparable passages in Bernart that the poet did deliberately what Raimon Vidal regards as a lapse. It is worth noting, though, that Vidal, though he did not know it, was observing a characteristic strategy of Bernart and of the courtly love lyric generally at this time. The false reasoning by which the singer extricates himself from his service marks the point when he begins to respond to the enemies. False reasoning is a sign that the singer is imitating "the vulgar ones"; it is the mark of carnality, and it always appears in great contrast to the strict consequence of true love.[14]

This dialectical technique of representing every viewpoint on love conceivable in courtly society worked well for the troubadour: it enabled him to identify courtly love as a fiction and at the same time to dignify it above every other love in order to fulfill his office. If this way of love is supposed to be the supreme condition of courtliness, then the singer must demonstrate that he chose it freely, when other ways were available. It is just by this technique that he proves that he can see a woman as his enemies see her, but still chooses to exalt her. The singer's awareness of the different viewpoints of carnality and courtliness is the clearest proof that the courtly lover's glorious lady owes her glory to the lover's will. And so the singer mocks himself in behalf of his enemies. No one was a better master at it than Bernart. In this strophe, for example, the singer's casual decision to become a great lover offers a double response to the vulgar element; as he tries to sound like one of them he only succeeds in corroborating their opinion of the courtly lover, whose love, as far as they can see, is never anything else but a solitary decision.

This alternation between courtly love and plain carnality makes perfect sense, in fact, because they are related as different modes of the same kind of love, which the troubadour's dialectical technique can render with perfect truthfulness. In one case, the desired woman is adorned with the defining qualities of a social class; in the other, she is altogether unenhanced and undemanding, momentary and compliant. In either case, the woman has no personal reality, no reality at all except as an object, which the lover endows with attributes according to his desire. Only her raw existence has the certainty of a fact; her qualities are all invented. She is adorned by the lust that dreams of her, the lust of Guillem's *leis de con,*[15] instinctual appetite conjuring up a woman ruled by itself; or the lust called *fin'amors,* lust that is trapped in a maze of exquisite social forms which deflect it from its object and which it must, of necessity, fulfill. The courtly lover is therefore close to his enemies, particularly those he calls the *fals amadors,* the "false lovers." He and they look and talk exactly alike; they are often indistinguishable in the lady's eyes, for the one difference between them is invisible: he chooses this way to love because he is a courtly man. The false lovers follow it only because they are required to, repeating amorous formulas like parrots. In this predicament where sincerity and hypocrisy have the same face and speak the same words, the one way out lies in the movement through all the perspectives of the audience. This technique, which is so perfectly suited for the representation of a love that can know only the object it has itself devised, is also the one way in which the true lover can distinguish himself from the counterfeits, for it enacts his freedom of choice, shows that he has chosen this way, though he could have chosen the other.

At least, that is what it is meant to show the singer's "friends." For it is only in their regard that the singer vindicates his role as a courtly lover, and it is for them that he steps out of that role, to prove that he is free when he chooses to return to it. When he steps outside that circle of joyous despair and witnessing friends, he steps into the world of his enemies. Once there, in the ordinary, actual world, he is, paradoxically, in "exile," because it is only that circle that identifies him. He may yet repudiate his enemies by continuing to sing of his hope to return "yonder," *lai enves Ventadorn:* even though he is in the world of his enemies, where he is just an ordinary carnal man, he will not sink down to their lust. But that does not always happen, as it does not happen here. Once he is no longer in the region where he is recognized, he is no longer controlled by the regard of the friends. In exile he is free to imagine anything he likes, his fantasy knows no limits. He can behold himself favored and loved and caressed by the lady, he can get her image to do anything he wants it to. There is no end to the pleasures he can imagine, because he is in a land without landmarks, and the image in his mind no longer depicts the moral ideals of the courtly class: it is only the female image in an erotic fantasy.[16] Again, this enactment of "exile" is ultimately a service he performs for his friends, for though he does not return to their circle in this song, he will in another. His friends are the audience of his entire music, and they hear each separate song as a strophe in the one encompassing Song of his career. He can refer to earlier times when he sang for them and can trust them to hear each utterance, even his fantastic boasts, as a fulfillment of the task of a dedicated man. This movement of exile and return is one of the patterns that are played out in the play of courtly love.

If we consider that total Song, we can see this pattern of exile and return. The entire corpus of Bernart's lyrics has a single theme: the courtly man loves the way ordinary men love (in "exile"), but that is not enough to satisfy him: he must also love with *fin' amor* (in the circle of courtliness).[17] Speaking in "exile," Bernart ridicules courtly love, as Guillem IX did, by punctuating the lover's gentle speech with outbursts of carnality. A masterpiece in this regard is *Era•m cosselhatz, senhor,* which touches every base in the course of its seven strophes. The lady has another lover, and the singer has to decide whether to give her up or share her. In the first of the *tornadas,* he stops playing the courtly lover and steps into another role:

Domna, a prezen amat
autrui, e me a celat,
si qu'eu n'aya tot lo pro
et el la bela razo.

Lady, in public love
the other one, and me in private,
so that I get all the good of it,
and he the beautiful conversation.

All that virtue and refinement gained through endless service and endless deprivation, the *bels digz,* the cultivated and high-minded conversation of which the courtly class alone is capable: give all that to the other man, I'll take your plain, unedifying body.

He derides the lover by exaggerating his posture of subservience, by making him say that it is good that she treats him unjustly, because then she will feel pity for what she has done;[18] or by making him brag about the one victory he can have, the conquest of her image.[19] One quite hilarious example of the courtly lover's determination to be dominated is in *Can vei la flor, l'erba vert, e la folha.* The singer begins by declaring himself on the question of *vassalatge* and *senhoratge:* in love, one should not be "lord" and make the other his "vassal," and whoever does so courts like a peasant (*vilanamen domneya*)—a telling incoherence, this last remark, since it is only the lady who manifests such "pride." Now he is resolved to be a fool no longer, the lover continues; he is finished with the lady who has lorded it over him. He will go to another lady, a certain one who once received him well but whom he treated with disdain. She will surely not treat him as an inferior. He will make up for his past neglect of her until she leads him to the place where she undresses. However, his posture as he speaks these words is astonishing:

> . . . eu sui sos om liges, on que m'esteya,
> si que de sus de chap li ren mo gatge;
> mas mas jonchas li venh a so plazer. . . .
>
> I am her liege-man, wherever I may be,
> and I offer her my pledge atop my head;
> with my hands joined, I come to serve her will.

The tears in his eyes, he continues, prove that he repents his folly in mistreating her, and he begs for forgiveness. And so, for all his talk of equality (*amdos d'un paratge*), he naturally resumes his former stance of an inferior, and he is back where he began.

What part of the audience is he responding to? It depends on the point of view. He imitates the false lovers, reciting vows of loyalty and subservience to a woman he disdains. He gratifies "the vulgar ones," even as he tries to sound like them, by impersonating the character they see when they regard the courtly lover: a fool who cannot stay off his knees for five minutes and concocts his martyrdom wherever he goes, even though he only wants what every man wants and a willing woman is there to provide. In the end he even satisfies the friends, for they, too, regard "the courtly lover" as an impersonation, a figure that comes forth in a kind of play, to be contemplated and admired but not emulated. He makes that figure ridiculous here, but they know that this self-mockery is a prelude to the singer's victory over his enemies.

Bernart even makes a mockery of one of the great sacred pieties of troubadour song—the singer's declaration that he must sing. This statement is heard repeatedly, as a response to the threat of silence. For in terms both of its object and its substance, the song is in constant danger of annihilation. The lady does not respond to it, nor does she distinguish it from those of the false lovers, and so it seems to be pointless. The false lovers debase his very language with their hypocrisy, for they say the same things he does, he shares all of the fixed elements with them: the "grid" upon which the song is composed. He has to find a way to escape from this obliterating silence, for the friends demand his song, and it must be a joyous song. The singer's silence now would amount to a betrayal, for they regard him as one of their own, as their voice, and his song as the anthem of their courtliness. He must find a way to overcome the lady's monumental unresponsiveness and the effect of the enemies' hypocrisy: he must sing, for the song will be a victory over those who deny courtly love.

This is the piety with which he begins his song, *Estat ai com om esperdutz,* "I was, for a long time, like a madman because of love." But now he has found himself: he has refused to sing, and now sees that he has been cruel to his friends. His mistake was to surrender himself to a lady who never loved him, and he saw too late that his waiting would always be in vain. Now he will follow *her* way and send love letters (*salutz*) everywhere and have an inconstant heart. Because she has another lover, he will be disloyal. In fact, he already loves another woman:

c'autre n'am plus bel' e melhor,
que•m val e m'ayud' e•m socor
e•m fai de s'amor esmenda.

For I love another one of them, a better one and more beautiful,
who does me good and helps me and relieves me
and makes amends to me with her love.

The sudden materialization of this "better" lady—everyone will think of the *gensor* and *bellazor* in Guillem's song "about nothing"[20]—and the fact that her love is to be "compensation" for all his pain and waiting, signify that this new love is no more real, in a personal sense, than his last. She is rather the denigrated image of woman, the image drawn by lust, perceived in exile, in contrast to the glorified image perceived in the circle of friends. In the world of exile all women are deceitful and full of tricks.[21] If we hear the singer's words as part of a performance, as a response to the perspectives of his audience, then we may even say that the first lady has betrayed him and taken another lover *because* he sees things from a viewpoint that cannot recognize fidelity and steadfastness.

In the *tornadas* he returns to the opening theme. He has found a way to end his silence: "I praise God that I can sing again,/ though it may irk my lady Dous-Esgar ["sweet, welcoming look"]/ and her lover." Now he can sing a joyous song, because he has found a woman that requites him: he can sing of the joys of fulfilled desire. He sings now in the service of the enemy Venus and thus completely twists the meaning of the lover's declaration that he "must sing." This particular opening statement announces a singer who builds his career on the dignity of longing, who proves his courtliness by his ability to keep faith with an image: that is what the friends demand and are now set to witness. The song that actually comes forth is a villainous parody of the one that was expected.[22]

Thus, the lover spends much time in exile. But in the career of that encompassing Song he inevitably returns home, to his place in the circle of friends and the role he enacts for them. Having followed the movement into exile, one can follow the movement of return in *La dousa votz ai auzida.* At the start of that song, the lady is "a false and vulgar/ traitress of base lineage/ [who] has betrayed me and is now herself betrayed,/ and cuts the branch with which she is beaten." And she deserves this beating because, while the whole world abandons itself to joy, he sees he is forgotten by love and therefore *fors del dreih viatge,* "off the right road." Finally he strikes the heaviest blow: he will leave her service. It is just at this point that the perspective changes: "And yet, when someone speaks to me of her,/ the words bring me pleasure." And because the singer has now turned to the friends, he returns to her. It was the *lauzenger,* the tale bearers, who made him speak those villainous words, but now he has recovered from their influence: "they are all liars/ who got me to say all those crazy things about her."[23] Now he has found his way back to the *dreih viatge: que tuih sei faih son enter,* "for all her deeds are perfect."

When he is on that "right road," it will always be like this—endlessly bound for her, mocked and bewildered by his enemies, bearing the hopes of his friends. The gaze of everyone in the audience is focused on him; he and they are bound together, as constituents and cocreators of the song. For the length of the performance, the song becomes their common life, the central act of their community, the basis on which each man's place and his relation to the others is determined. As a human creation to which every part of the audience contributes its own special aspect through the medium of the singer, the song is the aural image of the same reality of which the lady is the visual image. The enemies are those who affirm her ordinary lust, and who, in response to the singer's rapture, make him acknowledge carnality in his song. The friends are those who affirm her ideality and gracious concern, and who demand that the singer perform a song of praise. The sum of all these aspects, the form in which they are all united through the dialectical technique, is a song that celebrates the full range of courtly life, defined according to the different levels of love.

Ja mos chantars no m'er onors
encontra•l gran joi c'ai conques,
c'ades m'agr'ops, si tot s'es bos,
mos chans fos melher que non es.
Aissi com es l'amors sobrana,
per que mos cors melhur' e sana,
deuri' esser sobras lo vers qu'eu fatz
sobras totz chans, e volgutz e chantatz.

My song will never bring me honor
equal to the great joy I have won,
for however good it is, I always have a need
that my song be better than it is.
Just as love is supreme,
which keeps my heart whole and makes it better,
so the songs I compose should be supreme,
above every song, both conceived and sung.

The poet has set himself a goal that can never be reached: a Song beyond which nothing greater can be conceived. The remoteness of this goal, its inspiring vagueness, its irresistible incitement to a quest, are no different from the defining attributes of the lady. Indeed, there is no formal distinction possible between his longing for her and his longing for this unattainable song. If he achieves one, he achieves the other, and then he will have "conquered" something whose existence he senses now through his joy. Through the one victory he will experience, and through the other articulate, the harmonious unity of courtly life, the collective reality of the audience, who share with all human life a common base in lust but can soar to heights known only to these happy few.

He will never reach that goal, of course, but the dialectical technique brings him as close as it is possible to come. The performed song will always be sequential, the singer giving his voice now to the friends, now to the enemies; and the lady will never be possessed without being denigrated, nor exalted without being distant. That is why he can never stop singing and can never discover the final image of the lady: *er' ai leis, era no•n ai ges,* "now I have it, now I have it not at all." That is why, in the performance of his song, he never comes to rest in one perspective but turns his gaze continually from one sector of the audience to another, and why all his songs form one unending cycle.[24]

Within that cycle every vision is as real as every other, though at a certain moment courtly love is exalted above every other kind of love. In the next moment it may appear to be patently ridiculous, but then even that ridicule is part of the singer's strategy for victory over his enemies. That victory is essential; it is the object of the game that the singer plays with the audience, for courtly love is, after all its foolishness is granted, the highest love conceivable on the secular plane. The difference between the troubadours and the *Minnesänger* is that the troubadours return to this anchoring perspective in the course of an entire poetic career. Many of their individual songs end with the lover in "exile"; whereas the *Minnesänger* are concerned to signal this victory in every lyric.

If we have concentrated on Bernart to the virtual exclusion of the other troubadours, that is partly because of the very nature of the technique we have tried to describe: it cannot be shown at work except through a reading of each lyric in strophic order from beginning to end.[25] The meaning and structure of any love song consist in its manner of representing and then relinquishing in turn each perspective in a broad array. Therefore, we shall indicate briefly in a note some other poets whose lyrics lend themselves to the kind of reading followed here.[26] We have chosen to concentrate in this chapter on two of the greatest lyric poets in the Middle Ages, Bernart and Reinmar, representatives of the two languages in which the courtly love lyric reached its highest level.

Der lange süeze kumber mîn
an mîner herzelieben vrowen derst erniuwet.
wie möhte ein wunder groezer sîn,
daz mîn verlorner dienest mich sô selten riuwet,
wan ich noch nie den boten gesach [I.]
der mir ie braehte trôst von ir, wan leit und ungemach.
wie sol ich iemer dise unsaelde erwenden?
unmaere ich ir, daz ist mir leit,
so enwart mir nie sô liep, kund i'z verenden.

Wâ nu getriuwer friunde rât?
waz tuon ich daz mir liebet daz mir leiden solte?
mîn dienest spot erworben hât
und anders niht: ob ichz noch niht gelouben wolte,
joch waene i'z nu gelouben muoz. [II.]
des wirt och niemer leides mir unz an mîn ende buoz,
sît si mich hazzet diech von herzen minne.
mirn kunde ez nieman gesagen:
nu bin ichs vil unsanfte worden inne.

Daz si mich alse unwerden habe
als si mir vor gebâret, daz geloube ich niemer;
nu lâze ein teil ir zornes abe,
wan endeclîchen ir genâden beite ich iemer.
von ir enmac ich noch ensol. [III.]
sô sich genuoge ir liebes fröunt, sost mir mit leide wol.
und kan ich anders niht an ir gewinnen,
ê daz ich âne ir hulde sî,
ich wil ir güete und ir gebaerde minnen.

Owê daz alle die nu lebent
wol hânt erfunden wie mir ist nâch einem wîbe
und si mir niht den rât engebent
daz ich getroestet würde noch bî lebendem lîbe.
jô klage ich niht mîn ungemach, [IV.]
wan daz den ungetriuwen ie baz danne mir geschach,
die nie gewunnen leit von sender swaere.
got wolde, erkanden guotiu wîp
ir sumelîcher werben, wie dem waere.

Ein rede der liute tuot mir wê:
dâ enkan ich niht gedulteclîchen zuo gebâren.
nu tuont siz alle deste mê:
si frâgent mich ze vil von mîner frouwen jâren,
und sprechent, welher tage si sî, [V.]
dur daz ich ir sô lange bin gewesen mit triuwen bî.
si sprechent daz ez möhte mich verdriezen.
nu lâ daz aller beste wîp
ir zühtelôser vrâge mich geniezen.

Mac si mich doch lâzen sehen,
ob ich ir waere liep, wie si mich haben wolte.
sît mir niht anders mac geschehen,
sô tuo gelîche deme als ez doch wesen solte,
und lege mich ir nâhe bî [VI.]
und bietez eine wîle mir als ez von herzen sî:
gevalle ez danne uns beiden, sô sî staete;
verliese ab ich ir hulde dâ,
sô sî verborn als obe siz nie getaete.[27]

My long sweet suffering
for my beloved lady is renewed.

How could there be a greater miracle:
my fruitless service gives me no regrets,
and yet I have never once seen the messenger [I.]
that might bring me comfort from her, but only pain and unrest!
How shall I ever escape this torment?
If she is indifferent to me, that makes me grieve;
I would like nothing better than to be able to end it.

Where now is the counsel of loyal friends?
What am I doing, getting pleasure from what ought to grieve me?
My service has won mockery
and nothing else: if I refused to believe that before,
it seems I must believe it now. [II.]
I shall not be free of suffering till I die,
since the one I love with all my heart hates me.
There's no one who could tell me what to do.
I have become deeply disturbed within.

That she really considers me so worthless
as she pretends—I shall never believe that.
Now let her anger abate a little,
for I always await her grace at last.
I cannot and should not go from her. [III.]
If many others enjoy her love, that makes me sad and happy,
and if I cannot otherwise gain anything from her,
rather than go without her favor,
I shall love her for her goodness and demeanor.

Alas that so many alive
know well how I am about a woman
and do not give me counsel,
that I may have some comfort while I still live.
But it's not really my distress that I complain about, [IV.]
it's that faithless lovers have so much better luck than I,
those who never felt the pain of longing.
Would God that noble women understand
the courting of those fellows, what it really is.

One thing these people say upsets me
and I cannot be patient about it—
and now they say it all the more:
they keep on asking me about my lady's age
and talk of how old she must be [V.]
since I have served her faithfully all this time.
They say it to annoy me.
Now may the best of women let
me profit from their vulgar question.

May she yet let me see
what, if I *were* dear to her, she would do with me.
Since nothing otherwise will come my way,
let her act as though things were how they ought to be,

and lay me by her side [VI.]
and offer it to me a while, as though from the heart.
If it pleases us both then, let it go on forever.
But if I lose her favor there,
let it be nullified, as if she never did it.

The "long sweet suffering" that is now "renewed" sets this song at a specific point in the fictional pattern and strictly limits the direction in which the singer can continue. The audience knows all the formulas of progression that he can use after this opening and listens for clues as to which one he will use, as the choice will be determined by whatever segment of the audience has him under its influence. With his eye on the "friends" the singer will renew his vow of service despite all his grief, and thus enact the loyalty of a courtly man. With his eye on the "enemies" he will vow to quit her service and find a simpler woman, or will exaggerate his subservience until it sounds ridiculous and perverse.

Since this grief is "sweet," he is speaking to the friends, and so he says that his suffering brings him no regrets. With the first line of the *Abgesang* he once again "renews" his suffering; and this, too, is part of the same strategy. This new expression of pain and despair enables him to turn back to the friends, this time explicitly, at the beginning of the next strophe, with the motif of the *vriundes rât,* the appeal to friends for counsel. Thus, from the moment he begins his song, the singer is continually influenced by the fictional context and the dominant perspective: the fictional elements are like planets, the segments of the audience like the constellations they cross.

The words *dienest* (4) and *bote* (5) put the song into another kind of setting. *Dienest,* "service," means that his love is "courtly love"; it is the love of "vassal" for "lord," such love as can only exist in a courtly society. The *bote,* who travels from one place to another bearing messages, moves through a familiar terrain, the land in which the singer and his audience reside. The singer performs enclosed in the intimate circle of this audience, that circle itself enclosed by the court, the court by the castle walls, the walls by enormous barriers of privilege and wealth. But the very mention of the *boten* implies a certain demonstrative gesture that breaks through all these concentric circles. The messenger is to come—if he does come—*von ir,* from her castle, far-off, *there*. No poetry is so full of demonstrative gestures penetrating space as the lyrics of courtly love, for in the intimacy of the performance situation the singer has something significant to point to.[28] He enacts the fictional role of "the courtly lover," but the setting of that fiction is real; it is identical with the place in which the singer and his audience are gathered and extends to the boundaries of their region. This contrast between "here" (where the singer stands, whether in exile or surrounded by friends) and "there" (where she is, far away), expresses his longing and his "vassal's" attitude, and also defines a geographical distance, full of inhabitants.

Because the place of the performance is identical with the fictional setting, the audience is bound to play a role, or a number of roles. It cannot, in this circumstance, be a simple spectator: those who listen to the singer's fiction are involved in it as the inhabitants of its setting. They, or their figures, become characters; their responses to the singer's love become the points of view in his fiction. The roles they play are the familiar ones, and they are clearly designated in this song: they are the friends and the manifold enemies of the lover. The friends are called upon for help in the second strophe. "The false lovers," the *fals amador* of the troubadours, are *die ungetriuwen* of the fourth strophe; "the vulgar ones," the *gens vilana* of the troubadours, appear in the fifth strophe as *diu liute,* "the people," and ask their "vulgar question." And so, with his distant love, his land, his friends, and his enemies, the singer has acquired his full secular endowment.

The silence of his friends, in IV, sets him to considering the successes of his enemies. His real complaint, he says, is that faithless lovers have so much better luck than he does.[29] These *ungetriuwen* have never felt the pain of longing. They are the hypocrites who can fashion songs that sound sincere, and their successes inevitably imply a lack of discernment in "good women." These "faithless lovers" are the other poets, and they challenge him to redeem all those poetic formulas—the vow of service, the praise of the beloved's perfect courtliness—that they have debased with their hypocrisy. How can he make that language speak truly again?

His only way is to speak, for a time, the nonfigurative, specific, antipoetic language of the vulgar ones, the ones who deny that a love song ever refers to anything real, because there is no reality beyond the body's lust and the courteous manner of its disguise. If he can speak that language and find that something still remains unexpressed, then it must mean that there is something more in his heart than plain carnality: a love that demands an altogether different language. To this end, he turns to those whom he calls "the people," which means, not his whole audience, but one segment of it, a group of his enemies. To know who they are we must look for a moment at the way he treats them elsewhere in his poetry.[30]

His fullest account of them is in the song *Ein liep ich mir vil nahe trage* (MF 150, 1ff.), which begins with the singer's declaration that he will never falter in his devotion to his lady. A vow of this sort puts him immediately in mind of his enemies, and so he says, in the second strophe, that a man of sense will have good luck, and a good reputation, if he knows how to get on with "the people," *der mit den liuten umbe gât.* A courtly man should strive for every kind of good: there will always be those who envy him for that, but their envy is lightly borne. This leads into the final strophe:

Ez ist ein nît der niene kan
verhelen an den liuten sich.
war umbe sprichet manic man
'wes toert sich der?' und meinet mich?
daz kunde ich im gesagen, obe ich wolde.
ichn wânde niht deis ieman frâgen solde
der pflaege schoener sinne;
wan nieman in der welte lebt,
ern vinde sînes herzen küneginne.

Such envy can never be
hidden among the people.
Why do so many ask,
'Why is he being so foolish?'—meaning me?
I could tell them, if I wanted to.
I could not believe that anyone would ask this
who was of a noble mind,
for there is no one living in this world
who does not find his heart's queen.

These "people," his enemies, are thus characterized in a familiar way: they are envious, uncomprehending, and full of mockery. They reveal their ignobility by so questioning the lover, the man who strives for every good.

The same may be said about the people's "vile question" concerning his lady's age in the fifth strophe of *Der lange süeze kumber*. Here they are true to their role in Reinmar's songs, for they mean to imply that the poet is a liar: if he has courted the lady as long as he has claimed to, she would be an old lady by now. Earlier, in the second strophe, he wondered how he could get pleasure from what ought to grieve him: this brought his gaze immediately to these "people" and caused him to remark that his service had won him nothing but mockery. Now, with this terrible question, the full voice of that mockery becomes a part of the song and threatens to destroy it. For that question goes beyond the lady's age and challenges the singer to go on, if he can: what remains to be said after the voice of carnality has spoken? This is the most difficult challenge imaginable, because that voice speaks the literal truth: the lady does not exist, at least not in any way that "the people" could sympathize with—she is part of a fiction, and the poet is, from their point of view, a liar.

The singer defeats them by using the situation in which he performs. Once those vulgar insinuations enter the circle in which he sings and become part of a song, they are transformed into a lyrical theme. He sings about a lady it is sweet to suffer for, or so he says; and the "people" call out to him that after all these years she must be very old. He responds by begging the lady to listen to what they are saying and to take it to heart. Now that silences them: they cannot be heard from again in this song, except insofar as he imitates their voice in the final strophe. When they make fun of him for pretending to love a nonexistent lady, he responds by wishing that the lady would hear them too and perhaps be moved to reward him for his faithful service. They have to answer a question now: if she does not exist, how can he address her, how might she be stirred by their questions about her age? They do not believe in her; or they believe that she must be so old that the singer is lying in the things he says about her: but there he stands, reminding her that they have a certain point. It is unspeakable of them to ask about her age, but the truth is, nobody gets younger, time passes, all things decay: let him profit from their vulgar question.

All these "people," excluded from the circle of friends, call out their question standing in a world full of mortal anxieties, where things decay in ordinary time. Their question ought to spoil his song, for who can believe in a love, or in a beloved, that time cannot touch? That question originates in a part of the audience, but it is immediately taken up into the performance and transformed: it speaks no longer of human decay, but of love, it enlists the thought of decay into the service of love. It is no longer a vulgar question, for it is assimilated into an ancient theme, a literary theme heard in all love poetry. Those who stand outside will have to rub their eyes and wonder where the lady is whom this solitary figure seems to be addressing there, because instead of being struck dumb, the singer goes on to cajole her in their very words—he points them out to her and begs her to listen. He stands there solitary as ever, but his enemies have to wonder now. Is she actually there?

In what appears to be the final strophe—the strophic order of this song is uncertain—the singer assumes their voice and speaks in carnal terms about an imaginary love. He entreats his lady: Let us make love in the subjunctive. The mood is exactly right, since courtly love, although vividly experienced, is contrary to fact. The "people" do not understand this, so they try to prove by facts and figures that the singer is a liar: with their corporeal eyes they cannot see the subjunctive circle in which he stands, the only ground on which this play of courtliness claims to be true. Only the friends see it: it is for them that he has saved this song and redeemed the language of love.

Of all the great *Minnesänger,* Reinmar has been the most idealized and the most oversimplified. He is usually cited as the model of the bashful and introverted courtly lover: resigned, idealistic, passive, melancholy, more concerned with analyzing his fine desires than satisfying them.[31] It is amazing how well this lonely, sad, reflective lover who inhabits Reinmar's poetry has managed to conceal his smile from nearly everyone. And yet, he practically never stops laughing at the things he says. He talks a great deal about his unrewarded service and complains of the unjust treatment he receives, but these complaints in the mouth of "the courtly lover" are boasts of steadfastness. In fact, whenever he assumes a submissive posture, he does not hold it for very long.

In the first two strophes of *Nieman seneder suoche an mich deheinen rât* (MF 170, 36ff.), for example, he manages to declare four times over that he would never say a bad word about any woman: *si sint von allem rehte hêre,* "they are, by every right, superior." But he manages to hold to this courteous resolve for as long as it takes to get to the next strophe, which begins: *In ist liep daz man si staeteclîchen bite,/ und tuot in doch sô wol daz si versagent,* "They love to be endlessly entreated,/ and it makes them feel so good to refuse." It ends: "Whoever wants their favor,/ let him always be around them, full of praise./ That's what I do all the time: too bad it doesn't do me any good."

The performer's responses to his audience should be easy to trace. In the role of the courtly lover, and responding to the friends, the singer declares that he will never speak ill of women. Immediately, he hears the rebuke of his enemies: no man can endure such capriciousness from mere women and not speak ill of them. He then responds by speaking ill of them and concludes on a note of self-mockery, corroborating the enemies' opinion of the courtly lover.

Under the influence of this hostile perspective, he goes on to express his wish to be free of his love: *volende ich einest sende nôt,/ si getuot mir niemer, mag ichz behüeten, wol noch wê,* "If I ever come to the end of this distress of longing,/ she'll never do me ill again, or good, if I can help it." The *sende nôt* is a distress that comes from longing. Then *volende* means, "If I could attain what I long for"; and the whole line: "If I could come to the end of this distress by attaining what I long for." From one point of view, the one whose influence he is under at the time, this refers to her body: if he could once enjoy her body, she would lose all her power over him, and then he would be able to leave her. But the singer's moving vision is returning to its starting point, the sector of the friends, and these lines also have an alternative meaning: if he could be what he longs to be, if he could attain the perfect courtliness he sees reflected in her, then he would no longer need her. Possessed of the reality, he would no longer need the mirror, and he would finally be free. This image of his own longed-for perfection leads to the recovery of his vow in the wonderful concluding strophe:

Ich bin tump daz ich sô grôzen kumber klage
und ir des wil deheine schulde geben.
sît ich si âne ir danc in mînem herzen trage,
waz mac si des, wil ich unsanfte leben?
daz wirt ir doch vil lîhte leit.
nu muoz ichz doch sô lâzen sîn.
mir machet nieman schaden wan mîn staetekeit.

I am foolish to raise such a loud lament
and to want to make her guilty of my grief.
If I bear her in my heart without her consent,
what can she do, if I want to live a life of unease?
Perhaps it even causes her some pain.
Anyway, I must leave it as it is.
It is no one that hurts me, only my steadfastness.

The famous complaints of Reinmar can be seen, in a passage like this, for what they really are: quite audacious boasts. The generous and humble tone may obscure the self-praise that it expresses: the lady has nothing to do with his manner of loving her, for she is altogether unaware; it is his own nobility that inspires him to glorify her. At the same time, Reinmar's disposition to self-mockery, with its implicit denigration of the lady, is evident in this passage. Indeed, every single perspective seems to be exerting its influence at once in this final strophe.[32]

Every courtly love poet must, for the sake of his exalted theme, accommodate the hostile elements in his audience. The song is a pattern of the moves he makes to outmaneuver them, in order to save his song and to be a credible witness for the vision of his friends. These enemies, therefore, precisely because of their incomprehension and destructive intent, are an essential element in the lyric: the vindication of the friends takes the form of a triumph over the enemies.

Those whom the poets call "the vulgar people"—the *gens vilana, diu liute*—may not know very much, but what they do know is solid rock: they know what the human body requires, and so they know that no man with a living body can swear this consuming fealty to another human being, and woman at that, forever beyond his reach. When they behold the singer, they behold a fool, or a liar; or a man who is really one of them but who is putting on airs, as sometimes one has to do in court, much as "the false lovers" do.

These *fals amador, die valschen,* listen to the singer, hear his song as a strictly technical achievement, the mastery of a certain manner which, for them, is all that courtliness is. They hear the song as an advertisement of prowess addressed to a woman, or intended to impress the other false lovers, who are, in either case, too full of lust to bother about the question of sincerity. And so, when they behold the singer, they behold a man who is just like them, a hypocrite, and his resemblance to them is never more pronounced than when he claims to be different from them on the grounds that he really means what he says.

There are other enemies as well, or other aspects of these same enemies, the talebearers and spies, for example. They, too, are blinded and driven by their carnality, for they understand nothing of this love affair except that it is illicit, and they would like to expose it. All of these attending enemies come to the song with the intention of discrediting it. The singer uses his performance and the situation of his audience—rather than any of the fixed elements of the song, such as the music and the words—to triumph over them and save the play of courtly love from their hostility, disbelief and derision, to transform their destructive energy into a saving force.

He needs "the vulgar ones" because their outlook coincides with the facts and necessities of every day, which the courtly lover, in his rapture, effectively denies. The singer, the performer, shares a common ground with them, his flesh and blood are no different from theirs; when the song is over he returns to their ranks, for all the people in the world are "the vulgar ones," every man belongs to the carnal and undedicated world. The courtly man, who is capable of fidelity and esteem, differs from them because he is more than carnal; all others are under the rule of the body, which wanders from chance to chance. His song of courtly love is a celebration of this privileged devotion; and were it not for the jeers of the vulgar ones, forcing him to acknowledge his community with them, this exaltation would have no tie with man's carnality and be truly incomprehensible and even contemptible. He needs these enemies in his audience and their voice in his song, because the sweet chant of the nightingale will not sound genuine unless it is heard above the croaking of the frogs.

The singer needs them not only for what they contribute to the performance, but also for what they keep out of it. Their derision is a continual reminder of the literal truth: they are right, from their point of view, to jeer at the courtly lover, for courtly love has no existence in the world. It has no relevance outside the performing circle, no truthfulness except as play. Thus the incomprehension of "the vulgar ones" marks out the boundaries of the song's relevance, their disbelief defines his meaning. The effect of their presence is felt in the singer's self-mockery: he reveals, through his performance, how the figure of the courtly lover truly is absurd and unbelievable outside its performing context, when it is viewed from any perspective grounded in the ordinary world. Courtly love was not meant to be viewed that way; it has nothing to do with the demands of every day, with the life that goes on beyond its own noble enclosure. And so, the vulgar ones are necessary as the frame which separates the performance, which in their judgement lacks verisimilitude, from the ordinary world, which is the perspective they judge from.

The "false lovers" are necessary because they ensure that the full effect and the deepest meaning of the song will be expressed by the performance, and not by the words and music alone.

The singer, speaking in the role of "the courtly lover," describes the deadly effect of his enemies on his language: how can he prove that he means what he says, when these hypocrites say exactly the same things, with disconcerting skill? He is himself a great virtuoso, of course, but in his case the intricate fashioning of his song is part of its meaning as a celebration of the effects of love. But his virtuosity will not avail him in his effort to distinguish himself from these enemies, because, if they are not as skillful technically, they are at least skillful enough so that the lady cannot tell their songs apart from his, even though they do not know what love is.

The singer's way out of this predicament, as we have seen, is to represent in his song every perspective in his audience. This demonstration of his ability to regard himself, his lady, and his love, from every point of view proves that he freely chooses this way to love—the way of service, of adoration—when other ways are open to him. He is no hypocrite, therefore, when he praises the lady: he does not speak these formulas to flatter her or to conceal his contempt, because he is free to denigrate her, with equal truthfulness. He really means what he says because he chooses to say these things when he is able to choose not to say them. He is fully aware that his praise, from a certain point of view, is excessive, and that others speak this same praise, in these same words, without meaning it, in order to "get something." With this dialectic strategy he defeats these hypocrites by their own hypocrisy. Being hypocrites, committed to deception, they are not free to acknowledge their lust, and so their songs are all in the same elevated and formulary style throughout. But the singer, because he is sincere, has greater freedom: he moves continually between high and low. He asks the paragon of courtly virtue to take him to the place where she undresses, thus juxtaposing raw carnality with his ceremonious devotion, and making the unquestionable existence of the one authenticate the reality of the other. Those false lovers cannot avail themselves of this technique, which relates the singer to the community of the audience: imprisoned in the self-regard of lust, they sing in pure self-interest. But the singer, in all of his impersonations, sings in the service of his friends, voicing the ideal of their solidarity. Thus, from the performance situation there develops a practical aesthetic, which guided both the troubadours and the *Minnesänger:* the true lover's songs are better than those of his rivals, because each of his songs is composed on many different stylistic levels, in a sequence that is surprising and most often intentionally comic.

The false lovers, therefore, are depicted as the cause, the irritant that provokes the performer to develop a wider stylistic range. They have debased the language of love, which now can be redeemed only by the clear proof that it refers to something more than the language of lust can account for. The language that the enemies have corrupted was developed in a long tradition. The courtly love lyric shared with every other kind of medieval literature a common inheritance from classical, biblical, patristic, liturgical sources, from the entire European literary tradition, whose effect on the courtly love lyric has been explored. The *Natureingang,* for example, was part of a continuous development that went back to classical antiquity and included the early Christian hymns as well as the secular Latin lyrics of the early Middle Ages.

The false lovers are co-heirs, with the singer, of this tradition, which provided most of the fixed elements of the song: the cadences, the themes, the formulas of adoration, the melodies—the entire grid upon which the freer and more leisurely alternation of perspectives is plotted. Because they are all as good, or almost as good, in technique as the singer himself, it means that technical mastery of the fixed elements, including the sounding of that elevated tone, would never suffice for the composition of a courtly love song. The false lovers neutralize the entire literary tradition, whose wealth can now be used on behalf of lust and ignobility. Because of the false lovers, the fixed elements of words and music can never be sufficient to convey the true meaning and effect of the song apart from a concrete performance situation.

The literary tradition which provided the courtly lyric with much of its poetic material and its metrical techniques, contained nothing that the poets could use to make the lyric exclusively and definitively the genre of the courtly class. The clearest proof of this is precisely these false lovers, who are depicted as uncourtly but still adept at all the techniques that the tradition had to bestow.

Another way to demonstrate this point is to compare these lyrics with the songs of the trouvères, who completely, and probably deliberately, rejected the troubadour technique of audience perspectives. Their works, therefore, can put a perspective on what the troubadour lyric might have been, if it had relied exclusively on the literary tradition applied to the courtly milieu.

The differences between these two bodies of lyric poetry can best be revealed through their apparent similarities. The lyrics of the trouvères, for example, also require a performance; but only in the sense that in every song only a singer can realize the harmonies of its sounds. The songs of the trouvères, however, do not require a performance situation, or the image of an attending audience to which every single line refers. Similarly, the trouvère lyric is certainly not comprehensible except in the context of the court. It has the same fixed elements, the same immediate reference to a courtly scene, such as one finds in the songs of the troubadours and *Minnesänger:* the gesture of homage, the spies and talebearers, the ceremonies of courtesy, an indicative elegance of diction, and countless other details that are drawn from courtly life and make no sense except in that context.

This is all true, but only in the sense that every utterance, in whatever form, is truly understood only as part of a larger context. Though they were involved in similar scenes, the trouvères and the troubadours had entirely different poetic ambitions. The trouvères did not regard the performance of their songs as a celebration of courtliness before an assembled community of the courtly class. The French poets wanted to make their song independent of the conditions of performance. They sought to create a lyric that would not be restricted to the perspectives of an audience but would be free to explore and develop the possibilities of figurative language. We can get some sense of their ambition in the elaborate metaphorical system of Thibaut de Champagne's *Ausi conme unicorne sui,* for example, where each strophe, indeed each line, responds not to any audience or to anything else outside the verbal surface, but rather to the figures of speech and the suggestions contained in the other strophes and lines. This separation of the song from the perspectives of its audience is characteristic of the later lyrics of the courtly tradition in Germany and Italy as well; it provided the poet with the necessary conditions for the elaboration of figurative language.

The troubadours and the *Minnesänger,* in developing their songs, did not rely primarily on the stimulus of the verbal context. They relied, instead, on the extraverbal pattern of the audience, so that their song is an arrangement of continually shifting contexts. The situation out of which one passage is spoken is not exactly the same as that of the preceding or following passage, so that the context of each passage is a different segment of the audience. At the very end of the song, the whole audience has been heard from and, in its totality, exerts a retrospective influence over the entire song. The manifold appearances of the singer, each passage presenting him in a new perspective, are finally resolved into the ideal figure of the courtly man, and at the same time the audience is finally revealed as the epitome of courtly society.[33]

Thus it was the performance alone that made the troubadour love lyric "courtly" and therefore different from any other kind of love song. It was in the performance that the song achieved its intended effect, that it gave a voice to the various parts of the audience and became their song. For the trouvères, the performance was subservient to the song: a good performance would do justice to its literary and musical genius. But for the troubadours and the *Minnesänger,* the song was composed in order to reveal the meaning of the performance situation, of the confrontation between the singer and his audience. This transference of meaning from the song to the situation was deliberately intended by the early courtly love poets, and they achieved their purpose through the figures they called "the false lovers."[34]

What actually happened in the performance is practically anybody's guess. But having come this far, we can be sure of a few things. To begin with, we can take note of the regular occurrence in the troubadours and *Minnesänger* of words that imply a certain demonstrative gesture on the part of the performer (there is nothing comparable in the trouvères). *Seht!* says the *Minnesänger,* "Behold!" And it is no mere rhetorical underscoring but is meant to induce the audience to look where the performer is pointing.[35] For though the singer's love is fictional, its setting is real and specific: the land, the terrain, or the gathering place of the audience. Bernart continually plays on the contrast between *sai* and *lai,* "here" and "there." And though these words define a certain ethical relation—"here" in the realm of mortal faults, "there" in the residence of courtliness —they also designate a specific geographical location: *lai enves Ventadorn.* The "here" of the singer signified at once the place where, in the fiction, the courtly lover stood, and the place where the singer and the audience were gathered. Therefore, the fictional setting and the space occupied by the audience are identical; and the audience is involved in the song.

The singer begins—usually in that elevated, cadenced, literary language created and bequeathed by long tradition. This language comes forth under the influence of the friends' perspective, its formality and dignity reflecting the courtly quality of those who demand it. However, this is the language that the ignoble false lovers have also mastered. Suddenly, there is an astonishing change in the singer. "By the head of St. Gregory," shouts Guillem IX, spotting his old "companions in the audience of his courtly song.[36] "Let her lay me by her side/ and offer it to me a while," says Reinmar. And then the audience is drawn into even deeper sympathy with the singer; for each one, having identified himself as a friend, now casts the roles of the enemies and endows them with faces. Then the performer refers to another song of his, sung on an earlier occasion: "Now she shall see whether I told the truth when I said I would go away into a strange land."[37] And the atmosphere of exclusiveness and intimacy uniting the singer and his audience now extends over the intervening moments of ordinary life. The aim of the performance was to enlist the audience as a co-creator, to make the song their song. The attending audience played the role of the lyric audience, the "friends" and "enemies" in the song; those who heard this song gave faces, including their own, to all those sectors through which the singer's eye sweeps, and which demand, each in its turn, a certain language and a certain performing attitude.

With some imaginative effort it is possible to find at least a vestige of the joy that the courtly love lyric gave to those who originally heard it. The first moment of that joy must have come when they heard the routines of their life and their familiar territory translated into a literary form and thus perpetuated. But the height of that joy did not come from the words or the music of the song, but rather from the awareness that the performance situation, in which they were all included, was the truest image of courtliness.

The singer, by his technique of confronting the audience, exalted courtly love in service to the friends and enlisted the hostile elements into that same service, their carnality authenticating the idealism of that love, and their hyprocrisy intensifying the intimate community between the singer and his friends. The song was composed in order to reveal the meaning of the situation in which it was performed. The audience, before the singer confronts it, is an assemblage of conflicting perspectives, and he redeems it from this chaos. He transforms the destructive lusts of his enemies into forces that confirm the noble dedication of his friends. The singer's relation to the audience thus becomes an image of the ideal character of the courtly man, whose carnality reinforces a higher love capable of esteem and veneration, whose desires give their vitality to the dignity of his style.

This performance situation enacted the highest praise that the courtly class could give to its own life. Lust, envy, and malevolence were the heritage of all humanity, and they dominated all other classes. But here, in this chosen circle, they were deflected from their common paths and set in the direction of longing.

Thus the early courtly love lyric absolutely requires a performance situation in order to achieve its full meaning and effect—even if, today, that situation can exist only in the imagination of a reader who is willing to be the cocreator of the song. We who come to this lyric must read it as a performance, as the result of the singer's reactions to a live audience. We must set it in continual motion, follow its changes of tone and language as the singer scans the courtly circle; we must continually view the singer and his love with a different bias till we return, as he returns, to the *dreh viatge,* "the right path," finally to reaffirm, altogether aware of its foolishness, the supreme value of courtly love.

Notes

1. Guillem's ambiguous attitude toward the aspirations of courtly love is discussed by Leo Pollmann, *Die Liebe in der hochmittelalterlichen Literatur Frankreichs,* Analecta Romanica 18 (Frankfurt am Main: Vittorio Klostermann, 1966), p. 91 ff. Pollmann does not, however, consider the relation of these contradictory moods to the various audiences defined in Guillem's lyrics.
2. Cf. the chapter on "Style et registres" in Paul Zumthor, *Langue et techniques poétiques à l'époque romane (XI*[e]*–XIII*[e] *siècles),* Bibliothèque française et romane, series C, IV (Paris: Librairie C. Klincksieck, 1963).
3. Cf. Moshé Lazar, *Amour courtois et Fin'Amors dans la littérature du xiie siècle,* Bibliothèque française et romane, series C, VIII (Paris: C. Klincksieck, 1964).
4. One of the most beautiful expressions of this paradox is the "Venus lyric" of Heinrich von Morungen, *Ich wêne nieman lebe der mînen kumber weine;* text: *Des Minnesangs Frühling,* ed. Carl von Kraus *et al.,* 30th ed. rev. (Leipzig: S. Hirzel, 1950), 138, 17 ff. Herbert Kolb, *Der Begriff der Minne und das Entstehen der höfischen Lyric,* Hermaea, neue Folge, IV (Tübingen: Max Niemeyer, 1958).
5. Bernart de Ventadorn, *Chansons d'amour,* ed., Moshé Lazar, Bibliothèque française et romane, series B, IV (Paris: C. Klincksieck, 1966), Nrs. 3 (*Ab joi mou lo vers e·l commens*), p. 26 (*Can la freid' aura venta*), p. 36 (*Ja mos chantars no m'er onors*). All quotations of Bernart are from this edition.
6. Johan Huizinga, *Homo Ludens: A Study of the Play Element in Culture,* trans. R. F. C. Hull (Boston: Beacon Press, 1955).

7. Heinrich, *Des Minnesangs Frühling,* p. 137, 27 ff. Bernart, *Chantars no pot gaire valer.* Cf. Chapter 3, pp. 138.
8. Therefore, anything the lover can do to evade and deceive them is automatically honorable: Lazar, *Chansons d'amour, Per melha cobrir lo mal pes,* Nr. 21; *Be•m cuidei de chantar sofrir,* Nr. 13, which weaves together all the themes we have been discussing, the conspiratorial malevolence and debased poetry of the enemies, and the lady's uncertain resistance to their flattery; *Ara no vei luzir solelh* (Nr. 5).
9. They are already identified as such by Marcabrun and Cercamon. Marcabrun: among several examples, J.-M.-L.- Dejeanne, ed., *Per savi•l tenc ses doptanssa,* in *Poésies complètes du troubadour Marcabru,* Bibliothèque méridionale, 1st series, XII (Toulouse: Edouard Privat, 1909), with emendations by Kurt Lewent, "Beiträge zum Verstandnis der Lieder Marcabrus," *ZRP* 37 (1913): 313–337, 427–451; Aurelio Roncaglia, ed., *D'aisso lau Dieu,* "Il 'Gap' di Marcabruno," *SMed* 17 (1951): 46–70. Alfred Jeanroy, ed., *Cercamon: Puois nostre temps comens' a brunezir, Les poésies de Cercamon,* CFMA, 27 (Paris: Champion, 1922), strophes iv–v; cf. *Ab lo Pascor m'es bel qu'eu chan.*
10. Lazar, *Chansons d'amour, Lonc tems a qu'eu no chantei mai,* Nr. 19, strophe vi.
11. On the antithetical meanings of the mirror, see Frederick Goldin, *The Mirror of Narcissus in the Courtly Love Lyric* (Ithaca, N.Y.: Cornell University Press, 1967). On the ambiguous meaning of the figure of a lady regarding her image in a mirror, see Erich Köhler, "Lea, Matelda, und Oiseuse," *ZRP* 78 (1962): 464–469. On Bernart's deliberate ambiguity in the context of classical and Christian poetic traditions, see James J. Wilhelm, *The Cruelest Month* (New Haven and London: Yale University Press, 1965).

    The discussion on the audience in this chapter assumes a distinction similar to that which critics of the novel often make between the "inner" and the "outer" reader. The singer performed before an actual, historical ("outer") audience, not to be confused with the fictional ("inner") audience consisting of the characters mentioned in the song. The actual audience cooperated with the singer in the creation of the fictional audience.
12. Stephen G. Nichols, Jr., points out that the speaker himself is that "worst enemy" who made the mirror (p. 361), but does not take into account the denigrating effect of the mirror image: "Toward an Aesthetic of the Provençal *Canso*" in *The Disciplines of Criticism,* ed. Peter Demetz, Thomas Greene, and Lowry Nelson, Jr. (New Haven and London: Yale University Press, 1968), pp. 349–374.
13. *The Razos de Trobar of Raimon Vidal and Associated Texts,* ed. J. H. Marshall (London: Oxford University Press, 1972).
14. This holds true in the romance as well: see Chapter IV, pp. 144–145 and n. 10.
15. Alfred Jeanroy, ed., *Companho, tant ai agutz d'avols conres, Les chansons de Guillaume IX,* CFMA, 9 (Paris: Honoré Champion, 1927; reprint 1964). On the blind necessity of the "law" see Mario

Casella, "Il più antico trovatore," *Archivo storico italiano,* 96, pt. 2 (1938): 3–63; Casella is on much firmer ground for his reading of the earlier lyrics in Jeanroy's edition than for the later ones. On the consequent distancing of objective reality, see Theophil Spoerri, "Wilhelm von Poitiers und die Anfange der abendländischen Poesie," *Trivium* 2 (1944): 255–277, esp. 267 ff.; reprint in *Der provenzalische Minnesang,* ed. Rudolph Baehr, Wege der Forschung, 6 (Darmstadt: Wissenschaftliche Buchgesellschaft, 1967).

16. See Chapter VI, below, on Ulrich von Lichtenstein and Burkart von Hohenfels.
17. See Chapter III for the treatment of this theme by Walther von der Vogelweide and Neidhart von Reuental.
18. *Lo tems vai.*
19. *Tant ai mo cor.*
20. Jeanroy, ed., *Companho,* Nr. VI, strophe vi.
21. Cf. *Lancan vei per mei la landa.*
22. A lyric similar in meaning and strategy is *Tuih cil que•m preyon qu'eu chan* (Nr. 33), also concerned with the problem of finding a way to sing and the effect of his silence on his friends. The sudden outburst in strophe iv—"If I had love in my power,/ I tell you I'd do something cruel to it"—strikes an oft-repeated note in courtly poetry (cf. Friedrich von Hausen, n. 26, below) right through the *rime petrose* of Dante (*Cosi nel mio parlar voglio esser aspro*). He is all set to depart into exile, as he promised at the end of the *lauzeta* lyric; but suddenly a *bel semblan* from a lady "here" gives him hope again. Perhaps around this time Bernart had his *tenson* with a certain Peirol (*Peirol, com avetz tan estat,* Nr. 35), where he advises the disconsolate lover to do as he did in order that he might sing again: he left the lady with the lion's heart and found "a woman that I love more."
23. The recovery from the influence of the enemies is the theme of a lyric very similar to this one by Cercamon, *Ab lo temps qe fai refreschar,* ed. Jeanroy, Nr. II.
24. Erich Köhler, *"Observations historiques et sociologiques sur la poésie des troubadours," CCM* 7 (1964): 46.
25. The strophic order of the cansos varies among the manuscripts, but that is not so great an obstacle to the kind of reading proposed here as it might seem: the variations occur mostly in the middle strophes; there is usually a consensus regarding the two most important parts of each song, namely, the beginning and the end. The manuscripts almost always agree as to which strophe comes first, while the tornadas fix the final strophe, and these points determine the lyric's pattern.
26. The multivocality of the courtly love lyric can be seen developing in the poetry of Guillem IX. By the time he writes *Farai chansoneta nueva,* he punctuates the tone of obeisance and submission characteristic of the "new song," with carnal outbursts to accommodate the audience of the *Companho* lyrics. This is a device that Jaufre Rudel also uses effectively, for example in *Pro ai del chan essenhadors,* where he contrasts the *senhors* whom he calls on for

counsel with the "vulgar and jealous ones" he and his lady will have to evade (as she tells him) to have their joy in peace. He is sad because he cannot hold her *en luecs aizitz,* "in fine and private places." Jaufre has been spiritualized almost out of existence by many critics and scholars: suffice it to say here that he has more than a one-string fiddle. Giraut de Bornelh in *Qan lo freitz e·l glatz e la neus,* a song usually regarded as a veritable catalog of courtly love clichés, praises the beauty of his lady's body and concludes with an oath: may he be called crazy if he ever divulged one secret thing on the sly that she told him; he, lacking her strength, is like a lamb confronting a bear. No one shows how great a fool the courtly lover is as thoroughly as Peire Vidal in *Ajostar e lassar.* She has made an unwilling traveler out of him, and all he has ever "gotten" from her is a bit of ribbon and a kiss that he stole like a thief while she was sleeping; only Solomon, David, and Samson can be compared to him; he has to wait around like a Breton waiting for King Arthur to return, for he is in exile, having been driven out by *fals lauzengier gloto,* grubbing, lying slanderers. Indeed, the follies to which love drives him in his poetry are reflected in the mad stories told about him in the *vidas.*

An example from the *Minnesang* is Friedrich von Hausen's famous lyric, *Wâfenâ, wie hât mich Minne gelâzen.* The song begins by stressing the lover's passivity (note the several verbs indicating that he is acted upon—*gelâzen, betwanc, verwâzen),* but as it unfolds the lover becomes more and more self–assertive, a movement that reaches its climax after strophe iii, which beautifully suggests the ineffability of *Minne,* when the singer bursts out, "Minne, I would like to stick out that squinting eye of yours!" But immediately after this indulgence in the thought of revenge, he ends exactly where he began: "But right now I have to live beneath your power." A similar effective use of the threat of revenge occurs in Heinrich von Morungen's *Vil süeziu senftiu tôterinne,* where the singer "threatens" the lady, should she continue to withhold her body, with eternal submission and service after death. The same is true of Heinrich's *Hete ich tugende niht sô vil von ir vernomen,* where, after two marvellous strophes in a tragic mode, he vows to take revenge on her in his son: he will be so handsome, that she will break her heart longing for him. All of these examples could be multiplied until nearly every love lyric of the classic period would be included.

27. *Des Minnesangs Frühling,* 166, 16 ff. I have followed the strophic order of the C text.

28. Wolfgang Mohr, in the article cited in n. 34.

29. Lazar, *Chansons d'amour,* Nr. 23, strophe ii; Nr. 26, strophe iii.

30. Besides the following example, the *liute* appear elsewhere in Reinmar's poetry (*Des Minnesangs Frühling,* 177, 30; 176, 2; 181, 22). As a rule they are depicted as the ones who misinterpret the poet's words, or who are the source of misunderstanding and slander. He is going to be more careful in the future about what he says in their presence (*Des Minnesangs Frühling,* 175, 31 ff.).

31. See, for example, Gustav Ehrismann, *Geschichte der deutschen*

Literatur bis zum Ausgang des Mittelalters (Berlin: C. H. Beck, 1932–1935; reprint Munich, 1966), vol. 6, p. 240; Helmut de Boor, *Die höfische Literatur, Geschichte der deutschen Literatur,* ed. Helmut de Boor and Richard Newald, vol. 2 (Munich: C. H. Beck, 1960), 286 f.

32. The same graceful and illuminating movement of the lyric's focus through the audience can be observed in Reinmar's *Waz ich nu niuwer maere sage* (*Des Minnesangs Frühling,* 165, 10 ff.). The poet begins by depicting himself as the hostile part of the audience sees him, *die hôhgemuoten.* Reinmar uses this term elsewhere to imply sexual attainment (*Des Minnesangs Frühling,* 151, 12; 189, 9). In other words, the *hôhgemuoten* are those "who never knew the pain of longing." Strophe iv, about the two things disputed in his mind, is the clearest statement that the lady rules by the lover's deliberate choice; cf. n. 22. In the final strophe Reinmar presents a beautiful and moving defense of his moral decision and consequently of his poetry.
33. Xenja von Ertzdorff, "Das Ich in der höfischen Liebeslyrik des 12. Jahrhunderts," *Archiv* 197 (June, 1960–Feb., 1961): 1–13, shows how the various aspects of the "I" were integrated in the classic period.
34. On the importance of the performance situation in the *Minnesang,* see Hugo Kuhn, "Zur inneren Form des Minnesangs," in *Der deutsche Minnesang,* ed. Hans Fromm, Wege der Forschung, 15 (Darmstadt: Wissenschaftliche Buchgesellschaft, 1961), p. 167–179; *ibid.,* "Stil als Epochen-, Gattungs- und Wertproblem in der deutschen Literatur des Mittelalters," in *Stil- und Formprobleme in der Literatur des Mittelalters,* ed. Paul Böckmann, Vorträge des VII. Kongresses der Internationalen Vereinigung für moderne Sprachen und Literaturen in Heidelberg (Heidelberg: Carl Winter, 1959), pp. 123–129; *ibid.,* "Minnesang and the Form of Performance," in *Formal Aspects of Medieval German Poetry,* ed. Stanley N. Werbow (Austin, Texas and London: University of Texas Press, 1969); Wolfgang Mohr, "Minnesang als Gesellschaftskunst," *Der Deutschunterricht,* 6 (1954), reprint in *Der deutsche Minnesang;* and Paul Zumthor, *Langue et techniques,* especially pp. 205 ff.
35. See the discussion by Kuhn in "Minnesang and the Form of Performance."
36. Jeanroy, *Companho,* Nr. VIII, strophe iii.
37. See the note by Carl Appel to *Tuih cil que•m preyon* in his edition of *Bernart von Ventadorn: seine Lieder* (Halle a. S.: Max Niemeyer, 1915). Cf. n. 18; and Goldin, *Mirror of Narcissus,* Chap. III.

Bibliographic Note

I list here certain works which there was no occasion to cite in the notes but which have guided me in my study of the lyric and shed light on the background of the discussion in this chapter.

For the formal study of the Northern French lyric, the basic work is R. Dragonetti, *La technique poétique des trouvères dans la chanson courtoise,* Publications de la faculté des lettres de Gand, 127 (Bruges: De Tempel, 1960).

On the continuity of courtly literature, Reto R. Bezzola's monumental study is indispensable, although it is difficult to accept many of its literary judgments: *Les origines et la formation de la littérature courtoise en occident,* 5 vols. (Paris: Honoré Champion, 1958–1967). Bezzola's rigidly sociological interpretations of courtly literature have been criticized by Antonio Viscardi, "Le origini della letteratura cortese," *ZRP* 78 (1962): 269 ff.; 81 (1965): 454 ff.

The classical and medieval Latin backgrounds of the troubadour lyric have been discussed in several articles by Dmitri Scheludko: *Archivum Romanicum* 11 (1927): 273–312; *ZFSL* 52 (1929): 1–38, 201–66; *ZRP* 54 (1934): 129–174; 60 (1940): 191–234; *ZFSL* 60 (1936): 257–334. For the German lyric, Hennig Brinkmann, *Entstehungsgeschichte des Minnesangs* (Halle, 1926) and *Geschichte der lateinischen Liebesdichtung im Mittelalter* (Halle, 1925).

On the music of the courtly lyric, J. Chailley, *Histoire musicale du Moyen Age* (Paris: 1950), and *L'Ecole musicale de St. Martial jusqu' à la fin du XIe siècle* (Paris: 1960), both of which take account of previous studies.

On the later German lyric, Hugo Kuhn, *Minnesangs Wende,* Hermaea, neue Folge, 1 (Tübingen: Max Niemeyer, 1952; rev. ed. 1967).

On the manuscripts of the troubadours, "L'art d'éditer les textes lyriques," in *Recueil de travaux offert à M. Clovis Brunel,* vol. I (Paris: 1955): 463–475; and D'arco Silvio Avalle, *La letteratura medievale in lingua d'oc nella sua tradizione manoscritta* (Turin: Giulio Einaudi, 1961).

CHAPTER III

The Challenge to Courtly Love

Renata Karlin

The greatest poets, both in Provence and Germany, were well aware of the inherent absurdity of courtly love: a man longing for an invisible, often insensate lady, proud of being deprived, convinced at once of the lady's indifference and of her beneficial effect. By confirming the unrealistic nature of their stance, they managed to affirm the very ideality and efficacy of their quest. It is hard to think of a more noble and more ridiculous lover than Reinmar. Self-mockery for the sake of preserving an ideal, the involvement of the audience, the constant shift between ideality and reality, all these indications of self-awareness are carried through with such mastery by Reinmar that he appears to have exhausted their possibilities. It would seem that for the succeeding generation of poets there was nothing left to do but to repeat and modulate Reinmar's themes. But, the succeeding generations produced two of the greatest medieval poets who went far beyond the possibilities set forth by Reinmar: Walther von der Vogelweide (fl. 1180–1228) and Neidhart von Reuental (fl. 1190–1236).

It is with these two poets that, for the first time in German, the basic premises, the essentials of courtly love lyric, are challenged. With Walther and Neidhart the ideality of courtly love, and its absurdity, is put into question. What Walther sets out to explore, and what Neidhart elaborates on, is the possibility of a love relationship that is reciprocal but nevertheless courtly.

After writing a few early poems in the style of Reinmar,[1] Walther introduces the theme of reciprocity which becomes the dominant note in all his lyrics:

> minne ist zweier herzen wünne:
> teilent si gelîche, sost diu minne dâ:
> sol abe ungeteilet sîn.
> sô enkans ein herze alleine niht enthalten.
>
> [69, 10–13][2]

> *minne* is the joy of two hearts
> if they share equally then there is *minne;*
> if however it is not shared
> then one heart alone cannot contain it.

The poem begins with the question: what is *minne?* After the conventional statement that he does not know much about it, combined with an equally conventional appeal to the audience for help, Walther states unequivocally his definition of *minne:* it is love only if it brings joy; if it engenders pain then it cannot be called *minne. Minne* is the joy shared by two hearts; if the sharing is unequal, then there is no love. If it is unshared, as in the traditional poet-lady relationship, then it does not exist; one heart cannot contain it and the poet will not be able to sustain his love. Consequently Walther ends the strophe with a plea to his lady for help. What the nature of the help should be is then elaborated. Walther, in the traditional role of *Minnesänger,* carries too heavy a share. If the lady is to help him, that is, to reciprocate his feelings, then she must say so and he will become a free man, a man not bound by a feudal relationship.

Here Walther places himself squarely against the conventions of the courtly love lyric. There is nothing unconventional about the poet's threat to end the relationship, indeed it is a recurring theme in the lyric; what is unconventional about Walther's stance is his reason for quitting. While the traditional poet speaks of ending the relationship in order to emphasize the unbearable pain inflicted by his lady's inaccessibility and thus by this very gesture affirming the nobility of his stance, Walther wants to end the relationship unless he can make of it something entirely new: the joy shared by two hearts, a relationship based on mutuality and reciprocity. In this poem Walther avoids the question of whether such a mutual relationship could still be noble, although the warning to his lady that ends the strophe seems to imply that singing of the lady in these new terms would still be a superior way of praising her, thus, presumably, a noble endeavor.

In the last strophe Walther seems to want to soften the harsh remarks he has made; although the mood continues, the statements are vague and the images relatively weak. This becomes obvious when one compares the image of a man blinded, not knowing where to go in the fourth strophe, with the image of a man free and strong who proudly proclaims his independence and severs his vassal relationship in the third strophe.

In a poem dating from the same period, he further elaborates on the same theme:

Ich sanc hie vor den frowen umbe ir blôzen gruoz:
den nam ich wider mîme lobe ze lône.
swâ ich des geltes nû vergebene warten muoz,
dâ lobe ein ander, den si grüezen schône.
swâ ich niht verdienen kan
einen gruoz mit mîme sange,
da kêr ich vil hêrscher man
mînen nac ode ein mîn wange.
daz kît 'mir ist umbe dich
rehte als dir ist umbe mich.'
ich wil mîn lop kêren
an wîp die kunnen danken:
was hân ich von den überhêren?

[49, 12–49, 24]

Before I have sung for women for their mere greeting
and this I have accepted as reward for my praise.
Now if I have to wait in vain for a response,
let another praise there, whom they greet well.
Wherever I cannot earn
greeting with my song
I, a proud man, will present
the back of my neck or the side of my cheek.
This is the rule: 'I feel about you
exactly the way you feel about me.'
I will turn my praise to women who know how to reward;
what's there to gain from the proud ones?

If the love relationship cannot be mutual then the poet threatens to turn his love away from the proud courtly lady and turn towards "women who know how to reward."

There has been a great deal of discussion about that period in Walther's life during which he wrote poetry for and about "women who know how to reward." Scholars taking the terms from one of Walther's later poems customarily refer to the poetry of this period, as *niedere Minne,* "low love," as opposed to the *hohe Minne,* "high love," of the conventional courtly love lyric. The terminology is unfortunate because *niedere,* "low," has frequently been interpreted in a very narrow sociological sense: since the courtly lady could not reciprocate the poet's feelings, he turned to women of lower social status for whom the absence of conventional patterns would allow a more natural response.

There is absolutely no evidence that the woman, or women, Walther wrote about in his poems on *niedere Minne* were of any other social class than those whose praise he sang in his earlier poems. Whenever he addresses a woman in his poems on *niedere Minne* he addresses her as *frowe,* the conventional *Minnesang* term for lady, and the term that defines a married lady of the court. What distinguishes these poems from the conventional love lyrics is not the kind of woman who inspires the poet to write, but the kind of love these poems describe.

In the poems immediately preceding his period of *niedere Minne,* Walther stated that love must be mutual if it is to be sustained. Now he seeks to explore the possibilities of such a relationship. The most outstanding characteristic of this kind of relationship is the fact that Walther finds its justification in the cosmos. Such a relationship is possible, he argues, because it is within the natural order. In one poem he exuberantly describes the arrival of spring, and ends with a plea addressed to his lady to follow the example of nature by giving and receiving joy (52, 15–52, 20).

The acceptance of love as a natural process was a literary cliché by Walther's time. Making love acceptable by grounding it in the purpose of the cosmos first found poetic expression in the allegories of Bernardus Silvestris and Alanus de Insulis. Walther, who read Latin well, must have been familiar with these ideas which were a common intellectual tradition in his time.

It is interesting to note that the variety of nature descriptions for which Walther is praised begins at this period. In his earlier poems, nature either appears not at all or in a very conventional form. Walther is the first poet of courtly love to describe nature for its own sake rather than as a setting to the poet's feelings. In one poem of this period, Walther laments the arrival of winter, not because it signifies an end to love, but because the poet, being part of nature, suffers from the cruelty of nature as much as birds, flowers, trees, and the heath:

> Mîn herze swebt in sunnen hô:
> daz jaget der winter in ein strô.
>
> [76, 13–76, 14]

> My heart was floating high in the sunshine:
> and now winter chases it into a straw cot.

The image of the freely floating, self-generated heart, *swebt,* is juxtaposed with the image of the heart totally at the mercy of winter, *jaget,* and the infinite outdoor space, *sunnen,* is juxtaposed with the image of a narrow enclosure in which people huddle together in the straw to keep warm. In the last stanza, Walther draws the final analogy between himself and nature; he participates in nature by comparing himself to a pig (76, 15–76, 16). In this poem life is defined by nature, rather than by a courtly code.

A great deal has been written about Walther's poems on *niedere Minne* and yet one very important aspect has been completely ignored: that there are very few true love poems in this period. Most of them speak of love as a feeling harmonious with nature but do not refer to any specific woman or any specific experience on the part of the poet. Very few poems actually relate a love experience that could be analyzed in order to understand what this "natural love" meant to Walther. With one exception, none of the poems relates a sexual encounter. This poem, widely discussed and frequently quoted, *Under der linden,* speaks in an exuberantly happy and open way about a meeting of lovers on the heath (40, 1–40, 9). Although this poem speaks of a mutually satisfying love relationship within the realm of nature, what is frequently overlooked is the fact that this experience is not related by the poet, but by a young girl. And there is no indication whatsoever that the poet was the lover. It is the only love poem by Walther that is not cast in the conventional *canzon* form; indeed it has been related to the *pastourelle* tradition.[3] It is neither a *pastourelle* nor a *canzon*. The very freedom from conventional forms allowed the poet to express emotions that would be in conflict with the conventions of courtly love.

In all other poems on *niedere Minne*, if a love experience is mentioned at all it is only alluded to in veiled imagery and, what is more important, the experience is eventually exposed as a dream, as in *Nemt, frowe, disen kranz:*

> "sô zieret ir den tanz,
> mit den schœnen bluomen, als irs ûffe traget.
> het ich vil edele gesteine,
> daz müest ûf iur houbet,
> obe ir mirs geloubet.
> sêt mîne triuwe, daz ichs meine."
>
> [74, 22–74, 27]

> "You will grace the dance
> with the beautiful flowers on your head.
> If I had jewels
> they would be on your head;
> believe me,
> I assure you, I mean it."

The poem opens with an exchange of wreaths: a well-established symbolic exchange of love by Walther's time. It is significant that he addresses the woman as *frowe.* Thus, even though she is called a young girl in the second line, we are to assume that she has noble qualities. This is further emphasized by the fact that Walther assures her he would gladly offer her jewels to wear on her head, presumably because she would be worthy of such a headdress. The juxtaposition of wreath and jewels is not to be understood as a juxtaposition of nature and court, for nature reigns through the entire poem; rather, the jewels are introduced to establish her status as noble. The girl takes his gift, blushing and embarrassed. The poet stresses her innocence, honor, good manners, and beauty. Then he elaborates on his proposal, ending with an image which clearly suggests sexual union: *da suln wir si brechen beide,* "there let us break the flowers together" (75, 16).

There follows a most complex and surprising strophe:

> Mich dûhte daz mir nie
> lieber wurde, danne mir ze muote was.
> die bluomen vielen ie
> von dem boume bî uns nider an daz gras.

seht, dô muost ich von fröiden lachen.
do ich sô wünneclîche
was in troume rîche,
dô taget ez und muoz ich wachen.

[75, 17–75, 24]

It seemed to me that I never
felt happier than I felt then.
The flowers fell from the tree onto the grass.
Look, then I had to laugh with happiness
that I was so joyously
rich in my dream.
Then day came and I woke up.

Never has he been happier, says the poet, using an image that brings the sexual act into total fusion with nature: the man becomes a tree and the woman grass—earth fecundated by his blossoms. Once the poet establishes this image he proceeds to expose the entire experience as a dream. The poem ends in self-mockery, the dreamer searching for a trace of the dream in a reality that never contained it. To be sure, he searches and looks into every girl's eyes, but his vision is obscured; they are wearing *huete,* the headdress of the married court ladies which covers most of their faces. If they were wearing wreaths, maybe there would be some hope of recapturing the bliss he felt in his dream. The humor in this last stanza is like the humor of Bernart. By acting for a moment as if the poet's vision could be translated or equated with reality, the poet emphasizes the wide gap between reality and vision, and his self-mockery thus serves to emphasize the very ideality of his stance.

With the exception of *Under der linden* which stands apart also in structure and form, the natural, mutual love which Walther espouses is never actually experienced. It remains a dream. Thus Walther merely substituted his dream of natural love for the *Minnesänger*'s dream of perfection through service. The experience has to remain a dream because the poet cannot love that way and still remain noble. Walther attempts to solve this dilemma by emphasizing in almost all of the poems that the woman in question is noble. In this poem he mentions both her honor and her courtliness. In one poem in which he defiantly opposes the unrequited love of the *Minnesänger, si getraf diu liebe nie,* "they were never touched by love" (49, 35), with the joy experienced in a mutual relationship, *liebe tuot dem herzen baz,* "love soothes the heart" (50, 3) he wonders in the last strophe: *hast du triuwe und staetekeit,* "are you faithful, are you loyal" (50, 13). He concludes that he cannot love her unless she possesses these courtly qualities. What distinguishes Walther's noble lady from her predecessors is that her nobility is not a definition of class, rather it is an absolute and moral definition outside and beyond class distinctions. It is precisely her classlessness that feeds his doubt, for the traditional poet knows that his lady is the epitome of courtliness.

In this moral order in which Walther encounters his *frowe* he seeks to attain transcendence of his soul—moral exaltation through service to an idealized woman—and transcendence of his body—a union with nature, with the woman as intermediary endowed with consciousness. The opposite poles are clearly marked and Walther, once having set them, cannot bridge the gap. Torn between unattainable ideals, Walther finds that he has undermined his very identity as a poet and as a member of the courtly class. In the poem *Aller werdekeit ein füegerinne* (46, 32–47, 15), Walther states his dilemma. The poet begins with a plea to Lady Moderation to teach him to love in a well-balanced way, because both the high love and the low love are expressions of immoderation and thus lack the most essential of courtly virtues. High love lacks moderation in Walther's opinion because, while it is an ennobling force, it is at the same time deceptive, *reizet,* for it has to deny the reward it promises. Low love lacks moderation, for, while the feelings of the poet are reciprocated, *kumet diu herzeliebe,* the woman is removed from her superior position and love becomes "sick" love. There is no solution to this dilemma. Whichever way the poet turns he is misled and Lady Moderation cannot provide the answer.

From then on the poet indeed followed the beckoning of high love. He returned to the traditional role of the courtly poet-lover, writing a great number of poems which, although they are very skillfully fashioned, lack the vitality of the poems immediately preceding those poems of *niedere minne.* Some of his late poems are bitter, others are resigned like *Ich bin als unschedelîche frô* (41, 13–42, 15).

In this poem, Walther affirms the premise of the courtly poet-lover whose act of singing is the expression of his courtliness, an exemplary performance of knighthood. By serving the lady unfalteringly, he can experience moral exaltation, *hohen muot,* and joy. Although his service brings immeasurable grief, *herzeleides,* he has to maintain his joyful appearance in order to convey the nature of his love to other members of the courtly class. This is a theme which runs through a great number of his late lyrics, that the poet performs a chivalric act by taking on the appearance of joy:

> Bî den liuten nieman hât
> ze fröiden hovelîchern trôst denn ich:
> sô mich sende nôt bestât,
> sô schîne ich geil und troeste selben mich.
>
> [116, 33–116, 36]

> In this society no one
> consoles himself in a more courtly manner than I.
> When longing and pain obsess me
> then I seem joyful and console myself.

With this strophe Walther firmly places himself within the *Minnesang* tradition. The idea that the poet, although suffering immeasurable grief because of the lady's unattainability, feigns joy, but still performs an act of exemplary courtliness, is to be found in Walther's immediate predecessors:

> Manger der sprichet 'nu sêt wie der singet!
> wêre im iht leit. er têt anders dan sô.'
> der mac niht wizzen waz mich sanges twinget:
> nu tuon ab ich reht als ich tet aldô.
> do ich in leide stuont, dô huop ich si gar unhô.
> diz ist ein nôt diu mich leides verdringet:
> sorge ist unwert dâ die liute sint frô.
>
> [133, 21–133, 27][4]

> There is many a man who says: "Now look how he sings!
> If he were in pain he would do otherwise."
> He who speaks thus does not know what compels me to sing:
> when I act like this I act appropriately;
> when I act sorrowfully then I judge her to be unworthy.
> This is what compels me to drive my pain away.
> Sorrow is not worth much where people are joyful.

Reinmar, Morungen, and Walther not only assert the nobility of their endeavor to put on a joyful appearance, they further stress that this noble tour de force is misunderstood and misjudged by other members of their class, and that it is their endeavor that sets them apart from the reality of courtly life.

In the Walther poem under discussion the poet makes this point most explicit: *sô wil mir maneger sprechen zuo: sô swig ich und lâze in reden dar* (41, 8–42, 1), "many a person wants to give me advice: then I am silent and let him speak." The fourth strophe and the final strophe of the poem convey a mood of intense resignation, of total abdication of joy. Emphasizing the impermanence of joy, the poet seems to echo imagery of penitence sermons: no one can find joy; it vanishes like the flowers in the field.

If these lines are compared with one of his earlier poems, where he defines love as a mutual sharing of joy and proudly proclaims that, unless his service brings joyful requital, he will cease to sing for his lady, one can discern the long road Walther has travelled. Seeking joy he has tried to find alternatives to the one-sided servitude of the courtly poet. He thought that a mutually satisfying relationship could be found within nature, but this proved to be a dream, for his lady never left the court; she always remained the *frowe* endowed with courtly qualities such as honor, loyalty, and courtly manners. When he abandoned his dream, he affirmed more absolutely than before the one-sided vassal relationship of the courtly lover in which joy plays no part. To look for it would be to look for "false joys." He serves his lady unfalteringly without expectation of reward. More than ever before she becomes a frozen idol, a fiction of the poet's imagination in whose servitude he may be able to transcend his moral existence. But this relationship he knows to be unsatisfactory and this dissatisfaction is expressed in bitterness and resignation.

Neidhart von Reuental, about ten years younger than Walther, probably began his writing career at the time when Walther was composing his songs on *niedere Minne*. This seems probable because Neidhart's entire work is devoted to exploring the possibilities of *niedere Minne* and to exposing its fallacies. Neidhart's poems are divided into so-called *Sommerlieder* and *Winterlieder*, according to whether the opening stanzas acclaim the coming, or lament the passing of summer. The majority of Neidhart's *Sommerlieder* were composed during his first period of creativity;[5] all of the *Winterlieder* were written during the middle and late period of his life. While the *Winterlieder* are composed in the traditional *canzon* form, the *Sommerlieder* have a structure which is very loose and varied, and they are referred to frequently as *Reien* or dance songs.

In the *Sommerlieder* Neidhart took up Walther's ideal of natural love and explored its possibilities. In exploring a love within a natural setting, Neidhart altered the traditional nature description in an entirely original and dramatic way. A typical nature description of the *Minnesang* presents flowers, birds, grass, trees, well illustrated by Albrecht von Johannsdorf (90, 32–90, 36).[6] The notable feature of such description is its static, two-dimensional quality. The poet paints a colorful array of roses and clover under the linden tree, on whose branches he places singing birds. There is absolutely no action, no sense of space or time in this *paysage*. The nature *topoi* are frozen into a permanent state of summer.

With Neidhart, on the other hand, the static picture of nature explodes into movement. The elements of the summer *topos* are pulled out of their state of immobility and become active participants in a little scene presenting the arrival of spring:

Der meie der ist rîche:
er füeret sicherlîche
dem walt an sîner hende.
der ist nu niuwes loubes vol: der winter hât ein ende.

"Ich fröu mich gein der heide
ir liehten ougenweide,
diu uns beginnet nâhen."
so sprach ein wolgetâniu maget; "die wil ich schône enpfâhen."

"Muoter, lât ez an melde!
jâ wil ich komen ze velde
und wil den reien springen;
jâ ist ez lanc, daz ich diu kint niht niuwes hôrte singen."

[3, 22–4, 10]

May is powerful,
securely he guides
the forest by his hand,
covered with leaves now: winter has ended.

"I go rejoicing towards the heath
and the bright flowers
with which he is approaching."
Thus spoke a beautiful girl, "I will go and welcome them properly."

"Mother, I am telling you
I shall go to the fields
and dance the *reien.*
Indeed it has been long since I heard my companions sing."

Heath and Forest are companions to Spring, the great and powerful lord. In Spring's retinue, Heath and Forest are almost as important as Spring himself. In the second strophe, the human world, represented by the young girl, enters the scene and joins the procession emphasized by the preposition *gein,* "towards." Her statement "and dance the *reien*" appears in the same position in the strophe as "he is approaching" and "the Forest by his hand." Thus, by implication, the procession of Heath and Forest in Spring's retinue and the dancing of the young girl are presented as analogous acts of welcoming. The dominant theme of every *Natureingang* in the *Sommerlieder* is joy. Words of joy such as *vreude,* "joy," *vreun,* "to enjoy," *vro,* "joyful," abound, appearing forty-eight times in twenty-nine *Sommerlieder.*[7] Frequently, they appear in the conspicuous position at the beginning of a line or, occasionally, at the beginning of a strophe. Neidhart clearly experimented with, and emphasized Walther's idea that it is natural to be joyful in springtime. The personified nature-*topoi* express their joy by receiving Spring in a little scene. The human world participates in this little scene initiated by the nature-*topoi*; Neidhart allows them to become part of nature. Their emotions, their joy and love, are thus too brought into nature's domain and defined as being within the natural order.

Neidhart's nature descriptions appear to follow Walther's exploration of *amor naturalis,* "natural love." However, Neidhart plays through the variations of *niedere Minne* in a series of dialogues and demonstrates that such love, rather than being free and natural, becomes trapped by the burdens of family, neighbors, respectability, and marriage: *Ez meiet hiuwer aber als e* (7, 11–8, 11).

The poem consists of a dialogue between mother and daughter. The first strophe is spoken by the girl. There is an analogy between her condition and that of nature. Both she and nature are cured by spring's arrival, symbolized by the image of the dew,[8] and the same word, *springen,* is used to describe her activity, a dance, and that of nature, spring forth. The mother turns away from nature. Her advice to ignore the curative effect of spring and to turn away from love, coupled with the warning of winter's cold and all that it implies, is entirely against nature as described by the poet and in the words spoken by the young girl. But, it is a natural reaction for one conditioned by the rules of her class. Her warning, not to enjoy oneself because of the bad times that may come, indicates an attitude conditioned by the morality of the village. The mother's next line, "but if you do go to the dance," has a beautiful touch of irony and psychological insight. It reveals the frustration of a parent who, after a firm "No!" concedes in the end for the sake of peace. The mother gives in only to qualify her concession with a warning to be careful. Her warning, again, is petit bourgeois: watch out that you don't get pregnant, for if you do, "your joy will become infinitely small"—as small as a baby. And with this she comes back to her earlier warning, "remember the cold winter," which appears in the same position in the strophe as the earlier warning.

The function of the mother in Neidhart's *Sommerlieder* thus parallels the role of the *nîdere* in the traditional *Minnesang*. While the enemies of love introduce the uncourtly element —the world of ordinary people—and thus serve to emphasize the courtliness of the poet, the mother here represents peasant morality, common sense, and is contrasted to the natural order established in the *Natureingang*.

In this poem the name of the girl's lover is Merze, probably an endearing term rather than a name meaning literally "treasure." In all other *Sommerlieder,* the lover of the girl is the poet-knight who appears under the name of der von Riuwental. Their love, symbolized by their dance under the linden tree, is seemingly part of the natural process. However, after Neidhart has played through the welcoming scenes of spring, an essential element of every *Sommerlied,* he introduces the unnatural element that reveals the true nature of the love suit. The mother customarily interjects a warning of pregnancy, and this is at times heightened by the addition of "you know what happened to so-and-so,"[9] which reveals her love for gossip where others are concerned, and the fear of it for her own. In the poem, her statements frequently contain the implication that the girl was tricked into granting her favors.[10] The notion that love's consummation is brought about only through the trickery of men reveals her bourgeois outlook. At times the mother ends with the thought that the damage is done, so let's at least keep up a good appearance and avoid gossip.[11] The mother's chief objection to the knight-lover is that he is outside their class and is therefore unlikely to restore the girl's good name by a speedy marriage. There are several poems in which she tries to force the girl into consenting to a marriage, or at least a betrothal, with a peasant.[12]

The girl is revealed to be as materialistic in outlook as her mother. While the mother is concerned with appearances in the eyes of society, the daughter is concerned with what she wears and how she looks. It is of great importance that she is considered the best-looking girl in the country. This fact alone, she feels, is sufficient reason for the Knight von Riuwental to desire her.[13] Her quarrels with her mother invariably are prompted by arguments over her holiday attire, which she feels she needs to go to the dance.[14] Although the *Natureingang* establishes an analogy between the trees wearing their new foliage and the girls wearing their holiday attire to welcome spring, the emphasis on the girl's dress turns out to be, not a sign of her naturalness, but of her materialistic outlook. In one dialogue the daughter offers the following oath:

> ob er mich des lîbes ie gebaete,
> sô sîs unlange staete
> diu valde an mîner waete
>
> [6, 36–6, 38]

> If he ever asked me for my love
> then may the fold of
> my dress become rumpled.

The fold on her dress must be very important to her if she is willing to swear by it, and it is not unlikely that the correct fold was a matter of propriety. Thus the girl was offering her visible propriety as proof for a moral propriety. That clothing was considered a visible manifestation of a moral state by the society to which the girl belonged, is made clear in the following remark made by the mother:

> dîn wankelmuot ist offenbâr.
> wint ein hüetel um dîn hâr
>
> [24, 30–24, 31]

> Your wavering has become manifest.
> Put a hat on your head.

A *hüetel, hat,* was the sign of a married woman.

For the girl, the appearance of her dress is a matter of prestige. It is used as a visible sign of her superiority over her peers, manifested in the fact that she has a knight as her lover:

> mîn hâr
> an dem reien solt mit sîden sîn bewunden
> durch sînen willen, der mîn zallen stunden
> wünschet hin ze Riuwental.
>
> [28, 29–30, 32]

> My hair
> should be bound in silk for the dance
> on his account, who at all times
> wishes my presence at Riuwental.

Her statement, "on his account," reveals her gratitude to the knight, whose love she feels makes her superior to other members of her class, and allows her to wear silk, a material normally forbidden to the peasant. Also, bright colors could not be worn by the peasant.[15] And yet, the girl boasts that he gave her the stockings which she wears (21,16–21, 17), and sent her a wreath, which establishes the fact that the knight is her lover. It is not a secret love, for this girl proclaims her love boldly by wearing the wreath and the red socks. "What he asked me for, no one knows," can be understood only ironically. By wearing the wreath and the red socks she openly proclaims not only that he asked her for her favors, but also that he received them. These socks, both courtly and outlandish, were not only red, a color not suitable for a member of her class, they also came "from beyond the Rhine." With the wearing of these socks she sets herself apart from her class. The mother frequently comments upon her desire to catch the stupid knight (27, 30). In another poem, Neidhart speaks in his role as observer of the scene and states that she stole two red socks from the proud Knight von Riuwental and offered him a wreath while dancing (20, 30–20, 37). Thus, according to this observer, neither the wreath nor the socks were given her. It was she who offered the wreath, thus she was the one who initiated the love-suit, and the red socks she stole from the knight. Defying the rules of her class, she reached for the love of the knight and tried to acquire courtliness by force. She dresses herself in the externals of his courtliness from the silk ribbons in her hair to the red socks on her feet, but since they are only external manifestations of courtliness they are meaningless without the inner code of ethics.

The love of the *Sommerlieder* is thus not natural and free as Neidhart led us to believe in the *Natureinang*. For the girl, this love is a matter of pride and social ambition, not *amor naturalis* but *amor nobilitatis,* while for the mother it is a matter of grave concern, for it runs counter to the rules of propriety of her class. In short: in the *Sommerlieder* Neidhart demonstrates the pitfalls of Walther's natural love. In dialogues he plays through its possibilities and demonstrates what happens if a man from the noble class attempts to experience such natural love. This love is neither *amor naturalis,* sexual experience for the sake of procreation, as sanctified by the Church, nor is it mutual and joyful as Walther indicated. It becomes immediately entangled in the notions and prejudices of the morality of the village, where a girl cannot admit experiencing sexual pleasure and where thus the consummation of love is made out to be an act of submission on her part brought about only through the trickery of the man. A necessary corollary of this notion is the need to stabilize such a relationship through marriage and thus avoid the scorn of society brought about by an illegitimate child. The mother, deeply grounded in the notions of her class, wants her daughter to marry a peasant. The daughter, on the other hand, has ambitions of courtliness and hopes to marry her lover, the knight. Thus, the final destination of both the *amor naturalis* sanctioned by the Church, and this natural love experienced in the sphere of the peasantry is the safe harbor of marriage. If the knight consents to it, he has lost his sense of moderation as well as his identity as a member of his class. If he rejects it, then the love-suit must end or else it will be exposed for what it really is—*cupiditas.*

After rejecting the concept of *niedere Minne* as a workable alternative, Neidhart proceeded to reaffirm the concept of courtly love. In the *Winterlieder,* the poet proves his identity and serves his function as a member of the courtly class by serving his lady. Although his service is not rewarded, he continues to serve her because by his unfaltering service he can experience moral exaltation. Although her unattainability brings immeasurable grief, he has to present the appearance of joy, because that posture, as Walther also confirmed, is part of this service and thus an act of true courtliness.

Neidhart's return to the *Minnesang* convention is paralleled in his nature descriptions. Nature is no longer represented in a scene; once more nature is used in a static, two-dimensional way, as a foil for the poet's feelings. The harshness of winter reflects the harshness of his lady, and the suffering of nature is paralleled by the poet's grief.

The lady whom Neidhart serves is, however, not the courtly lady, but the wanton girl of the *Sommerlieder* and, while the poet serves her *âne lon,* "without reward," she bestows her favors freely upon his rivals who are referred to as *dörper,* "villagers." More than half of the space of the *Winterlieder* is devoted to descriptions of these *dörper.* In the convention of courtly love, the enemies of the poet, like their counterparts, the friends, remain shadows, nothing more than names, symbols for the outside world. Neidhart uses the inherent dramatic potentiality of the convention and demonstrates in a variety of scenic images both the *nît,* "envy," and the uncourtliness of his rivals.

What is immediately striking about Neidhart's villagers is the fact that they are defined as peasants, not by the presence of rural tasks in rural surroundings, but entirely by their lack of courtliness. They dance ungracefully, even jerkingly, and lack both control and moderation.[16] Most of all, their uncourtly moral state is revealed in their choice of dress, which is courtly to be sure, but foppish and extravagant. Like the girls in the *Sommerlieder,* these rivals are singularly concerned with their appearance, their hair styles and dress.[17] Not only do they dress like dandies, they also wear armor while dancing,[18] which as we know from Arthurian romances is an unforgivable offence against courtliness.[19] A knight was expected to appear in civilian clothes in the presence of ladies. Like the male pheasant, these rivals of the poet use their brightly colored attire and shining swords to attract the female. The animalistic nature of their urge is emphasized through Neidhart's use of images presenting them as animals.[20]

It is important to note that these rival-*dörper* behave in exactly the same fashion as the knight-lover behaved in the *Som-*

merlieder. Like the knight, they dance with the girls under the linden tree; like the knight-lover, they seek joy through sexual union; like him, they sing and lead the dance, and like him, they collect flowers for a wreath.[21] Thus, like the knight-lover of the *Sommerlieder,* these rivals seek to experience *niedere Minne* and so are granted intimacies by the girl. These intimacies were once the prerogative of the poet in his role as knight-lover of the *Sommerlieder.* In this sphere of *niedere Minne* he was unchallenged, as in the *pastourelle* tradition the sexual prowess of the knight is never questioned. Only when he returned to the role of the courtly poet-lover and attempted to relate to his lady on a sublimated, spiritual level, did his rivals appear. His lady, who was, so to speak, programmed in the physical sphere, fell easy prey to the *dörper* who simply took over the territory of the Knight von Riuwental.

Neidhart makes it quite clear that his *dörper* are only symbolic peasants, figures of lowered knights, men who, although they are members of the courtly class, behave in an uncourtly manner and are symbolically relegated to the sphere of the peasantry. The description of the behavior of these rivals, however, should not be read to reflect the reality of courtly life. The poet-lover, the lady, and the *dörper,* who in Neidhart's poetry are the *nîdere,* the enemies of courtly love, are merely *personae* within the play of *Minne.* The *dörper*-strophes are, after all, part of his *Minnelied* and thus part of his *dienst,* "service."

Occasionally, a *dörper* seeks to serve the lady in the fashion of the courtly lover but fails, lapsing back into his customary sensual pursuit of happiness. Here lies the tragedy that underscores the ludicrous *dörper*-scenes: *Minne* no longer exists. The poet seeks it, but his lady is keyed to sensual pleasure; his rivals occasionally seek it; however, the sensual disposition of the lady, as well as their own, prevents them from experiencing it.

The question posed and answered in Neidhart's lyric is not only "What is courtly love?" but "What is courtly?" As Neidhart points out, the difference between a peasant wearing armor and a knight lies not in their outward appearance; in that they are identical; the difference lies solely in their attitudes. In the hands of a *dörper,* a sword is misused as a *weibelruote,* "a stick for women," rather than as an instrument with which to serve the lady in a chivalric act. It is the commitment to an ethical code that unites the poets in presenting to their audience the image of ideal courtliness, an ideal which could never be fully realized but had to be aspired to, if the reality of their lives was to be justified as courtly. Neidhart's *dörper* are representations of the uncourtly man, the man who pursues sensual pleasures alone and fails to aspire to the courtly ideal.

Thus, more forcefully than Walther, Neidhart rejects the idea of natural love as a viable alternative and reaffirms the basic premise of courtly love. Stubbornly adhering to an ideal which is unattainable, Neidhart's late poems, like those of Walther, are dominated by a mood of despair and resignation. One late poem opens with a winter lament coupled with a love lament. The universal sadness produced by the absence of summer is paralleled by the personal grief of the poet. The unapproachability of the lady, states the poet, causes him immeasurable grief which is incomprehensible to others, and yet, in the tradition of Morungen, Reinmar, and Walther, Neidhart affirms that he has to put on the appearance of joy in order to make his service an expression of true courtliness.

After thus establishing his adherence to a courtly mode of conduct the poet then proceeds to describe the behavior of some *dörper:*

ine gewann vor mangen zîten ungenâde mêre,
danne ich hân von einem getelinge:
derst ist alsô getoufet, daz in nieman nennen sol
der ist an sîner strâze beidiu tretzic unde hêre.
langez swert alsam ein hanifswinge,
daz treit er alez umbe; im ist sîn gehilze hol.
dâ sint luoger in gemachet, zeine zîzelwaehe;
oben in dem knophe lît ein spigelglas,
dem gelîch alsô daz Friderûnen was.
dô bat er die guoten, daz si sich dar inne ersaehe.

sîne wolde iedoch in sînen spiegel nie geluogen:
daz versagtes im in einer smaehe;
si sprach verwendiclîchen: "daz ist immer ungetân.
ich bekenne iuch niht an iuwer hövescheit sô kluogen.
ê ez iu ze liebe an mir geschaehe,
jâ wolde ich ê verliesen slehtes allez, daz ich hân."
sî sprach: "liupper, heime ich hân noch guoter spiegel drîe:
derst mir ieglîcher lieber danne der."
schiere sprach er aber: "vrouwe, luoget her!"
alsô müete sî der gouch mit sîner hoppenîe.

hie mit disen dingen sî diu rede alsô gescheiden!

lât iu mêre künden mîner swaere!
die tumben getelinge tuont mir aller leideclîch.
swaz ich tuon, ich kan sî bî der guoten siht erleiden.
wessen sî, wie lîhte ich des enbaere,
si würben anderthalben, Gîselbreht und Âmelrich:
die hânt dîsen sumer her getanzet an ir hende
allenthalben, swâ man ie der vreude phlac.
hinne vür gelebe ich nîmmer lieben tac,
unze ich mînen kumber nâch dem willen mîn volende.

[59, 6–59, 35]

I have never seen such rudeness
as I have seen of a certain peasant.
His name is one which no one should know,
he walks along both stubbornly and proudly.
A long sword like a flail he carries
with him always, the inside of which is hollow,
precious rods are carved into it like little teeth
and on the handle is a mirror
like the one Friderûn had
and he asked the good one to look into it.

She, however, did not wish to look into his mirror,
she refused it disdainfully
and said proudly: "that will never happen,
I do not acknowledge your clever courtliness.
Before I would do you such a favor
I would rather lose everything I possess."
Then she said: "My dear boy, at home I have three good mirrors
and each one of them I prefer to this one."
But he replied: "come on, lady, look!"
Thus the fool troubled her with his insistence.

With this I shall cease speaking of them.
Let me tell you more about my troubles:
the stupid peasants give me great grief,
whatever I do, I cannot make them unattractive to the good one.
If only they knew how easily I can do without that
they would court differently. Gîselbreht and Âmelrich.
They have danced all summer on her hand,
everywhere, where joy was to be found.
From now on I shall never experience a day of love,
and shall complete my grief according to my own will.

It is noteworthy that the poet refuses to give the name of this rival while in all other poems their names are enumerated. Rather than describe any specific rival, the poet here appears to present the single rival, the uncourtly courtier. In the next two lines, the poet reveals both the pretense and the actuality of this rival in one image: he is stubborn and proud, and yet, the sword he carries is like a flail. The sword he wears to identify himself as courtier, however, is hollow, with precious rods carved into it, so that it cannot be used in actual combat, but is purely decorative. Like the other *dörper,* this one uses the sword as a *weibelruote,* "a stick for women," an instrument with which to impress "the good one." The mirror attached on the handle further emphasizes the purely decorative quality of the sword and reflects the uncourtliness of this rival. It is significant that the mirror is attached to the very sword that reveals both what he pretends to be and what he really is. It is the sword with which he identifies himself as a member of the courtly class and it is his handling of it that reveals his moral uncourtliness. The sword, thus misused, loses its function and thus its justification, and the bearer loses his courtly identity.

It is not surprising, therefore, that "the good one" refuses to look into his mirror. By so doing, she refuses to identify with his vision of courtliness: "I do not acknowledge your clever courtliness." Disdainfully and with an air of great superiority, "proudly," she contrasts his mirror with her own vision. However, the ideal she prefers is reflected not in one mirror but three. Thus, the poet seems to indicate that for her, too, courtliness is a masquerade, a matter of pretensions, and that the mirror or mirrors that reflect this courtliness are deceiving her with false visions of perfection. The significance of the three mirrors may become obvious from another *Winterlied* in which the number three is important: *Sumer, diner liehten ougenweide* (78, 11–79, 17). The first source of grief is the arrival of winter which brings universal sadness to the courtly world. The second cause for grief is that the poet's service has remained unrewarded. Thirdly, he is grieved "that the good one is not lying in my arms." This line with its sensual implications appears to speak of a different kind of reward than that envisaged previously. It appears to refer to the poet in his role as lover in the *Sommerlieder.* In this role, he received the tangible reward of the girl, now the prerogative of the *dörper.* Thus, the three kinds of grief the poet speaks of are: the universal and impersonal sadness produced by the arrival of winter and its implied absence of love; then, his unrewarded service; and lastly, unrequited sensual love which he experienced as Knight von Riuwental in the *Sommerlieder.*

These lines illuminate the meaning of the three mirrors of the good one by the three distinctly different images of the lady represented in Neidhart's poetry. First, she is the universal and idealized lady. Then, she is his *vrouwe,* the individual courtly lady whom he serves in his song. Lastly, she is the girl of the *Sommerlieder,* his personal love in his role as Knight von Riuwental. Each of these images must be reflected by a different mirror. It is not surprising that she prefers each of these mirrors of the poet to the mirror of the *dörper,* which can only reflect his pretentiousness.

The different images of Neidhart's lady reflected in each of the three mirrors correspond to the three aspects of love presented in his lyrics. First, there is the ideal and abstract *minne,* then, the individual poet's love for the courtly lady, and lastly, the love that belongs to the girl of the *Sommerlieder.* This gradation of love from the exclusively spiritual to the exclusively sensual level is reflected also in Neidhart's vocabulary which ranges from the lofty language of the *Minnesang* to the colloquial and even vulgar. Occasionally, the two extremes are juxtaposed in one phrase revealing the unbridgeable gap: *mîner ougen wünne greif er an den füdenol,* "she is the joy of my eyes and he touches her cunt" (65, 12).

How can the lady be both an object of lust and an object of worship and simultaneously grant sensual satisfaction and moral exaltation? She does so because she is a mirror, she is what the *persona* of the poet makes her to be. As such, she can reflect his sensuality or his ideal nature, lust or sublimation. By allowing the lady to be at the same time the girl of the *dörper* and the idealized lady, he points out that the lady is a purely fictional character. Whatever the "real" lady may be, as the lady in his lyric she can be spiritual or physical, inspiring or sensual, depending on what the poet makes her. For his rivals the lady is an object of sexual desire, while the poet maintains that she is the embodiment of the courtly ideal. Thus, although the poet is still in possession of the mirror that reflects true courtliness, for the *dörper,* the mirror of the courtly ideal is lost. There remains the hope that if the poet continues to serve the lady as if she were the ideal and holds the mirror before the eyes of his society, his rivals might accept the ideal it reflects so that their image of the lady and the poet's image would become united and be reflected

In the last strophe of the poem, the poet seemingly returns through the same mirror.

to the motif of the *dörper.* In reality, the strophe is an affirmation of his role as *Minnesänger,* by which he demonstrates his courtly identity, an identity which could and should also include his rivals. The first line of the strophe is a love lament, a stylistic mannerism with which Neidhart frequently bridges his *dörper* strophes. He first implies that what he is about to say has nothing to do with his previous statements, but goes on to say that the behavior of his rivals contributes significantly to his grief. His grief, it appears, is caused by the fact that they share an intimacy with the good one" which he himself would like to enjoy. However, "the last two lines of the *Aufgesang* bring the significant modification. If they knew, the poet assures us, how easily he can do without this intimacy, then these rivals would court her "differently." The nature of the "differently" is defined in the first part of *Abgesang* by contrasting it with the manner in which these rivals court her at present. The words "summer," "danced," and "joy," clearly indicate that they seek the love of the *Sommerlieder.* This type of love, the poet says, he can do without, indeed he has given it up long ago.

By allowing the enemies of love to enter the magic circle, he once more draws the line of exclusion, closer and more narrowly defined this time, and again excludes the *nîdere,* his *dörper,* from participating in the play of *Minne.* There is a ray of hope that these rivals might also reject the love of the *Sommerlieder* and come to appreciate the value of *Minnedienst* as exemplified by the poet, that they "would court differently." If so, they would cease to be *dörper,* and regain their courtly identity, and the poet, the holder of the mirror, along with his audience, who looks into the mirror, might again be united and allowed to enter the magic circle once more. However, at present, these rivals remain trapped in sensual love as indicated by their names: Gîselbreht appears to be composed of *gîsel,* "prisoner," and *breht,* "chatterer"; Âmelrich is probably composed of *amer, jamer,* "grief," or "despair," and *rich,* "rich." In the last lines, the poet parallels their sensual behavior with his own mode of conduct. Refusing the love of the *Sommerlieder,* he chooses to continue his exemplary service "according to his own will." The poem began in the mood of the traditional *Minnesang* but ends in an elegiac mood, affirming the poet's adherence to this tradition.

Both Walther and Neidhart first rejected the conventions of

courtly love and experimented with the possibility of *amor naturalis.* Realizing that the possibility of *amor naturalis* in a postlapsarian world turns out to be *cupiditas,* they reaffirmed and restated the conventions of courtly love lyric more intensely and in a more complex way than ever before.

The poets who succeeded them failed to understand the true significance of their experimentation. For a poet like Burkhart (see Chapter VI), for instance, courtly love is the adherence to a ritual whose significance is lost to him and consequently his poetry becomes an enumeration of images that cloak a ghost. For a poet like Geltâr, who tries to imitate Neidhart's *Sommerlieder, amor naturalis* is nothing but the pursuit of sensual pleasure, what Neidhart exposes it to be, *cupiditas.*

Geltâr failed to understand the nature of Walther and Neidhart's quest. The reasons for this failure are very complex. There is a general decline of awareness among the poets of the thirteenth century. For most of them the pursuit of courtliness degenerated into a ritualistic adherence to a fixed code (see chapters II and VI) with the result that the poetry appears to be an enumeration of clichés. Along with this comes the disappearance of the interplay—the magic circle—between the audience and the poet, between the *personae* of the lyric and the audience from whose ranks the *personae* are drawn. It is possible that this disappearance of an audience to whom the poets could address themselves accounts for the general decline of lyric poetry after Neidhart.

Neidhart was not only one of the great poets of courtly love, he was also one of the last, a fact he seems to be aware of in one of his late poems (32, 6–32, 35), possibly his last one. In this poem, he not only reviews his own definitions of love and courtliness, he also echoes those of other poets and reviews concepts which had become defined during the twelfth century.

The first lines of the last strophe of the poem supply its date: it must have been written in the spring of 1236, when *die Diutschen* (32, 30) consisting of Bishop Ekbert of Bamberg, Bishop Rüdeger of Passau, Duke Otto II of Bavaria, Count Otto of Brandenburg, and the Beheim, King Wenzel of Bohemia, threatened to invade Austria as executors of the imperial decree proscribing Duke Frederick II, Neidhart's patron at the time. They invaded Austria in the fall of the same year and, since no reference to this event can be found in Neidhart's poetry, we may assume that he died or stopped composing lyrics at that time. Thus, like Walther's *Elegie,* this poem must be regarded as one of the final utterances of the poet, the expression of a man who has lived a long life in the service of an ideal and who, we may expect, will attempt to define his relationship to the ideal and to the society for whom he performed his exemplary service. Neidhart clearly sets his concept of love in opposition to Walther and Gottfried. Walther states in *muget ir schouwen* that his lady acts against nature if she refuses her reward and fails to bring joy to the poet, while the entire world, nature and mankind, rejoices over the arrival of spring. Thus, by implication, he defines courtly love as unnatural.

The first strophe is spoken by the poet in his role as poet-lover. In the tradition of the courtly poet, he laments the unattainability of his lady and contrasts his inner emotions to the conditions of nature. The second strophe is spoken by a girl who gives us an exuberant exclamation of joy over the arrival of spring and its curative power. Her emotions are in harmony with nature and in contrast to those of the poet.

The third strophe, spoken by the girl's companion, immediately brings the characteristic turning away from nature:

> "trûtgespil, nû swige, hiht verlius dîn lêren!
> ob ich dir noch hilfe dîne vröude mêren,
> wer mêret mit die mînen? man eint niht in êren,
> daz si tougen unser minne gern;
> ich wil von in valscher minne enbern:
> die site wellent sich verkêren."
>
> "Friend, be quiet, don't waste your advice.
> Should I help you to increase your joy,
> Who is going to increase mine? Men are not honorable
> When they love to avoid our love.
> I will gladly do without their false love,
> For the customs truly have changed."

Her complaint, that she cannot partake in the joy because she is not loved, is presented in *Minnesang* vocabulary, *minne, êren,* and *tougen;* however, every one of these terms is misunderstood and misapplied. *Tougen* is used as a verb, whereas, in the *Minnesang, tougen* appears as an adjective modifying *minne* as Neidhart used it in Strophe I.

The girl's companion uses *tougen* to mean "avoid" or "not desire." She laments that men do not desire her and other similar unfortunate ones. Connecting her lament with the *Natureingang* by the use of *vroide,* "joy," Neidhart reveals that what she desires is not *minne* but natural love. She completely misapplies the word *êre,* "honor," by her statement that men are dishonorable if they avoid her love, *tougen.* A *Minnesänger' êre* is heightened by the proper conduct of *tougen minne.*

In the fourth strophe, the girl continues the use and misuse of courtly vocabulary initiated by her companion in the previous strophe:

> Sâ dô sprach diu ander: "man sint underscheiden:
> die mit triuwen dienen wîben unde meiden,
> die selben lâ dir lieben und die boesen leiden!
> ist uns iemen âne herzen holt,
> dem ist kupher lieber danne golt:
> gehoenet werde er von uns beiden!"
>
> Whereupon the other answered: "Men are not alike.
> Those that serve faithfully ladies and young girls
> Let them serve you, and avoid the evil ones.
> He who loves us without his heart
> He loves copper more than gold
> And he shall be cursed by both of us."

Seemingly answering her companion's lament she differentiates between men "who serve faithfully" and the "evil ones" who love without heart. These words echo Gottfried von Strassburg's famous discussion on true and false *Minne, Tristan und Isold* (12183ff.). In it, Gottfried argues that it is not *Minne* that is at fault but the people that take part, for they lack *staete vriundez muot,* "the heart of a constant friend" (12269) and *triuwe,* "faithfulness" (12336ff.). The last two lines also echo Gottfried's condemnation of King Mark, who could not always distinguish between Isot and other women (12666–12671). Although the girl uses Gottfried's vocabulary and images, she starts out from very different premises and thus completely misuses the images. She connects the word *triuwe* with the *Minnesang* word *dienen.* After the love potion, the relationship between Gottfried's lovers does not resemble the relationship of vassal and lord as in the *Minnesang;* rather, it is a union of two equal individuals. Gottfried makes it quite clear that the true *Minne* of which he is speaking is mutual, and that the purity and intensity of the experience depends on the ethical and emotional commitment of both partners. This girl in her ignorance combines Gottfried's concept of full emotional commitment—avoid those that love *ane herzen*—with the *Minnesang* tradition, where the lady remains distant and passive and the commitment is largely on the part of the poet, *die selben lâ dir dienen.* She continues in this vein in the sixth strophe, where she defines *valsche minne* as love without emotional commitment, *liebe.* However, her true feelings are revealed in the words *dô si bî herzeliebe gerne lâgen,* "when lying close to those they loved." To her, love means physical consummation only, and thus her use of courtly vocabulary is another sign of her pretensions of courtliness. The use of the word *liebe* and especially the word *herzeliebe,* which seems to refer to Walther's *"Aller werdekeit ein fuegerinne"* (46. 32ff. 1. 47, 12) shows that she would like to make this relationship mutual. The *sous-entendu* is that if the relationship were mutual, that is if she were considered the knight's equal, as she is in other *Sommerlieder* by herself, her mother, her friend, and the knight, then she would have achieved her social ambitions. Her use of the words *hôhe minne, herzeliebe, bî ein ander lâgen,* all intertwined, neatly express her contradictory and confused premises, which in the end all reveal true desire and ambition.

The concern of her companion is of a completely different nature:

die den wîben hochgemüete solden machen
unde in in diu lôsen ougen solden lachen,
die habent sich bewollen mit sô vremden sachen,
daz hie bevor den Tiutschen wilde was.
ja ist er niht der wîbe spiegelglas,
der sî ze vrevel wil geswachen.

[32, 18–32, 23]

Those that should have lifted women's hearts
And should have laughed into their loose eyes,
These have undertaken such strange things,
Which were formerly completely foreign to the Germans.
Indeed, is he not the mirror of women
Who wants to reject them for the sake of his perversity.

The use of the word *hôchgemuete,* "joy," with *in diu lôsen ougen,* "into their loose eyes," reveals that what she desires is the natural love as indicated in the *Natureingang.* Neidhart uses it similarly in other poems (12, 13–16; 22, 17–23). The natural love does not exist, she complains, because men are concerned with *vremde sachen,* "strange things." Critics have suggested that this strophe makes reference to the practice of homosexuality. That it does so, but in an entirely different sense than the usual interpretations,[22] can be demonstrated by a comparison with the *De planctu naturae* of which many echoes can be found in this poem.[23]

Among the themes of Alanus's allegory are the necessity of replenishing the ranks of mankind depleted by death, and the heinousness of man's departures from normal sexual life, including such deviations as homosexuality. Following is a passage from Alanus to which Neidhart's poem appears to make special references:

Humanum namque genus a sua generositate degenerans, in conjunctione generum barbarizans, Venereas regulas invertendo nimis irregulari utitur metaplasmo. Sicque homo a Venere tiresiatus anomala, directam praedicationem in contrapositionem inordinatem convertit. A Veneris ergo orthographia recedens, sophista falsigraphus invenitur. Consequentum ergo Dioneae artis analogiam devitans, in anastrophem vitiosum degenerat (Wright, p. 462).

The human race degenerates from its high position, commits barbarous acts in the union of genders, perverts the immutable rules of love by employing a most irregular practice. Thus man is made into a Tiresias of abnormal passion, turns the predicate into direct contraposition against all rules. Through Venus he deviates from the rules of writing and becomes a false writing sophist. Consequently he deviates from the proper art of Dione and degenerates into vicious perversion.

Neidhart's "strange things" appear to echo Alanus's *in conjunctione generum barbarizans,* and so does the word *wilde,* "barbarous," "wild," which is but another translation of Alanus's *barbarizans.* With the word *Tiutschen,* Neidhart appears to give, in humorous fashion, the reference to his source. These barbarous acts were lamented, thus presumably committed, not by *den Tiutschen* but in the land of the author Alanus. The word *wilde* serves as a double pun: such acts are *wilde,* thus foreign to the Germans; they are also *wilde,* that is, barbarous as Alanus says. The last two lines of the girl's lament are a puzzle. Judging from the context, a reasonable translation of these lines seems to be: "is he not the mirror who wants to reject them for the sake of his perversity." The word *vrevel* with its implication of impropriety, irregularity, appears to echo the words of Alanus such as *irregulari, inordinatem, devitans, venereas regulas invertendo.* The idea that a man who practices homosexuality becomes the mirror of woman in that he acts like a woman, but is only a reflection of her not her true substance, appears to echo the lament with which Alanus begins his allegory.

In retrospect, the words of the girl in the third strophe acquire an additional meaning. The men whom she complains about truly *tougen,* "avoid," and *geswachen,* "avoid," the love of women, and they have lost their "honor" in the double sense of having fallen from the courtly code, as well as having fallen from a general ethical code.

This lament of Alanus finds an echo in the *Natureingang*-strophe spoken by the girl. The use of anaphora is most unusual for Neidhart; indeed, this is the only poem in which this rhetorical device is used. The anaphora of joy over spring's arrival, its curative power and the love it brings, echoes in reverse the anaphora of lamentation over sexual aberrations by Alanus.

Thus, by the reference to homosexuality, as well as by the rhetoric of the *Natureingang,* Neidhart reveals his source. Once more, as in all his *Sommerlieder,* he takes this natural love as glorified by Alanus and exposes it as *amor un-naturalis* and *amor nobilitatis.* In the last two strophes of the poem, he speaks up in the role of the poet, laments the loss of true courtliness in his society and reaffirms the courtly values. While Alanus is concerned with the aberrations of society from the rules of love as decreed by nature, Neidhart concerns himself with the aberrations of society from the rules of courtliness. In this last strophe, he expresses the fear that the Germans might invade Austria before the spring planting. Their lack of concern for the innocent population that would suffer from starvation would be proof of their lack of *largitas.* This statement is immediately followed by a lament that there are "certain lords," his *dörper,* who wear "clothing unfit to be worn in the presence of ladies." Neidhart ends his poem with the statement that if these violations of the rules of courtliness would cease, then, and only then, could he function as a poet: *dâ von wolde ich singen unde sagen,* "then I would indeed write and sing."

This then is the only *Sommerlied* in which the poet speaks in the traditional role as *Minnesänger,* a role in which he presents himself in the *Winterlieder.* It appears that the mature poet returned once more to the poetical form of his younger years in order to elucidate his earlier creations. While the *Sommerlieder* clearly demonstrate that in Neidhart's opinion "natural love" is not a workable alternative to the poet's dilemma—on the contrary it adds new problems which threaten to undermine his identity as a member of the courtly class—they do not present a reaffirmation of the courtly values as do the *Winterlieder*.

One of the most striking and powerful features of this poem is its circular structure. Strophes are elucidated and acquire a second level of meaning through statements made in succeeding strophes. Thus, the seemingly traditional sentiments expressed in the first strophe acquire a new and profound meaning after the reading of the entire poem. Unlike preceding poets who cannot succeed in attaining their lady's love because of the conditions of the convention, Neidhart, it becomes clear, cannot attain the love of his lady because neither she nor his audience exist any longer. He speaks in a vacuum and the magic circle, which formerly contained and protected him and made his service a noble endeavor, has disappeared. He stands alone in a world where his words can no longer be understood. There is nothing left for him to do but lament and yearn for the past when his audience still existed, for then he would still have a function in society: "then I would indeed write and sing."

Walther and Neidhart tested the limits of the courtly love convention. Seeking a love in a new setting outside the conventional court, they found that the essence of the convention, its ennobling force, was inextricably linked to its courtly setting and that the poet cannot love in a perfectly noble way outside the magic circle which he himself has erected. Consequently, they return to the courtly setting and reaffirm the value and necessity of a select audience, with whose help true courtliness alone can be experienced.

The narrative poets are not so fortunate. They must test and apply the convention within a realistic setting in which the *personae* of the narrative move. They cannot maintain the balance between the physical and the spiritual as do the lyric poets because, ultimately, love in the narrative must be confronted with society; and the dilemma of the narrative poet is that this love proves to be inapplicable to a courtly world.

Notes

1. To establish the date of a Walther poem I have followed Carl von Kraus, *Walther von der Vogelweide. Untersuchungen* (Berlin and Leipzig: W. de Gruyter, 1935). The scholarship on Walther is enormous, but a summary of the most important publications in recent years is provided in Kurt Herbert Halbach, *Walther von der Vogelweide* (Stuttgart: Metzler, 1965).
2. The edition used is Carl von Kraus, ed., *Die Gedichte Walthers von der Vogelweide,* 12th ed. (Berlin: de Gruyter, 1959).
3. Compare W. T. H. Jackson, "The Medieval Pastourelle," *PQ* 32, II (1952): 156–176.
4. Heinrich von Morungen in *Des Minnesangs Frühling,* ed. Carl von Kraus, 32nd ed. (Stuttgart: Hirzel, 1959).
5. In dating the poems I have generally followed Edmund Wiessner, *Kommentar zu Neidharts Liedern* (Leipzig: 1954). Use was also made of Wiessner's *Vollständinges Wörterbuch zu Neidharts Liedern* (Leipzig: 1954). The edition of Neidhart's lyrics used was by Edmund Wiessner, *Die Lieder Neidharts,* Altdeutsche Textbibliothek, no. 44 (Tübingen: Max Niemeyer, 1955). The quotations in this chapter are from the second revised edition by Hanns Fischer, which appeared in 1963. Neidhart scholarship is almost as immense as the scholarship on Walther. For a summary of the history of Neidhart see Eckehard Simon, *Neidhart von Reuental. Geschichte der Forschung und Bibliographie* (Cambridge, Mass.: Harvard University Press, 1968).
6. von Kraus, *Des Minnesangs Frühling.*
7. See 4, 1; 5, 12; 5, 37; 9, 28; 10, 25; 14, 33; 16, 10; 17, 19; 19, 27; 28, 36; 29, 32; etc.
8. Neidhart frequently uses the image of dew as a resuscitating agent, e.g., 7, 18–19; 28, 15–21. There is a striking similarity between Neidhart's use of dew and that occurring in Jewish literature, where it is frequently used as a sign of resurrection; see Louis Ginzberg, *The Legends of the Jews* (Philadelphia: The Jewish Publication Society of America, 1909–1938), 7 vols.: I, 10; II, 334; III, 95; IV, 197.
9. See 7, 27–8, 3; 21, 6–12.
10. See 6, 29 ff.; 7, 27 ff.
11. See 17, 39–18, 2.
12. See 24, 14 ff.; 29, 9 ff.
13. See 4, 27–30.
14. See 10, 27 ff.; 22, 24; 24, 33 ff.
15. We can gain some information about sumptuary laws from two contemporary literary sources: Eduart Schroder, ed., *Die Kaiserchronik eines Regensburger Geistlichen,* MGH, I (Hanover:, Poeschel, 1895) and Joseph Seemuller, ed., *Seifried Helbing,*

(Halle: Waisenhauses, 1886). In the *Kaiserchronik* it is stated explicitly that the peasant is permitted to wear *rupfin tuoch* "coarse material" (14800), and the author of *Seifried Helbing* states that a "peasant and his wife" are to wear only material of *guoten stampfart* "of durable quality" (2, 71). Both authors stress that the wearing of strong colors was forbidden to the peasant (*Kaiserchronik,* 14792–94; *Seifried Helbing,* 2, 71–72).

16. See 60, 16; 89, 1–2; 96, 21; 98, 21.
17. See 60, 11–17; 68, 4–7; 74, 13–14; 75, 13; 86, 17–21.
18. See 52, 3–11; 54, 34; 55, 38–56, 1; 59, 6–15; 61, 8–15.
19. Compare Wolfram von Eschenbach, *Parzival,* 164, 1–5 and *Willehalm,* 312, 12–14.
20. See 51, 18; 68, 16.
21. See the knight-lover dancing: 3, 5–7; 16, 31–36; 21, 2–5; 27, 13; the *dörper* dancing: 52, 5; 59, 32–33; 62, 21–22; the knight-lover singing: 6, 24–28; 21, 2–3; 26, 7–14; the *dörper* singing: 96, 14; 96, 26; the knight-lover collecting and wearing garlands: 17, 12; 19, 10–16; 20, 35; the *dörper* wearing flowers: 57, 5–9; 62, 26–33; 96, 12–13.
22. Most critics approach Neidhart with a *mimesis* interpretation. Thus, in this case they argue (see Wiessner, *Kommentar,* p. 76) that the poet himself deplored the practice of homosexuality, whereas, as will be shown, the reference to such *vremde sachen* serves as a literary allusion.
23. One of them is the frequently recurring image of spring giving new foliage to the trees and giving grass and flowers to the fields in order that they may be properly dressed for his welcoming, an image which is used by no other *Minnesänger* except Walther. Alanus uses the same image twice except that it is not Spring that is received but the personified *Natura* (Wright, pp. 447–449). Another stylistic feature is Neidhart's frequent use of dew as a curative, rejuvenating, even resuscitating agent, which can be found in no other *Minnesänger.* Dew appears twice in the work of Alanus, and it is used there in a strikingly similar way (Wright, p. 448). Thus, echoes of Alanus seem to be present in Neidhart, and it is not surprising that in the poem under discussion echoes of Alanus are unmistakably present and play a significant role in the meaning of the poem.

Renata Karlin

Bibliographic Note

These additional works have also been helpful.

On Neidhart: Brill, Richard. *Die Pseudoneidharte. Eine Stiluntersuchung.* Thesis, Göttingen, 1903; Boueke, Dietrich. *Materialien zur Neidhart-Überlieferung* (München: C. H. Beck, 1967); Fritz, Gerd. *Sprache und Überlieferung der Neidhart-Lieder in der Berliner Handschrift,* germ. fol. 779 (Göppingen: A. Kümmerle, 1969); Keinz, Friederich. *Nachtrag zur Neidhart-Ausgabe* (München: C. Wolf, 1884); Mack, Albert. *Der Sprachschatz Neidharts von Reuental.* Thesis, Tübingen, 1910; Meyer, Richard M. *Die Reihenfolge der Lieder Neidharts von Reuental.* Thesis, Berlin, 1883; Osterdell, Johanne. *Inhaltliche und stilistische Übereinstimmungen der Lieder Neidharts von Reuental mit den Vagantenliedern der Carmina Burana,* Thesis, Köln, 1928; Schürmann, Ferdinand, *Die Entwicklung der parodistischen Dichtung bei Neidhart von Reuental,* Beitrage des Programmes der Oberrealschule, 3, Düren, 1898; Simon, Eckehard, *Neidhart von Reuental: Geschichte der Forschung und Bibliographie* (Cambridge: Harvard University Press, 1968); Weidmann, Walther. *Studien zur Entwicklung von Neidharts Lyrik* (Basel: B. Schwabe, 1947).

On Walther: Burdach, Konrad. *Reinmar der Alte und Walther von der Vogelweide* (Leipzig: S. Hirzel, 1880); Burdach, Konrad. *Walther von der Vogelweide* (Leipzig: Duncher, 1900); Jones, George. *Walther von der Vogelweide* (New York: Twayne, 1968); Kraus, Carl von. *Walther von der Vogelweide. Untersuchungen* (Berlin: de Gruyter, 1966); Lieres und Wilkan, Marianne von. *Sprachformeln in der mittelhochdeutschen Lyrik bis zu Walther von der Vogelweide* (München: C. H. Beck, 1965); Marsh, Christopher. *Walther von der Vogelweide: A Glossary of Ethical Terms.* (Durham: Duke University Press, 1970); Mohr, Ferdinand, *Das unhöfische Element in der mittelhochdeutschen Lyrik von Walther an.* (Tübingen: Laupp, 1913); Scholz, Manfred G. *Bibliographie zu Walther von der Vogelweide* (Berlin: Schmidt, 1969); Schönbach, Anton E. *Walther von der Vogelweide. Ein Dichterleben* (Berlin: E. Hofmann, 1895); Schulte, Massimo. *Walther von der Vogelweide, poeta moderno* (Napoli: Artigianelli, 1961); Wilmanns, Wilhelm. *Leben und Dichten Walther von der Vogelweide* (Bonn: Weber, 1882).

CHAPTER IV

The Conflict of Lyric Conventions and Romance Form

Joan M. Ferrante

Lyric poets, as late as Neidhart, felt the need to preserve the idealizing, striving aspect of courtly love, despite its artificiality, despite its denial of very real physical wants, because it gave them a spiritual and social identity as noble men. Poets writing in narrative genres were equally aware of the positive force of courtly love and did their best to preserve it in their works, but they faced different and perhaps insoluble problems. Since their primary interest was in the knight's service to his society, they could accept love as a beneficial force only when it strengthened him in that service. In the romances of antiquity, which are concerned with the fate of historical peoples, not of individuals except as their actions affect the destiny of their nations, little is made of romantic love. The personal concerns of the hero must be subordinated to public responsibility. Love is tolerated if it does not disturb the social order; otherwise, it is condemned. Arthurian romance shares the social concern of the classical romances, but focuses on the individual. On the assumption that the man best fitted to serve his society is one who has achieved a harmony in his own spirit, a balance between personal desire and public duty, Arthurian poets attempt to integrate the hero's love-service with his other commitments. Such a balance, however, is almost impossible to achieve outside the lyric.

Lyric poetry describes emotions; narrative poetry relates actions. The lyric lover can vacillate forever between hope and despair, renunciation and desire, in the pursuit of an unattainable ideal, but the hero of a romance must act—he must achieve his goals or be overcome in the attempt. He faces real problems, for which he must find a solution, real people to whom he owes service and loyalty. The lady he loves is not a creation of his fantasy, aloof or yielding as his mood demands; she is a woman with her own desires, ties and responsibilities, that may not always be in harmony with his. In serving her, he may find himself neglecting other duties, even betraying other loyalties.

The poets of courtly love were not unaware of the problems it posed in the real world. They created another world in their works, not a reflection of this one, but an ideal exemplar of it; a world in which the restrictions of reality are removed, in which rules are tacitly set up and observed. This is true not only of the lyric, but of a certain kind of romance as well. Arthurian romance posits an ideal world, in which the normal laws of time and space do not operate, in which a moral problem can be posed and resolved without the complications of external evils or of chance. It is a world without an historical context, the only setting in which courtly love could function successfully; but even in this ideal world, the demands of the narrative form place a strain on the serious treatment of courtly love conventions. Courtly love is, as we have seen, a kind of game. It differs from the Ovidian game of love, which both men and women can play, employing any means, however deceptive, that will achieve their goal—possession of the beloved. In courtly love, playing the game properly is its own reward. The goal is to better oneself in the striving. This game cannot be won or lost; it must not be played out, as the narrative demands, because playing it out means having to face the illusions inherent in its rules and conventions. The lyric poet can straddle the line between illusion, or the game, and reality; the narrative poet cannot. The lyric poet studies the effects of love on himself alone—he is his own hero; the narrative poet must show the effects of love on many characters and events.

Since courtly love is almost inevitably at odds with its society in the romance, there is no way, ultimately, to distinguish between courtly love and the destructive passion of classical love.

Both traditions are at work in medieval romance—the long-suffering but ennobling devotion of the courtly lover and the overwhelming physical passion of lovers in classical poetry, who sacrifice honor and duty, who destroy themselves and their dependents, to satisfy their desires. We shall see that the two views of love clash in Arthurian romance, and that the destructive passion finally drives out the ennobling force. But in the medieval reworkings of classical material, only the destructive aspect is seriously considered. Although the French romances of antiquity were written in the twelfth century, when courtly love dominated the lyric in Provence and Germany, they present love almost exclusively as an obstacle to social responsibility and knightly glory. Since these romances occasionally betray an awareness of courtly motifs, we must assume that the authors consciously rejected the possibility of love serving as a beneficial force. If they use the courtly conventions, it is only to criticize or ridicule them. They choose to present love in the tradition of classical poetry.[1]

Against the backgrounds of the Theban and Trojan wars, love, when it is given any importance, becomes a destructive force. Not even Eneas's love for Lavine,[2] the one apparent exception, exerts a positive force over the hero in the *Eneas*. Eneas falls in love so long after he has taken on the war against Turnus, that love cannot be considered the motivation for his action—on the contrary, it almost renders him incapable of fighting. The main function of the Lavine episode seems to be to counterbalance Eneas's affair with Dido which interfered with his historical destiny, while this union furthers it. For the most part, the love affairs in the *Roman de Troie* are of the Dido-Eneas sort, distracting men from their public responsibilities, and threatening their honor. In the *Roman de Thèbes,* love is rarely permitted to intrude on the political and military issues. The few moments the author accords it, perhaps in deference to his audience, the court of Henry II and Eleanor,[3] reveal some influence of the new lyric tradition, but have no importance for the plot.

Though there are several potential love stories in the *Roman de Thèbes,* little is made of their possibilities from which one can infer a lack of sympathy, if not tacit criticism. The poem begins with a prologue, not found in Statius, that tells the story of Jocaste and Edyppus, which influenced Chrétien in the similar Laudine-Yvain situation.[4] Although Edyppus has killed her husband, Jocaste allows herself to be maneuvered into marriage with him when he solves the riddle of the Sphinx. She may suspect his part in her husband's death, but she avoids having to refuse him on that account. When she questions Edyppus about the event, she promises not to hate the as yet unidentified murderer: "What good would it do me to hate him?/The dead cannot be restored" (ll. 429–430). Her justification has a certain proverbial wisdom, but it is hardly natural for a woman whose husband has just been killed. Although the marriage is treated as a political necessity, Jocaste apparently feels a strong attraction for the stranger. The poet may well be criticizing her for allowing personal preference to influence her public decisions, in light of the disaster the marriage is to bring on the land.

Since the only other romantic episodes in the poem are built around the children of Jocaste and Edyppus, one wonders if the propensity to love did not follow from the perverse union that gave them birth. The more serious of the two brothers, Pollinices, does not engage in love.[5] His brother, Ethiocles, is susceptible to romantic encounters of different kinds. He rides a horse given to him by one of his loves, Galathea, whose legs he has had painted on his shield "as a joke," *par gaberie* (l. 6273), a gesture that recalls a story about Guillaume IX,[6] but hardly courtly love. Like Guillaume, Ethiocles is also capable of a more courtly devotion, but the social effects of that devotion are questionable. When the daughter of an accused traitor comes before him to beg for her father's life, he hesitates because she has shown no mercy to him despite his long service to her (l. 8054 ff.). He is eventually moved by her tears, however, and grants her request, but this act is not well received by his courtiers, some of whom had made the same request and been denied. One complains not that Ethiocles freed the traitor, but that he did so at the request of a girl, when he had refused his barons; another replies, "so it is in love and chivalry,/you may hold it villainy,/for us it is courtesy" (ll. 8111–8114).[7] The effect of this "courtly" decision is not to restore harmony to the court, but to increase resentment within it.

The two daughters of Edyppus and Jocaste, Anthigone and Ysmaine, also engage in love; the French poet introduces the romance of Anthigone into the story, but makes little of it, and extends the story of Ysmaine, which ends sadly for the lovers. Both stories contain superficial elements of courtly love, but accord it no moral or ethical force. The knights perform feats in honor of the ladies, not to win their love, which seems to be mutual from the beginning, but to indicate their devotion. Anthigone's lover sends her a horse with the message "I performed my chivalrous deeds for her" (l. 4598), but we hear little of their love. Ysmaine's knight performs chivalric feats in her service, but they are reckless and eventually fatal, an indication of his youth and brashness rather than of his love: he takes on two men at a time because she is watching him and gets away with it, but when he begins to fight without his hauberk, taunting his enemies to attack him, he is killed. Ysmaine remains faithful to him, asking her brother to build an abbey in his memory, to which she will retire as a nun. Like Sigune, in Wolfram's *Parzival,* Ysmaine moves from adolescent delight in her lover's prowess to life-long devotion and denial after death. There is a criticism of love-service in both stories: the French poet deplores knightly endeavor that serves no purpose but to impress the lady, while Wolfram attacks the lady for pushing her knight too far, only for her own vanity.

Love is attacked more directly in the *Roman de Troie,* where it has some effect on the plot. Illicit love is responsible for the beginning of the Trojan war and for the deaths of many heroes in the course of the war. It is, for the most part, a passion that leads to illicit relationships and interferes with duties and loyalties. When men succumb to it, love destroys their reason and their social responsibility. They relinquish "belief and faith, father and lord, lands and territories" (ll. 18455–18459).[8] Love is disastrous for the heroes, even for Achilles, who falls in love with a blameless woman, Polixena, destined to die an innocent sacrifice on his tomb. Not only does he suffer the worst torments of love, and scarcely a metaphor in the Ovidian tradition is omitted from his long monologues,[9] but he is torn between the desire to win his lady and his honor and loyalty to the Greek cause. He can have Polixena only by withdrawing his help from the Greeks; he does, at first, rationalize his refusal to fight by questioning the purpose of the war—what is the point of getting Heleine back if all the kings of Greece are lost (l. 19620 ff.)? Love not only robs men and women of their sense, but also makes them especially skillful in false logic.[10] But despite his questions, Achilles cannot deny his duty completely. He sends his Myrmidons to fight and finally goes himself, eventually killing Troilus and bringing on Ecuba's revenge. It is surely not accidental that the three major lovers are brought together in this dishonorable event: Achilles is ambushed and murdered by Paris to avenge Troilus's death. He falls into the trap because "love took away his sense" (1.22117) as it had done to both the others.

The women who inspire love are for the most part condemned, individually by their own acts and collectively by the poet's comments:

> A feme dure dueus petit;
> a l'un ueil plore, a l'autre rit.
> Mout muent tost li lor corage.
> Assez est fole la plus sage.
> Quant qu'ele a en set anz amé
> a ele en tries jorz oblié.
>
> [11. 13441–13446]

> A woman's grief does not last long;
> she weeps with one eye and laughs with the other.
> Their hearts change very quickly.
> The wisest of them is very foolish.
> What she has loved for seven years,
> she forgets in three days.

The figure of Fortune seems to have inspired at least the second and third lines of this passage, which suggests that the author puts love on a par with worldly goods and position, to be won by caprice rather than merit, and generally to be despised. Pausing briefly for the perfunctory praise of a virtuous lady, presumably his patron, Benoît caps this harsh passage with a reference to Solomon on the unlikelihood of ever finding beauty combined with chastity or loyalty in a woman.

There are some loyal women in the poem, notably Andromacha and Penelope, who are praised by the poet, but neither has a central place in the story; and Andromacha, a faithful wife and innocent victim of the war caused by Heleine's lust, eventually becomes the mistress of Orestes. A great deal, on the other hand, is made of the love affairs of Heleine and Briseida, who show only superficial feelings for the men they give themselves to, but are quite adept at rationalizing their actions. Medea, whose story is told early in the poem, is far more straightforward in her acts, and more intense in her feelings, than either Briseida or Heleine. However, she gives in to the same impulses, abandons her family and land, throws herself at a man who makes courtly-sounding but empty promises, who accepts her love and then betrays her. Her lust sets the pattern for the other women in the poem.

When Heleine first sees Paris, she is attracted to him (11. 4345–4346), which he is quick to perceive and take advantage of. She only pretends to be distressed when he carries her off, *faiseit semblant/ qu'ele eust duel e ire grant* (11. 4639–4640). She accepts his comfort and his love, saying she would not have chosen this, but if it has to be, she will make the best of it, a common (within this poem) female justification of self-indulgence under the guise of fatalism. Heleine remains emotionally uninvolved throughout the poem, assuring Paris it is right for him to hate and fight Menelaus if Menelaus hates him, but telling Hector that she loves both of them when they are fighting over her. She laments her own guilt in bringing all this distress on the world when Paris dies, and offers herself for Trojan revenge, but this is really a successful ploy to gain their sympathy. Indeed, she is recaptured by Menelaus at the sack of Troy and restored to her home and her honor, the immediate cause of the war and destruction, but none the worse for it. This is perhaps the strongest condemnation of women in the poem—so far outside the sphere of morality that they are not even punished for their actions.

Briseida's shift in affection is even more blatant than Heleine's. Despite her vows of eternal love to Troilus, and the great show of distress when she is forced to leave him, she does not discourage Diomedes' advances. She refuses him at first, fearing to appear light and fickle, but softens her refusal with praise and the assurance that, though she has no desire to love *aparmains,* "immediately," if she were to love, she would hold none dearer. He does not miss the implication—"being wise . . . he understood from the first words/ that she was not too hostile to him" (11. 13681–13683)[11]—and bides his time. Like Paris, he sees through this thin veneer of respectability that covers the woman's lust. Diomedes is caught, however, in love's snare; he frets and loses sleep, and Briseida treats him all the more harshly, the more he is in her power. Although this has the outward appearance of a lyric situation, the motives are different; he is not ennobled by his suffering, she is simply indulging her vanity. Women are like that, the poet observes (1. 15038 ff.). When her affair with Diomedes becomes known, she worries for a moment about her reputation: "a good story will never be written about me, nor a good song sung" (11. 20238–20239), but she justifies herself without difficulty: "the wisest and cleverest men are deceived by words" (11. 20253–20254). In any case, she says, she would never have gotten involved, had she not been alone and friendless (1. 20283 ff.)—she had, of course, come to the Greek camp to join her father. There's no use repenting now, she concludes, but at least she can be loyal to this one. After all, he helped her when she needed it; "let him slander me for it/ who came late to comfort me" (11. 20301–20302). By these last lines, she has so far talked herself out of remorse that she can challenge those who might condemn her and, far from the fear of scandal with which she began, she ends in scorn of public opinion (11. 20303–20304). She shows, like Heleine, a readiness to make the best of her circumstances and very little real feeling.[12]

The last part of the poem tells of various murders and plots resulting from adultery, the revenge of Greek wives on their errant husbands when they return. Even Ulixes, who struggles hard to get home to his patient and faithful wife, is killed by a son he had unknowingly begot while under the enchantment of Circes. Love is clearly given its due as a powerful force in the *Roman de Troie,* but it is condemned for its antisocial effects.

Because love is potentially harmful in the *Eneas* as well, the hero is allowed to feel only the kind of love that will not interfere with his destiny. Dido gives in to a passion which endangers her city, threatens the founding of Rome and leads to her own destruction, but Eneas, although he is the willing object of her attentions, never expresses or feels love for her. When he falls in love, it is with Lavine, a love in harmony with his fate and Rome's. The French poem makes a good deal more of this love than Vergil had, presumably to offset the hero's affair with Dido. Dido is the victim of passion and the machinations of Love (Venus), but her own excess makes her vulnerable. Although both she and Eneas "drink the fatal poison" of Ascanius's enchanted kisses, Dido indulges in them far more: *c'est Dido ki plus fole estoit/ ele i a pris mortel ivrece,* "Dido was the more mad; she became fatally drunk" (ll. 820–821).[13] Nonetheless, she needs the encouragement of her sister to renounce her vow of loyalty to her dead husband. The sister offers Dido the most persuasive motive, the good of the kingdom. Up to this point, Dido has been an effective queen who won her land by a clever stratagem, and governs it well, but now, ironically, she lets everything go for love, with no thought to the consequences: *ne li chalt mais que que l'en die,* "she no longer cares what will be said" (l. 1536). Her epitaph will read: "she loved too wildly/ her wisdom was of no use to her" (ll. 2143–2144).

Eneas shows no signs of love for Dido, although he is happy enough to indulge hers for him, and he would have stayed with her if the Gods had allowed him to, because he was comfortable (ll. 1654–1655). His lack of feeling is shown, in the French version, by the ease with which he gives away tokens of her love: he sends Latinus a ring Dido had given him "for love," and clothes Pallas's body with a robe she had presented when she fell in love with him. The gifts to Latinus, in Vergil's poem, are a bowl that belonged to Anchises and various objects of Priam's, all redolent with authority and piety. The French poet replaces them with Dido's ring and a goblet from Menelaus, each of which evokes thoughts of illicit and destructive love. They are used here presumably to show that Eneas renounces all connections of that kind and is preparing himself for the pure and proper union with Lavine. There is even some suggestion that Eneas is forced to fight this war because of his idyll with Dido. Latinus is willing to accept Eneas as his son-in-law, but his queen is favorable to Turnus and will not let her husband forget the Trojan heritage of false love. She reminds him that Troy was destroyed because Paris stole Menelaus's wife, and that Eneas himself abandoned Dido, as she predicts he will do to Lavine when he gets her land. In the French version, it is the queen who sends for Turnus to prevent Eneas from having her daughter; in Vergil's poem, the gods incite Turnus to fight.

Lavine is completely innocent of love until she sees Eneas. Her mother tries to arouse some feeling for Turnus in her and to explain what love is, but she has no desire to look for trouble and pain. As soon as she sees Eneas, however, she knows all there is to know of love: *Amors a escole m'a mise/ en poi d'ore m'a molt aprise,* "love set me to school and taught me much in a short time" (ll. 8183–8184). She argues with herself at first, but then accepts her love and even decides to reveal it to him. Once again it is the woman who takes the initiative, but in this case the man responds—the mutuality of feeling, of suffering and doubt, is probably the most positive aspect of their love. Eneas suffers the same pangs and argues with himself in the same way, while he tries to keep his mind on his combat with Turnus. He draws a careful distinction between this love and his affair with Dido: if I had felt for her what I do for Lavine, I would never have left her (l. 9039 ff.). When the lovers are finally brought together, their joy is as great as Paris's and Eloine's (ll. 10109–10110), but its outcome is quite different. Paris and Eloine destroyed a world with their love—Eneas and Lavine begin one.

The medieval versions of these stories show greater interest in love than their classical sources, but it is almost as if the love had been introduced only to be condemned. In Arthurian romance, on the other hand, with the focus on personal and moral problems rather than historical or national issues, courtly love assumes more importance, and its ethical possibilities are explored. If love inspires a man to embrace the highest moral values of his society in order to be worthy of his lady, then it should provide the ideal motivation for action in the romance, where the man is expected to serve society by defending those values. In fact, however, this rarely works out.

In early Arthurian romance, an attempt is made to adapt the inspirational force of courtly love to the service of society. Arthurian poets were well acquainted with Ovid and with the romances of antiquity on which they drew for incidents and characters, but they did not, at first, share the classical attitude towards love. In *Erec,*[14] his first extant romance, Chrétien de Troyes (fl. 1170–91) suggests that his lovers, when they are reconciled, have surpassed the destructive kind of love represented by Dido and Aeneas, whose story is depicted on the saddle of the horse Enide is given to ride. But, although Chrétien begins, in *Erec,* with a love that is eventually made to serve a social purpose, or at least not to hinder it, he ends, in *Perceval,* having his hero reject earthly love to seek the Grail. Chrétien ridicules the love conventions in different ways in all his works, particularly in *Cligès,* where the pursuit of love is actively antisocial. Even in *Erec,* Chrétien reverses the normal courtly relationships: when the man becomes aware of his own imperfections, he withdraws from his lady, tests her, and eventually restores his favor to her. Only once, in *Lancelot,* does Chrétien come to grips with the basic problem of courtly love in the romance genre—how to allow the love to be consummated without sacrificing its beneficial effect —but he leaves it hanging. He brings the narrative up to the physical union, describes the immediate social effects and then, unwilling or unable to solve the problem, refuses to finish the poem.[15] In any case, Chrétien's treatment is ambiguous. In the last romances, he avoids the problem entirely: Yvain's relations with his lady take second place to the gratitude and sense of responsibility he feels for, and inspires in another lady, not to say a lion: and Perceval is motivated first by thoughts of his mother and then by the Grail. Chrétien seems, finally, to have little faith in the social benefits of courtly love. As his thoughts about life grow more complex, it becomes increasingly difficult for him to handle courtly love positively within the romance genre. This will become apparent as the romances are discussed in their probable chronological order, and contrasted, where relevant, with the work of Hartmann von Aue and Wolfram von Eschenbach.

Chrétien tries every conceivable approach: love in marriage, love in adultery, a serious presentation of mutual love and a parodistic one, but he cannot find a satisfactory setting. In *Erec* (c. 1170), the lovers share a strong and constant attachment that is superficial and selfish at first, but builds in mutual trust through the poem so that, whereas in the beginning Erec misunderstood Enide's spoken words, by the end he is able to read her unspoken thoughts. But his love for her is not the source of action or correction. Erec's problem, his tendency to avoid action and commitment, is apparent before he meets Enide. He appears in the queen's company, neither hunting like other men of the court, nor equipped to protect the queen from insult when it occurs. The insult rouses him to cautious action—he takes care not to catch the offender until he is properly armed —but once he has avenged it, and incidentally won Enide, he again falls into inactivity. He has only shifted his service from the queen to Enide—not a real shift since Enide takes her function, along with her clothes and her name, from the queen. Again, he must be roused by a kind of insult, and this time he does not go off alone to avenge it; he takes Enide with him, but she is simply a snare to attract adventures. She is described as the ideal lady, a beauty created perfect by Nature, in whom one could see oneself as in a mirror. When they depart on adventures she presents the physical appearance of the inspiration to action: dressed in her best gown, mounted on a fine horse, she rides before him, literally leading him into encounters. Nevertheless, she is not the ideal lyric lady; she does not withdraw her favor from him because he is unworthy of her, she only complains to herself that she is being blamed for his failures. She must learn to respect his courage and ability, which he feels impelled to prove, not because of her displeasure, but because of his own anger at her lack of faith in him. What he wins from his action is not so much her approval as the respect of his enemies, as well as his friends, and finally the official recognition of the Arthurian court. His failure was not simply in devoting himself to Enide, but in not taking his social responsibility seriously enough. He discharged it in a superficial way by equipping his men to fight, but refusing to get involved himself. Yvain's error will also be to confuse the superficial glory to be won by unnecessary fighting with the real purpose of knighthood, to defend the just cause, to engage in active support of good.

Erec works his way from defensive adventures, in which he simply protects his possessions, to offensive adventures which he seeks on his own initiative in order to rescue others.[16] The defensive adventures, in their essentially selfish concern, represent the period of chivalric inactivity when Erec paid other knights to discharge his responsibilities but did not engage himself directly. The offensive adventures look to the time when he can assume his proper place in society, not only by acting, but by accepting a commitment from others. He refuses Guivret's friendship the first time he meets him, and he refuses the hospitality of the Arthurian court; both later come to him and force themselves upon him, drawing him out of his self-imposed isolation, which is simply another facet of his self-centeredness. When he completes the offensive adventures and accepts the company of Guivret and Arthur's court, he is able to be an example to other knights, to rescue them from a predicament similar to his and restore them to society, as he does in the *Joie de la Cort* episode.

The lovers of the *Joie* are an example of courtly love working against social responsibility: the service the lady demands of her knight not only bars him from human society, but also makes his only contacts with it destructive. He has promised her that he will remain inside their pleasure garden, fighting all who approach, until he is defeated by another knight. The very real consequences of the senseless fighting and killing this promise entails—the heads of the defeated opponents—are displayed on stakes set up around the garden.

The *Joie de la Cort* is a distorted reflection of the Erec-Enide situation. Erec's refusal to carry out his responsibilities to society directly does not produce so dramatic an effect as the knights' heads on stakes, but it is antisocial and meant to be condemned as equally harmful potentially. He indulges his own desires and makes up for his inactivity by paying others to act in his place. Maboagrains also indulges himself, using the promise to his lady as his excuse. He accepts his isolation, not because he does not wish to act—on the contrary, his promise involves him in continual fighting—but because he has a superficial and selfish sense of chivalric honor. He continues to fight and destroy others, rather than accept defeat or refuse to fight, even though each victory simply prolongs his imprisonment. His promise to the lady is as much an expression of his own desires as Erec's decision to withdraw from knightly activity.

The ladies who cause the knights, whether by design or not, to withdraw from society, are not themselves without fault: Enide's cousin exacted the promise from Maboagrains because she did not have sufficient faith in his love and loyalty and wished to bind him to her at whatever cost to his real honor. Enide does not demand a show of Erec's devotion, the traditional love-service, in the same way, but she too lacks a perfect faith in him and is moved to some extent by selfish concerns. When he first asks her father for her, she is pleased to know she will be a rich queen; and in the early adventures she worries about her own fate, should anything happen to Erec, but she learns both to put his safety first and to respect his courage. It would, of course, be foolish to expect a romance heroine to be as perfect as the abstractions of the lyric, but if Chrétien had intended to preserve the lyric conventions, he could have had her exert far more influence over her lover. She does not inspire his action, even though, by riding before him on the adventures, she leads him into his encounters; nor can she be said to have awakened him to his fault intentionally, as a courtly lady should, and to have withdrawn her favor. It is he who withdraws his, and then tests her repeatedly, even as he is proving himself, and when he is convinced of her loyalty and perfect love, he pardons her. It is only at that point that he puts himself "entirely at her command" (11. 4888–4890).

Hartmann pays no more attention to Enite in his *Erec* (c. 1185) than Chrétien had, but he does allow her greater indirect influence and presents her as nearly faultless. Her loyalty is never in question, her devotion perfect. When they are reconciled, Erec asks her forgiveness for what she has had to endure (11. 6771–6813).[17] She does give him support and guidance. When he revives from apparent death, she shows him the way back, a symbolic acknowledgement of her proper function. The mere thought of her inspires Erec in his fight with Mabonagrin, while his opponent must draw his strength from the physical presence of his lady. From the questions Erec asks him, "Why did you live such a life alone with her, *women don't like it?"* (1. 9409 ff.), we can assume that he has accepted Enite's reproof as just. He has understood that to serve her worthily, he must serve society. He has acted on her criticism, and because she is good and desires only his good, it has served him well. Mabonagrin, acting on the courtly belief that her will is his, that if he were not to do as she wished, he would harm himself (1. 9508 ff.), has been led astray, because his lady does not incarnate the proper values.

That love can be a strong force for bad, as well as good is clear not only in Mabonagrin's situation—and Hartmann emphasizes the harm by having the innocent victims, the eighteen widows of his opponents present at the *Joie*—but, in the actions of the men who fall in love with Enite and are driven by the power of that love to commit acts of treachery against Erec. Their love, however, is totally uncourtly; not only do they not offer service to Enite, they attempt to force their love on her despite her objections. Even Erec falls prey to the destructive power of love, though only temporarily. Unlike Chrétien's hero, Hartmann's was an aggressive knight, before he married and his thoughts turned to love, and he is restored to that same aggressive spirit after his adventures. His attitude towards the *Joie* combat is almost recklessly bold, though he now attributes his manhood to Enite (11. 8864–8867). The moral problem is simpler here than in Chrétien: Hartmann's hero is temporarily distracted by love from his duty, but the lady is not, in herself, a bad force and can, therefore, lead him back to his proper self. The opposition is essentially between self-indulgence and social action, not between degrees of social commitment as in Chrétien.

In both versions of Erec, the love between husband and wife is a strong mutual devotion, presented seriously and positively. In *Cligès* (c. 1176), on the other hand, though the feeling of love is strong on both sides, its value is questionable. The parents think about it a good deal--the monologues of Alexandre and Soredamors dominate the first section of the poem—but they are incapable of action. They describe their love with every possible figure, they analyze every aspect of their feelings, but they take so long to decide how to declare their love that they lose the opportunity. If the queen did not act and speak for them, it is unlikely they would ever come together.

It has been suggested that the parents are precourtly, not quite adept even with the metaphors, whereas the young lovers are more at home in the tradition and manage it better.[18] Certainly they have much less trouble declaring their love to each other, but their situation is complicated by Fenice's marriage to Cligès's uncle. This creates, on the surface, a courtly atmosphere: the lover can serve her in hopes of reward, while she is in a higher sphere and essentially beyond his reach. Indeed, she refuses to be his as long as she lives with his uncle, unwilling to belong, like Ysolt, to two men, but Chrétien does not mean us to admire her rectitude. Her solution is to leave her husband and live in hiding wtih Cligès, thereby avoiding public disgrace but not the act which would incur it.[19] The complicated machinations of the lovers, Fenice's potions and false death and Cligès's tower with frescoed walls and hot water but no visible entrance, point up the artificiality of their position, which Chrétien must condemn in any case because it cuts them off from society. Like the wall of air surrounding the *Joie de la Cort* in *Erec,* which represents a self-imposed imprisonment, the wall around the garden of Cligès's retreat is easily scalable, as we learn when Bertran blunders in. The entrance to the tower is cleverly hidden, but the garden is open to any who chance by, a comment on the lovers' ludicrous attempt to preserve their honor by hiding themselves from public view. Honor is, after all, a question of public attitude; it is irrelevant in a state of isolation. Secrecy is a facet of courtly love, but it too only makes sense while the lovers remain in society.

Did Chrétien intend in *Cligès* merely to show how ridiculous courtly love conventions are when one attempts to live by them, or was he condemning them as a set of false values that force lovers into deceptive and hypocritical action? It is not altogether clear in the poem whether he meant to amuse more than to shock. It is perhaps even more difficult to determine Chrétien's attitude towards love in *Lancelot* (1177–81). Here we are faced with various problems: a hero who can be both a courageous, devoted knight, willing to face terrible risks and suffering to rescue his lady and her people, and an absentminded fool for love, knocked off his horse because he is too absorbed in thoughts of his lady to notice another knight attacking him. Chrétien sets his hero an almost impossible task and lets him accomplish it, but then, he cannot hide his dissatisfaction with his own work and refuses to finish it. It is curious, moreover, that this is the one poem in which Chrétien presents a nearly perfect courtly love situation, and seems to treat it seriously for the most part. Up to the near-completion of Lancelot's mission—he frees the prisoners but does not destroy the real threat to the Arthurian world, the evil Meleagant—the love has been a force for good, enabling the hero to do what no other knight could. But once that task is accomplished, the conventions of the love are left empty of purpose. Lancelot turns his attention from the object of his mission to the inspiration for it and pursues the physical satisfaction of his love for Guenievre. The love situation now degenerates until, by the tourney of Nouauz, the whole effect is reversed and the love becomes an antisocial force.

Lancelot's real task in the romance is to save the Arthurian world, not just its inhabitants imprisoned by Meleagant, but its values and ideals, perhaps even its viability as a literary setting for the author. After *Erec,* Chrétien seems to find the genre of Arthurian romance less and less adequate to express the problems that concern him.[20] In *Lancelot,* he makes the court's problems the focus of the story. His attempt to save Arthur's court in this poem may well be an attempt to save the genre of Arthurian romance for himself. It will fail, and in his next work, *Yvain,* he preserves the form, but at the cost of betraying his hero. In his last work, *Perceval,* he will move into a new sphere, the Grail world, for which he will have to stretch the form of Arthurian romance. Whether or not he would have succeeded one cannot know, since he left the poem unfinished.

The Arthurian court, in *Lancelot,* is threatened not only by Meleagant's challenge from without but also by disintegration at the center. Kes's selfish concern with his own superficial honor, to which he does not hesitate to sacrifice the honor of his king and the safety of his queen, is a threat to the court, which cannot be adequately protected by its other official representative, Gauvain. He accepts the task but refuses to take the risks necessary to achieve it; faced by a choice, he always prefers the safer and surer way to the more direct, if more dangerous, path Lancelot follows. And it is no accident that while Gauvain is pursuing this, for him, futile adventure, his own responsibilities to family and friends must be discharged by yet another knight, Yvain. Neither Kes nor Gauvain can cope with Meleagant, who represents the antithesis of Arthurian values—lust, envy, greed, deception; he would possess the honor of Arthur's world and its queen, not by being worthy of them, but by force and fraud.

Lancelot's real mission is to destroy Meleagant; freeing the prisoners is only a temporary measure. That Meleagant must be killed is made clear by the episode of the knight who insults Lancelot when he first enters the kingdom of Gorre; Lancelot defeats and would spare him, according to chivalric conventions, but a girl demands his head, claiming he is the worst knight that ever lived. This sets the tone, or should, for what happens inside Gorre. We know it is a different world, a land of the dead, from the omens in the cemetery and from Guenievre's appearance on a bier in a funeral procession. We see that its prince is evil beyond recall. Different conventions must operate here; evil must be destroyed. But Lancelot is distracted by the queen and both are caught up in their courtly conventions; the queen asks Lancelot to spare Meleagant for his father's sake, and he does, for her sake. Meleagant is thus free to pursue his plots to destroy the good of the Arthurian world, now in the person of Lancelot. Lancelot becomes a prisoner of Meleagant, not only physically—like the wall of air of the *Joie* in *Erec,* Lancelot's tower can be left at will, as we discover when he talks his way out of it to go to the tourney of Nouauz—but spiritually. He is imprisoned by his own lust for the queen. Having given himself over to Meleagant's power, he cannot, of course, destroy it, and since there is no one else in the Arthurian world who can, the solution seems hopeless. Chrétien probably could not find a satisfactory solution and therefore declined to finish the poem. His follower, Godefroiz, resorts to the *deus* or *dea ex machina,* the girl who had demanded the other knight's head, who searches for Lancelot, rescues him and sends him off finally to kill Meleagant. This ends the story, but it does not resolve Lancelot's problem or Chrétien's.

In his attempt to preserve the Arthurian court as the center of the highest social values, to save it from itself, Chrétien focuses on the highest lady of the court, Guenievre, and the finest, least worldly of its knights, Lancelot. Arthur is trapped by his own conventions, as he was in *Erec,* and unable to assert any power; Gauvain calls his acquiescence to Kes childish (l. 226), and the poet comments that Arthur is unable to say no (l. 5395). In *Erec,* the queen helped to save the court by postponing the contest that threatened to disrupt it until a solution offered itself, but in *Lancelot,* she is the immediate victim of the court's deficiencies. She is handed over to the protection of a thoroughly inadequate defender, Kes, because he has tricked the king. Guenievre incarnates both the values and the defects of Arthur's court in this romance. She takes her responsibility seriously, carrying out Arthur's wishes even when they endanger her life. It is worth noting that in *Perceval,* where Chrétien rejects the worldliness of the Arthurian court in favor of the Grail, high tribute is paid to the queen for her beneficial effect on her subjects (l. 8176 ff.); although it is Gauvain who speaks the praise, there is nothing in the words to suggest ironic overtones. Certainly she inspires Lancelot to achieve the great feat prophesied in the cemetery, so awesome it frightens all who hear of it. But she too, like the king, is caught up in a set of conventions, the forms of courtly love, which when followed for themselves, without the purpose for which they exist—to inspire the man to noble action—have a destructive effect. Guenievre continues to test Lancelot long after he has proven himself and carried out his task; the results are disastrous for them and for those who depend on them.[21]

From the first Lancelot himself is as perfect a knight as Chrétien can draw within the Arthurian sphere. In his dedication to his love and his pursuit of the task the love imposes on him, a task that is of enormous importance to his whole world, he is never deterred by selfish concerns: he climbs on the cart with little, though unfortunately some, hesitation, accepting the shame it visits on him because it will take him where he must go, and he crosses the sword bridge, scarcely noticing the wounds, because that is the most direct route. Gauvain refuses to ride in the cart, and prefers to cross the water bridge, because he is guided by reason while Lancelot is moved by love. Lancelot, therefore, succeeds against almost insurmountable odds and Gauvain keeps missing. Only Lancelot's selfless devotion can save the values the queen represents. The others, in whose care they have rested, have endangered not only the queen but also the people of her kingdom, many of whom are now imprisoned in the land of death. Lancelot reaches them, inspires their revolt, fights to free them and is blessed as their deliverer. At every step, it is his love for Guenievre which motivates him. Although his preoccupation with that love causes him to be thrown into the water (whence he emerges to conquer his opponent, while the sensible but uninspired Gauvain falls in on his own and has to be pulled out), and to faint at the sight of a few strands of her hair, still it is that love which, because it makes him forget himself, moves him to choose the nearest horse rather than the best, and the straightest road rather than the surest. Love, the poet says, with no apparent sarcasm, rules only the hearts she values (ll. 1233–1234); those who don't know love, the hero complains, turn honor to shame (l. 4354 ff.). It is not insignificant that Lancelot's capacity for love encompasses Christian charity, that he can be moved to acts of mercy by the thought of God (l. 900 ff.).

All this is not to deny the humor that runs through this work. Chrétien is never lacking in humor, not even in *Perceval,* and there are many instances of it here: the hero's falling into the water, or fainting over the queen's comb and having to be held up by the lady he is escorting, fighting with his back to the enemy so he can look at his lady in a tower, trying to commit suicide by sliding off his horse while no one is looking. These reveal the author's ironic attitude towards his subject, but at the same time they point up the potentially self-destructive nature of Lancelot's devotion. It is no accident that Lancelot attempts or contemplates suicide several times in the course of the poem: when he looks down from a tower and sees Guenievre being carried on a bier, he wants to throw himself down; later, when he hears she is dead, he tries to hang himself. One of the dangers Chrétien sees in courtly love is the denial of self which results from total dedication to the will of another human being. This may enable a lover to rise to great heights in order to serve and be worthy of the subject of his love, but it also robs him of the self-love that is essential to his own survival, moral, perhaps, as well as physical.

Lancelot's high-minded devotion is also contrasted with the empty forms of love service: a lady who invites him to bed but expects him to fight his way in through an armed guard; a knight who makes high-flown speeches, but intends to win his lady by fighting and refuses to acknowledge her indifference. Lancelot himself fails in only one thing; he hesitates to enter the cart, and his lady, like a proper courtly lady, calls him to task for it. He himself, like a courtly lover, accepts her chastisement, not daring to ask why, but believing completely in his own guilt and her perfection. However, there is a slight fault in Lancelot's perfect devotion to love; he thinks the queen is angry because he rode in the cart, mistaking the demands of worldly honor for the requirements of perfect love. But the queen's action, although justified within the courtly code, is excessive; indeed, it is not even honest. She feigns anger as she later admits: I went too far, I had intended it as a joke (l. 4205). By apparently exulting in her power and his success, she has pushed her role too far and from this point on, the nature of the love changes. It becomes harmful, first to them, then to others. She hears rumors of his death and regrets her action; he hears the same rumors of her and attempts suicide. In both cases, Chrétien's treament suggests something false in their actions: the queen says that her refusing to see and speak with him were the two blows that killed him; Lancelot says he should have died when she rejected him, both of them using figures of conventional love imagery, but playing with real death.

To make up for her mistreatment, the queen now moves too far in the other direction. There is nothing for her to do but bestow her favor on Lancelot and reward his devotion. However, since this reward is precipitated by her need to expiate her abuse of him, rather than by the successful completion of his mission, the results are not good. Instead of destroying Meleagant, that is, the evil he represents and the danger it poses to Arthur's world, Lancelot becomes Meleagant's victim—his love turns to lust. The queen now admits her love, receives Lancelot openly, and invites him to visit her at her window, but Lancelot is not satisfied with that. He breaks through the bars in the window, mutilating two fingers, and enters the chamber. These wounds cause far more trouble than all the wounds he suffered on the sword bridge, for they leave traces of blood in the queen's bed. It is significant that neither of them notices the blood; indeed, we are told that Guenievre thinks her sheets are still white and lovely (11. 4742–4743), that is, she does not recognize the implications of the change in their relationship. Blind to the social consequences of their love, she continues to operate in a sphere of conventions now empty of meaning. Henceforth, the effects of the lovers' actions are negative. When Lancelot hears the queen is attending the tourney of Nouauz, he talks his way out of prison to get there—a prison effective only while he allows it to be—and Guenievre, to test him, twice demands that he do his worst, that he make a public fool of himself. Since he has already proved his devotion beyond question, even submitting to worldly disgrace, this is pointless. The result of Lancelot's activities at this tourney, which had been called to arrange marriages for the young ladies of the kingdom, is that the young ladies decide they can marry no man but Lancelot and therefore go away unmarried; his presence thus thwarts the whole purpose of the tourney, and he returns to his prison where Chrétien leaves him.

Chrétien is not concerned in this romance with the question of adultery. Even when the love is consummated, it is not the wronged husband, who never finds out, but the jealous and rejected lover, Meleagant, who objects. What Chrétien does seek in this work is to rescue the ideals and the literary life of the

Arthurian world by having its noblest figure, inspired by selfless devotion, destroy the false values that threaten it, in the person of the ignoble Meleagant. After this romance, Chrétien puts aside the idea of courtly love or even of the love of man for woman as an inspiration to socially beneficial action. In *Yvain* (1177–81), the devotion to friends, Gauvain and Lunete, to whom Yvain is bound by ties of gratitude and affection, is more important than the devotion of husband or lover. The hero of Chrétien's last romance, Perceval, is disengaged altogether from human commitments; he moves from concern for his mother to the service, not of another person, but of the Grail.

One can see how much Chrétien's attiude towards love has changed from a contrast of the emblematic adventures in *Yvain* and in the much earlier *Erec.* In *Erec,* the story began with the interwoven episodes of the white stag and the sparrow hawk, both established to recognize the union of the loveliest lady with the finest knight. The union of prowess and beauty, symbolizing the harmony of personal feeling and public responsibility, is accepted as right and possible. By the time he writes *Yvain,* Chrétien has given up the idea of sexual love as a proper motivation; the opening adventures of the fighting bulls and the wild storm at the fountain herald the pointless violence of the knights, which will be counterbalanced, not by the hero's love for his wife, but by his devotion to his friends, Lunete and Gauvain. Lunete is bound to Yvain for a kindness he did her before the poem begins, and in return, she saves his life and wins his lady for him; later, he must save her life and she must once again win him his lady. It is significant that she is rescued by her friend, Yvain, while her lover, Gauvain, fails to appear. At the end of the poem (1. 6695 ff.), they are still arguing about who has done more for the other, still feeling gratitude and indebtedness. There is a charming echo of the theme of reciprocal service and devotion in Yvain's relations with the lion:[22] he rescues the lion from the serpent, then the lion rescues him from various opponents; both Yvain and the lion are wounded again and again in each other's defence.

The defense of the helpless and oppressed, not the pursuit of empty glory, is the proper motivation of adventure, as Yvain must learn. The Arthurian court, particularly in the person of Gauvain, has lost sight of this. The hero himself acts dishonorably, sneaking out of court alone in order to steal the adventure of the fountain, which he pursues recklessly, afraid his word will not suffice to convince the court of his victory, until he is caught in a trap like a rat. He falls in love with his victim's widow, who is persuaded to marry him ostensibly because she needs a protector for her fountain, but he leaves her and the fountain soon after at Gauvain's insistence, to go off on adventures which have no purpose except to increase the fame of the heroes. The vanity of the knights is emphasized by the fact that they camp apart from the court and expect the king to come to them. When the helpless are really in need of a knight, Gauvain is absent, rescuing the queen from a situation she should never have fallen into but for the inadequacy of the king and his seneschal. And when he returns, Gauvain engages in the defense of a woman he knows to be guilty, only because he will not refuse a fight. He is, however, ashamed enough of his position to hide away until the fight occurs.

Yvain is able to achieve real honor and restore his knighthood in a series of adventures in which he combats various kinds of injustice and exploitation. But his restoration is undercut by the fact that he must return at the end to Laudine, and in order to fulfill his commitment to her, must devote his life not to worthy adventures, but to riding out to fight whenever someone pours water over that stone. We are left at the end with a hero who has learned through difficult adventures the true meaning and purpose of chivalric action; he has learned to serve justice rather than fame, has become an ideal knight, but he is forced, because of the error of his first exploit, to go back to a life of meaningless adventure, where he will be at the mercy of any reckless fool who comes along. The pessimism of this conclusion is extreme. It is as if Chrétien had betrayed his hero in order to preserve the form of the romance. To have an ending and not leave the story to someone else to finish, as he had done with *Lancelot,* Chrétien must bring his hero back to where he started, a better man, but unable to put his higher consciousness to use. He is trapped by the circumstances of his life, as he was trapped in the portcullis at the beginning of his adventures.

Yvain's love for Laudine is a key part of the trap. This love is an echo rather than a counterbalance to his problem, and therefore serves no function in his moral development.[23] When he first sees her, she is in a wild rage, screaming, tearing her hair, and ripping her clothes (11. 1148-1161), yet he falls in love with her.

It seems unlikely that her beauty could attract him in such a mood, but it is fitting that this reckless knight, wildly seeking revenge, should fall in love with a raging woman. Indeed, his love is described as a kind of revenge for her husband's death. The situation is a literal working out of many love clichés: Yvain is literally and figuratively her prisoner; his beloved is also his enemy, seeking his death. Lunete, who is practical and devoted, is able to manipulate both the hero and his lady, first to bring them together and then to reunite them. But their union is always based on deception: a trick coupled with political necessity induces Laudine to accept Yvain in the first place and then to forgive him and take him back at the end. Yvain, even after his ennobling adventures, must "force" her to make peace with him, by using the fountain. There has been no real development in their relationship as it appears at the end of the poem from what it was at the beginning. Yvain ends in a situation not very different from the *Joie de la Cort* in *Erec*. This is the problem inherent in courtly love. Whatever the qualifications of the hero, whatever he achieves in the lady's service—and certainly Yvain is a far better man by the end of the poem—once he possesses his lady, the moral value of his love is lost.

Hartmann, unlike Chrétien, does not become disillusioned with the concept of a balance of love and chivalry as the knightly ideal. He is less critical of fighting in his *Iwein* (c. 1200), and less ironic in his presentation of the love.[24] He criticizes the abuses of the chivalric ethic, but not the ethic itself. The honor Iwein and Gawein seek is a good thing, not the false glory that Chrétien rejects. They seek it improperly, at first, and therefore lose it—it is much worse, Hartmann says, to win *êre* and then lose it than never to win it—but *êre* itself is not in question. And the love between Iwein and Laudine is treated as a real force. The first meeting is described in terms designed to make it seem more plausible: Laudine's fury is not excessive, and Iwein's love gives him both the courage to face her and the hope that she too may be moved by love (1. 1621 ff.). When they meet at the end, each begs the other's pardon; the reconciliation is real. Love between man and woman is still a viable symbol, perhaps even an essential first step in man's move from self-love to service and devotion to others.

Hartmann comes closest to a successful presentation of love as a positive social force, because he believes in the value and compatibility of love and social responsibility, of personal morality and worldly honor; and because he limits himself to a simple situation, an overbalance in one direction or the other which can be restored. Even in his other romances, which are more like legends of saints than chivalric tales, Hartmann preserves the courtly atmosphere and goal of the man and woman joined in love and service to society. Arme Heinrich is saved from himself and his leprosy by the example of a young girl, whom he calls his "little spouse"; she is good as an angel and inspired by the Holy Spirit to seek martyrdom and save the hero, but she shows the self-confidence of a courtly lady in her attacks on all who oppose her desire. Heinrich is finally moved by her beauty and courage to refuse her sacrifice and assume responsibility for his own problem; that brings about his cure and restoration to his people. The poem ends with the marriage of the hero and his young inspiration. She would have preferred to be a martyr, but Hartmann is insistent on service in the world. Even *Gregorius,* the tale of the good sinner who becomes a great pope, ends with the pope and his erstwhile lady, who is also his mother, working together, bound by a chaste love, for the good of all men. Although the sin that dominates this romance is incest, first between brother and sister, then mother and son, and although both situations are described in the clichés of courtly love and love-service is performed, Hartmann does not condemn courtly love. His concern is with the possibility of salvation through sincere repentance, despite the horrendous nature of the sin. His main characters, mother and son, renounce their lust, but they are united at the end of the poem in a purer love and, like the couples in all his romances, their union serves others.

But for Chrétien, neither courtly love nor chivalry can overcome the limitations of their conventions and benefit man or society, so he rejects them both. In his last work, *Perceval* or the *Conte del Graal* (after 1181), he turns to religion for a set of values that are not bound by worldly conventions. He begins the poem with a contrast between the vainglory and hypocrisy of the world and the charity preached in the gospels. This opposition is echoed in the two spheres Perceval moves through, the Arthurian and the Grail worlds. In Arthur's realm, religion is confused with chivalry: knights are taken for angels, ladies' tents for churches; the worship of God is feudal service that expects its rewards. And this is the setting in which courtly love is presented. Perceval himself never really engages in it. His sexual encounters are simple and swift; he steals kisses and a ring from the lady in the tent, comparing her favorably with his mother's maids; he takes the almost nude Blancheflor into bed with him to comfort her, lying *bouche a bouche,* "mouth to mouth" (l. 2065), all night, and enjoying "much pleasure" (l. 2067); he promises to fight for her in return for her love (ll. 2103–2105), but he soon leaves her to find his mother. There is little in the poem to suggest that he will return; he will be momentarily entranced by the blood on the snow, which reminds him of Blancheflor, but he seems to forget her again when it disappears.[25]

The only situation that in any way approximates love-service is Perceval's pursuit of the Grail, which preserves all the steps in the courtly system: the Grail embodies the highest ideals; Perceval serves it long and faithfully in the hope of reward; he gets some recognition, but it is withdrawn when he fails to live up to it; and, a distance is maintained between him and his object as long as he remains unworthy. This is not coincidental; Chrétien means us to see the Grail as the proper object of his hero's devotion in contrast to the courtly situations which are presented in the Arthurian sphere. Gauvain moves from one such encounter to another, and it is significant that the most "courtly" of these, in the sense of typical love-service, involve women who are far from ideal: the elder sister who demands proof from her lover, even a tourney against her own father, her lover's vassal and guardian, pitting his devotion to her against his honor as a lord and friend; and the lady Gauvain himself serves, who abuses him, as she has abused other knights—she is called *pire que Sathanas,* "worse than Satan" (l. 7456), and seeks nothing but the death and dishonor of any knight who serves her. Both women demand and get service, but neither does it to perfect her knight; one wishes to feed her own vanity, the other to achieve revenge.

Wolfram repeats most of these encounters in his *Parzival,* (c. 1205–10), but his attitude towards courtly love is less negative. He does present several characters who have indulged in the excesses of love-service and who suffer for it: Belacane and Sigune, who tested their lovers too far and lost them; Trevrizent and Anfortas, who should not have engaged in such love at all. But, he also describes instances of love-service coming to a good end: Gawan and Orgeluse, Gramoflanz and Itonje, and Obie and Meljacanz, whose love is set right by Gawan's innocent love-service.

It is not by accident that courtly love works properly in the Arthurian sphere and not in the Grail world, where it can have only a destructive effect. Although Parzival loves his wife and claims to seek her throughout the poem, he does not serve her; it is really the Grail he is pursuing, and it is to be worthy of the Grail kingship, not of her, that he perfects himself. Indeed, it is only when he surrenders to God's will and attains the Grail that he can be reunited with his wife. She is kept offstage for most of the poem, so that she has little opportunity to make demands or to reveal her human weaknesses, whereas Gawan's lady is a classic example of the exacting and capricious courtly lady. Her effect on her lovers shows the difference between love in the two realms: in the Arthurian world, Gawan can do good in her service, but when Anfortas, who belongs in the Grail world, tries to serve her, he becomes an invalid and brings suffering on his land and his people.

In the courtly sphere, Gawan is able to accomplish what Chrétien's Lancelot was meant to do: in the service of the demanding and haughty Orgeluse, Gawan frees the Arthurian world, represented by the imprisoned ladies, from enchanted love. The ladies are one generation behind events in the poem; they are contemporaries of Parzival's father, Gahmuret, who was unable to integrate the three worlds he wished to serve—chivalry, represented by Amphlise, Christianity in Herzeloide, and love in Belacane. His sons, Parzival and Feirefiz, do accomplish such an integration, but outside the courtly sphere. Gawan, who remains within it, is able to rise to the highest worldly achievements, but he never serves the Grail. He experiences instead all the facets of courtly love-service—service without reward for Obilot, love without service for Antikonie, and service rewarded by love for Orgeluse.[26]

Orgeluse herself, who has been responsible for the suffering of many knights, including Anfortas, has a reason for her action. She seeks revenge for her dead lover and will use anyone and any means that might achieve it for her. She represents courtly love for Wolfram in its positive and negative functions. To Anfortas, her love means physical pain and anguish, because it does not belong in the Grail world; to Gawan, it causes worldly shame but eventual glory. In her service, Gawan frees the enchanted castle, through the symbolic adventure of the magic bed which represents all courtly love adventures. Riding the bed, Gawan faces and overcomes every conceivable kind of attack: stones, arrows, a huge peasant and a lion. Gawan then wins Orgeluse's love by challenging Gramoflanz, the object of her revenge, in a scene that is filled with sexual imagery: after he has won the castle, he looks out the window and sees Orgeluse crossing the meadow in the company of a knight, Turkoite, who rides with his spear erect; when Gawan defeats Turkoite, Orgeluse sends him to get her wreath from Gramoflanz; to reach him, Gawan must force his horse to jump a waterfall, which he does not quite manage, and Gawan must pull himself and his horse out with his spear. This imagery suggests that, having proved himself worthy, in chivalric adventure, Gawan wins her finally by physical attraction. We are told later, in any case, that Orgeluse's anger was diminished by Gawan's embraces (Book XIV, 723, l. 7 ff.).[27] There may be some irony in the fact that Orgeluse is connected with Clinschor, the enchanter of the castle, so that by freeing the castle from his power, Gawan may also be destroying her powers.

Gawan wins Orgeluse although he never accomplishes the task she had set him, to defeat Gramoflanz. He can disenchant the castle while he serves her, but he cannot avenge her dead lover, because for Wolfram, revenge is not a proper motivation for a knight. Instead, Wolfram has two revenges cancel each other out, for Gawan, we learn, has killed Gramoflanz's father. Gramoflanz is also in love with Gawan's sister, whom he has never seen but serves faithfully. This love is a purer form of love-service than the kind Gawan performs for Orgeluse, which is dominated by the physical presence of the lady. Though the two knights are caught up in the same chivalric cycle of death and revenge, they are at opposite ends of the spectrum of courtly love-service. It is worth noting that before either one can be married to his lady, Parzival, who is neither an Arthurian knight—the Round Table accepts him, but he moves beyond it—nor a courtly lover, must come and fight both knights, each in the other's name.

Parzival's service to the courtly world is of this tangential nature throughout the poem. He wins nothing for himself; when he fights, he is always in the outer army and is only mentioned in passing. He actually appears very rarely in the courtly sphere. The only service he performs regularly for a lady is the sending of his defeated opponents to Cunneware, a service which has no overtones of love, but is simply an acknowledgement of her faith in his knightliness, for which she suffered when he first came to Arthur's court. The lady Parzival actually loves, Condwiramurs, is never the object of love-service. He fights for her before he loves her and she marries him and grants her love immediately, or as soon as he is able to take advantage of it. When he first saw her, he could not distinguish her from Liaze, whom he liked but left, in order to fight, as his father had done with his ladies. But by the time Parzival leaves Condwiramurs, he feels real love, not courtly love but a deeper feeling which awakens in him a sense of human responsibility. He departs not to fight, but to find his mother, which he accomplishes in a sense, by coming on the Grail. Henceforth, he will be driven by his love for Condwiramurs and desire for the Grail, the latter always the stronger impulse (see Book IX, 441, ll. 10–14). Although her name means "lead to love," she does not literally lead him to anything; on the contrary, it is only when he finds the Grail and fulfills his mission that he is able to find Condwiramurs. But it was his love for her that set him on the right path originally, not to Arthurian adventure, but to his mother and the Grail. Wolfram has changed the name of his heroine from the common romance name, Blancheflor, redolent of courtly love, to the allegorical Condwiramurs, and has kept her out of the action as much as possible so that she need do nothing to mar her perfect image. Condwiramurs, unlike courtly ladies, represents love in marriage and devotion to family and society, united in the Grail community.

In the Grail world love is not in conflict with duty. Feirefiz, who had been serving a pagan love in the courtly fashion, falls in love with Reponse de Schoie when he first sees her, and through his love for her he is able to see the Grail. There is no question of love-service to win the lady, any more than there was with Parzival; Feirefiz marries her and then serves the Grail. Love, in this case, not only leads him to the right life, but enables him to carry Christianity back to the East and, through his son, to convert the heathens. Although his own conversion is carried out with amusing dispatch, the point is significant—one is led to the Grail by love. But, in the final analysis, what the hero has fought and suffered to achieve throughout the poem is really not his wife but the Grail. That is his inspiration and his reward, the service to which he gives his life.

The Grail offers a possible substitute for courtly love, a religious rather than secular inspiration for action and one which cannot fail the knight who serves it. It does not, however, solve the problem posed by courtly love but simply evades it. It is not a coincidence that the two writers who defend the ideals of chivalry and love, Wolfram and Hartmann, were both knights themselves;[28] they had a stake in preserving the aspirations of their class. Chrétien and the major Tristan poets are caught up in more complex views of social and moral problems and, as a result, their attitude towards courtly love, as well as chivalry, is less positive. Although they draw on many of the lyric conventions, they turn them upside down or introduce variations significant enough to change the entire effect.

It is in the Tristan stories that the problem is given its fullest treatment in romance. Here the double nature of love is at the center of the story; it is both a refining force, which raises the hero far above other men, and a sensual force, symbolized by the potion, which can destroy him and his society. The lyric conventions are given full play. Because Isolt is married to someone else, the lovers can remain in the lyric state of desire, rarely fulfilled, accepting their suffering as a part of the price they pay for their love. They are threatened by external enemies who envy their moments of joy, the *niedere* and *losenger* of the lyric, and are raised above all who surround them by the spirituality of their devotion. But the physical aspect of their love is so strong that it clouds the moral; the lover's yearning is not morally efficacious, and the woman's desires prevent her denying or withdrawing her love. The separation of the lovers, when it occurs, is a result, not of her dissatisfaction with him, but of circumstances beyond her control. In other words, the basic moral force of courtly love is lacking. And the very fact which enables the poet to preserve the lyric condition of yearning—the adulterous nature of the love—places the lovers in conflict with their society and threatens their honor, because to give in to it they must betray other commitments, to king, husband, uncle, friend. In these stories, the love cannot be replaced by higher claims, glossed over or ridiculed, for it is the essence of the main characters; the only solution to their dilemma is death. Thus, although most of the poets who treat the Tristan material are sympathetic to the lovers, they cannot avoid the tragic conclusion that love imposes on them. In its final effects, then, there is little distinction between the ideal, inspiring lyric love and the immoral, destructive classical love.

The realistic view of love, morality, and worldly honor distinguishes the Tristan story from Arthurian romance, which cannot deal with insoluble conflicts of ideals and loyalties. For its conventions to function properly, the author must believe that worldly honor can be achieved without moral danger, indeed that honor and virtue are not only compatible but inseparable. Chrétien, as we have seen, is increasingly unable to maintain such a belief and moves further and further away from the Arthurian court as the center of values. In the Tristan stories, there is no attempt to present the courtly world as an ideal setting; the lovers must cope with the evil around them as well as with their own passions and loyalties. Normally, the story is not told within an Arthurian setting, although Arthur's court is sometimes mentioned, but in the prose romances, Tristan's love is coupled with Lancelot's. His tragedy is allowed to affect the Grail quest and thus, indirectly, to destroy the Arthurian world which, conceived as an ideal realm, cannot contain it.

Originally the Tristan story was a tale of adultery between a queen and the king's nephew; their love was the tool of an adverse fate which forced the hero to betray his honor and duty. This is still true in Eilhart's poem, while the other twelfth-century romances that tell the story show the influence of contemporary courtly-love attitudes.[29] Eilhart's is the one version of the story which is in no way sympathetic to the love. His hero had won great honor by fighting in his uncle's service, but he loses it when he becomes involved with Isalde. Throughout the poem, his action as a knight is set in opposition to his activities as a lover, the high points of one career coinciding with the low of the other. The almost impossible feat of winning the unknown bride for his uncle is quickly offset by the potion and the beginning of a love affair which leads Tristrant to commit "the worst betrayal ever committed" (ll. 2838–2839), to sleep with his uncle's wife while his uncle is tricked into sleeping with her maid; and the expiatory services he performs for Arthur and Havelin are offset by his returns to Isalde. The disguises he assumes on his visits to her indicate the shame of his involvement: he comes as a leper, as a minstrel, and finally as a fool. The only actions he performs in her service are unknightly: he fights lepers, he hunts to sustain their outlaw existence in the woods, and he wins a sporting event. When he lives apart from her, he is able to restore peace to several lands, Karahes and his own, and to fight in Gawan's company as a member of Arthur's court, but his love pursues him even there, to the harm of his friends. When Isalde visits Arthur's court, Tristrant is wounded paying a visit to her bed, and all of Arthur's knights have to wound themselves in order to protect him. Tristrant is aware of his sinful existence and tries to get absolution from a hermit, but he cannot free himself from the love until the potion wears off, and even then, although he returns Isalde to her husband, he is unable to keep away from her. That is, once he has succumbed to that love, he cannot be saved from it.

In Béroul, however, when the potion loses its power over the lovers, they repent their existence, confess to the hermit, and Iseut promises that there will be no more intercourse between them, despite the fact that the love still exists. Tristran will visit her later, presumably just to talk; in any case, nothing else is mentioned. Their sense of guilt seems to be removed, for, from this point on, in the extant portion of the poem, they are vindicated, publicly by Iseut's ordeal, and privately by the death of their enemies (l. 4427 ff.). God seems to be with them throughout the poem. He protects them in the scene under the pine; He allows Tristran to escape his execution and Iseut to proclaim her innocence before all; and, He enables them to avenge themselves on all the barons who have set Marc against them. The potion, not the love, is responsible for the sinful excesses of the lovers in this poem. Once they are freed of its power, they remember their social duties: Tristran regrets his life in exile, the loss of chivalry and adventures, the love of his uncle and the life of the court; Iseut thinks of her name and of the people who depend on her patronage (l. 2168 ff.). When they return to court, Tristran offers his services once again to Marc, who would accept them, but for the ill will of the jealous barons, the slanderers. Once these are gotten out of the way, presumably, Tristran can return to a life of chivalry and guiltless love.

Béroul presents a superficially courtly situation, with slanderers and spies who try to keep the lovers apart, with enforced separations and with an insistent denial that their love is shameful. But, it is in Thomas and Gottfried that we see a love which approaches the lyric concept. The portion we have of Thomas's poem (c. 1170), seems like the narrative version of a lyric: the lover vacillates between jealousy and love, doubt and recollection of former joys; in his distress he turns to another love, a lady who is more accessible, more able to reward him, but she is simply another aspect of his old love, a new Ysolt; he cannot be satisfied with her, so he returns to his ideal, to the image he has created of her (a statue in this case—in a lyric, it would be a mental image). He is later rejected by his lady, through a misunderstanding and Brengven's ill will, until he has done penance and service to win back her favor, avenging himself on Kariado, the man who had slandered him. But there is little to suggest the exaltation that a lyric lover experiences at times. It is difficult to say how much of this there may have been in the missing part of the poem, in the cave episode, for example, but, in the part we have, the only strong declaration of faith in the love, of a perfect union of two souls, is made by Ysolt when she thinks she will die before she reaches Tristran:

Vus ne poez senz moi murrir,
Ne jo senz vus ne puis perir,
Se jo dei em mer periller,
Dun vus estuet a tere neier.

[Douce, 11. 1641–1644]

You cannot die without me,
nor can I perish without you.
If I must die at sea,
You must drown on land.

For the most part, Thomas's attitude towards women is not flattering. The three main characters, the two Ysolts and Brengven, are capable of violent and destructive fury: Ysolt's attempted murder of Brengven, the exchange of insults between the two, Brengven's anger at Tristran, and Ysolt-as-blanchesmains's vengeful lies to her dying husband. Women are not presented as ideals to inspire men to great nobility, but as human and imperfect objects of passion, who destroy, wittingly or not, the men who love them. The men may create, in themselves, a higher kind of devotion and remain loyal to it, but it cannot give them happiness.

Thomas is the only Tristran poet who is not at all concerned with the social effects of Tristran's feelings. Although it is said of the hero at his death: *Tristran li pruz, li francs est mort/ A tut ceus del rengne ert confort,* "Tristran the brave, the good is dead; he was a comfort to all in the kingdom" (Douce, ll. 1791–1792), there is little in the poem to indicate a social commitment. The poet concentrates on the psychological state of the lover, on his doubts, suspicions and torments. Love is a disease, a poisoning, which only the lady can cure, but Tristran, like a lyric poet, is never sure that she cares enough to help him. What is the use of all this suffering, he keeps asking, if she fails me now (Sneyd, l. 39 ff., Douce, l. 1261 ff.)?

Thomas emphasizes the suffering rather than the joy and exaltation of love. It is only Gottfried (c. 1210), who can maintain the lyric mood of love, the continual movement from joy to pain, from mystical ecstasy to sordid passion, who can realistically present the conflicts love creates and still preserve the vision of a perfect love, shared by two ideally-suited spirits. The moment of love which Tristan and Isot share in the Minnegrotte is the fulfilled dream of lyric poets, the aspiration that preserves their love and devotion and ennobles them, despite the knowledge that it cannot ever be fully theirs. But Gottfried did not finish his poem; it is likely that the fullest expression of lyric love in the romance was possible only because the form was not preserved.

Love raises Gottfried's hero to intellectual and spiritual heights, but at the same time, it cuts him off from society, and therefore it is no longer courtly love. The only act Tristan performs directly in Isot's service, the winning of Petitcreiu, is an indication of the unusual nature of their love. He wins the dog to relieve her suffering, not his own, but she, in turn, sacrifices the dog's bell because she will not be comforted while he suffers. It is their mutual devotion, the necessary and complete sharing of pain as well as joy that makes their love what it is and distinguishes it from courtly love. The total dedication to one another that such love demands makes it impossible for that love to exist within society. Although Tristan's actions often have a beneficial effect—by killing the dragon to win Isot, he saves Ireland, and by killing Urgan li vilus to win the dog, he rescues Duke Gilan's land—that effect is accidental. Tristan is not motivated by public responsibility, by a desire to save society. Indeed, there is a strong suggestion that his attempts to preserve his position within society are a mistake. The only times the lovers can enjoy their love without obstacle or intrigue are on the boat and in the cave, but each time they choose to return to Cornwall for their honor. Once there, they are forced to practice sordid and degrading deceptions in order to fulfill their desires.

Clearly, the only way for Tristan and Isot to be faithful to their love is to leave the world for good, that is, to die. The love cannot subsist within the world because the world is incapable of understanding it. The lovers cannot rise above adultery as long as they remain in society. Once they have tasted the life of paradise in the cave, the renewal of the affair is wrong. Gottfried describes it as the fall of Adam and Eve. Henceforth they will live a life of suffering and penance, apart, until they can be united in the death they had hesitated to accept.

The French and Italian prose romances of Tristan in the thirteenth and fourteenth century preserve the sense of love as an ennobling force, but they attempt to contain it within the social context.[30] Knights are expected to be lovers, as long as the love inspires them to go off on adventures that serve society. Tristan and his companion, Lancelot, spend most of their time fighting evil and injustice in various forms, but they cannot refrain from visiting their ladies, not even while they seek the Grail. Eventually, they come into conflict with the jealous husbands, their kings, and all the good they have accomplished is undone by their excesses, which result in the general destruction of their society. In the *Tavola Ritonda* (early fourteenth century), the world of Cornwall, full of corruption, jealousy and intrigue, is contrasted with the Arthurian world, where goodness and justice prevail almost to the end. Tristano and Isotta should, for their virtues, be part of the Arthurian world, and they do move into it from time to time, but they are tied to Cornwall and cannot leave it permanently. The evil inherent in Cornwall must eventually undo them, and through them, indirectly, the Arthurian world as well.

Many of the elements of courtly love are still present in this version, but only in a superficial way: the ladies, Isotta and Ginevra, are the most beautiful in the world and inspire men to great deeds. The union of prowess and beauty is the subject of many adventures, most notably the Island of Evil Custom, where Tristano and Isotta are forced to marry before he takes her home to Marco (chap. XXXVI). Love is a prerequisite of a good knight. He cannot act without it; he fights better when he is in love. Arthur brings the ladies of his court to watch his battles so the men will be inspired (chap. VII). A knight is rewarded with his lady's favors when she is pleased and rejected when she is not. This is truer of Ginevra than of Isotta, who is always understanding, even when Tristano marries someone else. One wonders if there is some connection between Isotta's uncritical devotion and the fact that Tristano is prevented by his lust from seeing the Grail, which, in every other way, he is worthy of. Lancilotto, who incurs Ginevra's displeasure from time to time, gets closer to the Grail, at least in visions, although he too is unable to see it. Attractive as this thought is, however, there is little in the material to suggest that Tristano is less good than Lancilotto because Isotta is less demanding than Ginevra.

Tristano's love is doomed, not because of his lust, but because the world that houses it, Cornwall, is so corrupt. Marco is a villain by nature, jealous of his nephew long before Isotta appears. Knowing Tristano is worthier and more popular, his uncle is afraid he will usurp the kingdom, so he sends him for Isotta, hoping he will be killed (chap. XXVI). Marco is not at the mercy of slanderers in this version, he is one of them, and it is he, finally, who kills Tristano with a poison spear. Although Tristano's excesses in love prevented him from seeing the Grail, his death is a severe blow to the forces of good in the world. He had managed to do a good deal of fighting for the right cause, and his loss is felt not only at Arthur's court, but in the papal court as well (chap. CXXXIII). Once he dies, chivalry begins to degenerate even among the Arthurian knights; Lancilotto, missing his companion at arms, thinks only of his love. In the confusion that ensues, Morderette tries to make love to the queen, and the Arthurian world is consumed by the resultant struggles.

Malory (c. 1469), retelling the Arthurian story from the prose versions of Tristan and the Grail well over a century after the *Tavola Ritonda* was written, could still find some good in the now obsolescent ideals of courtly love. This is all the more striking since he was strongly influenced by the *Queste* tradition, which condemned courtly love as an absolute evil that distracts man from God's service and threatens his soul. In Part IV of the *Morte Darthur,* Sir Gareth of Orkeney, Malory treats a courtly situation quite sympathetically: Gareth is at first scorned by his lady, but when he proves himself, she accepts his love, though she imposes a further restriction, that he wait a year to marry her. Even in Part VII, Launcelot and Guinevere, the fourth chapter begins with May, the time of love, and an account of virtuous love which maintains a proper balance, reserving first "the honoure to God and secundely thy quarrell must com of thy lady." In the days of Arthur, the author comments, men could love without lust, in truth and faithfulness, but nowadays they cannot love without rushing to satisfy their desires.

Malory does not condemn love out of hand, but he does finally reject the courtly conventions that go with it. Launcelot is prevented from seeing the Grail by his sins, but they are sins of pride, as much as lust, and they come from his inability to put aside his courtly code for religious teaching. It is because he instinctively goes to aid the weak, who are not always in the right, that he is struck down. He helps the black knights of Argustus, instead of the white knights of Eliazar (chap. IV, the Quest of the Holy Grail), because the black are being defeated, and Launcelot reacts as a knight who is committed to helping the weaker side. He is wrong because the knights in black represent the world clothed in sin, while the white knights have chosen chastity and virginity. It is pride that makes Launcelot act by the chivalric code instead of religious faith. He makes the same error when he goes to aid the old priest holding up the eucharist in the castle of Corbenic (chap. VIII). He continues to see with worldly eyes, so he fails to perceive the miracle. Here, finally, we are faced with the statement that the chivalric code, which includes courtly love, is incompatible with the Christian code. It is not because Tristram and Launcelot love immoderately, although that is so, that they fail, but because they love by the wrong rules.

It is interesting that although Malory is more concerned with Launcelot's pride and worldly values than with Tristram's lust, lust is, structurally at least, at the center of his work. Not only is Tristram's story, Part V, set in the middle, between the secular ideal of love-service, Gareth, and the religious devotion of Bors, Perceval and Galahad, but it is further enclosed at one remove by the story of Launcelot, so similar to Tristram's, and at a second remove by the story of Arthur, whose own birth, in Part I, is the result of deception and adultery, and who also begets a son in adultery, Mordred, who helps to destroy him (Part VIII):

Part I, II	Arthur			
III		Launcelot		
IV			Gareth	
V				Tristram
VI			Grail	
VII		Launcelot and Guinevere		
VIII	Arthur's death			

In the late prose romances, as in the early classical romances, love is finally a socially destructive or distracting force. It endangers society because it fosters disloyalty and thus disorder. Courtly love is not, however, rejected, not even by Malory, without some sense of loss. The belief that love could be a force for good if properly directed and controlled does not die; but the increasing awareness that such love can only operate in an ideal world and that in the real world it becomes distorted and dangerous, destroys the efficacy of the courtly love system for literature. As we have seen, once that system is taken out of the lyric form and forced into a narrative genre, it begins to give way. It is based on a delicate balance of the lower and higher impulses of man's nature, a balance that can only obtain in his mind. When the lover becomes the hero of a romance and acts out his impulses, he may achieve great feats on the inspiration of the higher impulses, but he will eventually be undone by the lower. An action, once performed, cannot be erased; however sublime a hero's worship of his lady may be, once he has slept with her, their relationship changes. The romance hero must cope both with the lady's continuing desires, once he has aroused them, and with the reactions of other people, enemies, a jealous husband, solicitous friends. He cannot turn his back on the social consequences of his action or on the conflicts that will necessarily arise from it. Instead of being raised to great heights by a noble devotion, he is trapped by his passion. The more central the love story is to a romance, the more difficult it becomes for the author to find a comic solution to his story. Chrétien's *Lancelot* and Gottfried's *Tristan* were both left unfinished, and Chrétien's continuator, Godefroiz, ends the poem without resolving the crucial question of the love affair between the hero and the queen. When that problem is squarely faced, as in the complete Tristan poems and the prose romances, the ending must be tragic. There is no other solution. Unless the author chooses to ignore the dangers of love, to avoid the problem in order to concentrate, unrealistically, on his hero's social commitment, he must eventually face the tragic implications of secular love. Courtly love, which is meant to be a force for good in society, instead destroys society. In the later prose romances, the social consequences of uncontrolled passion become less important, and the religious values of individual morality take over, but society is destroyed in any case. As early as Chrétien, who was primarily concerned with social problems, there was a move away from romantic love towards friendship, and finally to religious love, a rejection of a secular code in favor of a religious one, which proved to be a foreshadowing of the development of the entire romance tradition.[31]

Notes

1. See R. R. Bezzola, *Les Origines et la formation de la littérature courtoise en occident* (500–1200), IIIe partie, *La Société courtoise: littérature de cour et littérature courtoise* (Paris: Honoré Champion, 1963), I: 284.
2. Names of the characters will be spelled as they appear in the text being discussed, with the single exception of Arthur, whose name will not vary.
3. See G. Raynaud de Lage, in the introduction to his edition of the *Roman de Thèbes,* CFMA, 2 vols. (Paris: Honoré Champion, 1968), pp. xxxi, xxxv. All subsequent references will be to this edition.
4. See F. Whitehead, "Yvain's Wooing," *Medieval Miscellany presented to Eugène Vinaver,* ed. F. Whitehead, A. H. Diverres, F. E. Sutcliffe (Manchester University Press, 1965), p. 324.
5. He is married without fuss to one of the two daughters of his host in exile, while the other girl is given to his companion, Thideus. Although the girls are described from head to toe in the best rhetorical tradition, Pollinices is unmoved, but Thideus is attracted to the younger sister. In order to get her for himself, he makes the gesture of offering the elder to his prince, a wry commentary on the power of sexual attraction over even the most loyal of men (1. 1050 ff.).
6. William of Malmesbury reports that William IX had a woman's picture painted on his shield so that he could carry her in battle as she carried him in bed. *Legitima quoque uxore depulsa, vicecomitis cujusdam conjugem surripuit, quam adeo ardebat ut clypeo suo simulachrum mulierculae insereret; perinde dictitans se illam velle ferre in praelio, sicut illa portabat eum in triclinio.* T. D. Hardy, ed., *Gesta Regum Anglorum,* 2 vols. (London: English Historical Society, 1840), Bk. 5, § 439, p. 671.
7. ". . . Si vet d'amie/ d'amors et de chevalerie;/ se le tenez a vilannie/ nous le tenons a cortoisie."
8. Benoit de Sainte-Maure, *La Roman de Troie,* ed. Leopold Constans, SATF, 6 vols. (Paris: Firmin Didot, 1904–12), vols. 52, 55, 57, 62, 66, 67. All references will be to this edition.
9. There are many lyric conventions in Achilles' monologues (11. 17638–17746 and 11. 18028–18100): the lady's features are inscribed and painted in his heart; she is his *vie* and his *santé, esperital, enluminee,* a *resplendor;* he pleads for *merci* and hopes for *joie,* alternates between hope and despair; he resembles Narcissus, who loved his own shadow, hence his own death.
10. The ability to rationalize their desires is a trait shared by some of Chrétien's lovers, particularly Yvain and Laudine. On the reverse correlation between the quantity of analysis and the quality of the feeling in Chrétien's lovers, see W. T. H. Jackson, "Problems of Communication in the Romances of Chrétien de Troyes," *Medieval Literature and Folklore Studies: essays in*

honor of Francis Lee Utley, ed. J. Mandel and B. A. Rosenberg (New Brunswick: Rutgers University Press, 1970), pp. 39–50.

11. The same line is used to describe Paris's perception of Heleine's feelings for him (l. 4352). The women are transparent in their desires.
12. There is some question whether the men in each case are to be trusted any more than the women. Diomedes tells Briseida that she is his first love, but we learn at the end of the poem that he has a wife at home. Paris makes the same claim to Heleine, presumably ignoring Oenone.
13. J. J. Salverda de Grave, ed., *Eneas,* Roman du XIIe Siècle, CFMA, 2 vols. (Paris: Honoré Champion, 1925, 1931, reprint 1964). All references will be to this text. Compare Isot's drinking the potion in Gottfried's *Tristan, ungerne und über lanc,* "unwilling and too long" (l. 11683).
14. Chrétien's works will be referred to by short titles throughout the chapter. The dates given follow A. Fourrier, "Encore la Chronologie des Oeuvres de Chrétien de Troyes," *BBSIA* (1950): 69–88. These dates are generally accepted although doubts have been raised about the validity of dating by historical events (see J. Misrahi, "More Light on the Chronology of Chrétien de Troyes," *BBSIA* (1959): 89–120). The chronological order followed in the discussion is also the more widely accepted one, i.e. *Lancelot* and then *Yvain* (see Misrahi, "Chronology," p. 118). Fourrier, "la Chronologie" (pp. 81–88) suggests a concurrent composition of the two poems. The editions used in this study are: Chrétien de Troyes, *Erec et Enide,* ed. Mario Roques, CFMA (Paris: Honoré Champion, 1955); *Cligès,* ed. Alexandre Micha, CFMA (Paris: Honoré Champion, 1957); *Le Chevalier de la Charette* (referred to herein as *Lancelot*), ed. Mario Roques, CFMA (Paris: Honoré Champion, 1958); *Yvain (Le Chevalier au Lion)*, ed. T. B. W. Reid, based on critical text of W. Foerster (Manchester University Press, 1942, reprint 1952); *Le Roman de Perceval ou Le Conte du Graal,* ed. William Roach (Genève: Droz, 1956).
15. F. D. Kelly, *Sens and conjointure in the Chevalier de la Charette* (The Hague: Mouton, 1966), makes a convincing case for Godefroi's carrying out Chrétien's plan for the romance. Though this may well be true, we are still left to explain why Chrétien chose not to finish the poem himself.
16. Bezzola calls these sets of adventures *l'aventure subie* or *lutte pour le "moi," l'aventure acceptée* or *lutte pour le "toi"* and the final episode of the *Joie, l'aventure cherchée* or *lutte pour le communauté.* R. R. Bezzola, *Le Sens de l'aventure et de l'amour* (Paris: La Jeune Parque, 1947).
17. Hartmann von Aue, *Erec,* ed. Albert Leitzmann, Altdeutsche Textbibliothek, 2nd ed. (Tübingen: Max Niemeyer, 1957).
18. P. Haidu, *Aesthetic Distance in Chrétien de Troyes* (Genève: Droz, 1968).
19. The hypocrisy of Fenice's position is evident in the religious imagery used to describe her situation. She is a saint and martyr

of courtly love; her "God," the only doctor who can help her, is Cligès, and to join him she undergoes a false death and a very real martyrdom of beatings and hot lead; she pretends to follow Saint Paul, though she distorts him to serve her purpose: "If you can't be chaste, be discreet" (1. 5264 ff.).

20. The Arthurian conventions are already strained in *Erec;* Gauvain points out the dangers of the White-Stag contest, but Arthur is unable to break with established tradition. In *Yvain,* the court is in a disordered state at the beginning—the king stays overlong in his wife's bed; the queen eavesdrops; the knights gossip and insult one another—and at the end, Arthur is hindered in the performance of justice by Gauvain's promise to fight for the wrong sister.
21. According to A. H. Diverres, Guenievre is "more concerned with exercising her authority over her lover than with her true duty to encourage him to attain a higher degree of chivalrous perfection." "Some Thoughts on the *Sens* of *Le Chevalier de la Charette*" in *Arthurian Romance, Seven Essays,* ed. D. D. R. Owen (Edinburgh and London: Scottish Academic Press, 1970), p. 30. I agree with many of the points in this recent article, although I am not convinced that Chrétien was critical of the love from the beginning. D. C. Fowler, in an article published after this chapter was written ("Love in Chrétien's Lancelot," *RR* 73 (1972): 5–14), points up the difficulty Chrétien had with the problems of love in this story and notes the "high comedy and high seriousness" of the work.
22. This is, of course, not the main importance of the lion in the romance, but his symbolic relation to Yvain's problem is not relevant to this discussion.
23. As W. T. H. Jackson says, "Chrétien's version of the Yvain story demonstrates with full irony the difference between service and love." "Faith Unfaithful—the German Reaction to Courtly Love," *The Meaning of Courtly Love,* ed. F. X. Newman (Albany: State University of New York Press, 1968), p. 58.
24. *Iwein,* ed. G. F. Benecke and Karl Lachmann, rev. L. Wolff, 7th ed. (Berlin: Walter de Gruyter, 1968). W. H. Jackson has suggested that even Hartmann was somewhat uneasy with the ending of his *Iwein,* that he is "less convinced than the narrator of *Erec* when he comes to look back on the entire story, of its exemplary truth." "Some Observations on the Status of the Narrator in Hartmann von Aue's *Erec and Iwein,*" Owen, *Arthurian Romance,* p. 79. H. Sacker, "An Interpretation of Hartmann's *Iwein,*" *GR* 36 (1961): 5–26, points out that it is only when the hero draws away from the ideals of the Round Table that he can achieve "a measure of inner peace, marital harmony, and service to others" p. 25).
25. The drops of blood melt into the snow, which suggests that Perceval's desire for Blancheflor will also disappear. In Wolfram's poem, they are temporarily covered by Gawan's scarf; that is, Parzival must be momentarily distracted from his desire for Condwiramurs, but that desire remains with him until he is reunited with her.

26. These distinctions are based on B. Mergell's *Dienst ohne Minneerfüllung, Minneverlangen ohne Dienst,* and *Gleichgewicht von Dienst und Minne,* put forth in *Wolfram von Eschenbach und seine Französischen Quellen,* II Teil. *Wolframs Parzival,* Forschungen zur deutschen Sprache und Dichtung (Münster: Westf. Verlag der Aschendörffschen Verlagsbuchhandlung, 1943).
27. Wolfram von Eschenbach, *Parzival,* ed. Albert Leitzmann, Altdeutsche Textbibliothek, 3rd rev. ed., 3 vols. (Halle: Max Niemeyer, 1947, 1948; Tübingen: Niemeyer, 1955) nos. 12, 13, 14.
28. So they tell us in their works: Ein ritter sô gelêret was/ daz er an den buochen las/ swaz er dar an geschriben vant:/ der was Hartman genant,/ dienstman was er zouwe (*Arme Heinrich,* 11. 1–5); schildes ambet ist mîn art (*Parzival,* Bk. II, 115, 1. 11).
29. The works cannot be dated precisely. Béroul's poem was written between 1165 and 1191; Eilhart's between 1170 and 1190, but the original exists only in a few fragments, and we derive the story from a later reworking: Thomas's poem c. 1170, and Gottfried's c. 1210. The poems are available in the following editions: Béroul, *Le Roman de Tristan,* ed. Ernest Muret, CFMA, 4th ed. rev. L. M. Defourques (Paris: Honoré Champion, 1957); *Eilhart von Oberge,* ed. Franz Lichtenstein, Quellen und Forschungen zür Sprach und Kulturgeschichte der Germanischen Völker (Strassburg: K. J. Trübner, 1877), no. 19; Thomas, *Les fragments du Roman de Tristan,* ed. Bartina H. Wind (Genève: Droz, 1960); Gottfried von Strassburg, *Tristan und Isold,* ed. Friedrich Ranke, 4th ed. (Berlin: Weidmannsche Verlagsbuchhandlung, 1959). For a comparative study of the Tristan romances, see J. Ferrante, *The Conflict of Love and Honor* (The Hague: Mouton, 1973).
30. For a summary of the Paris manuscripts of the prose romances, see E. Löseth, *Le roman en prose de Tristan* (Paris: E. Bouillon, 1890). The *Tavola Ritonda* is used as the example of the prose tradition both because it has a fairly clear structure and because it is available in print: Filippo–Luigi Polidori, ed. *La Tavola Ritonda,* Collezione di opere inedite o rare dei primi tre secoli della lingua (Bologna: 1864).
31. Professor Robert Hanning was generous enough to read this paper and offer very useful suggestions for which I am most grateful.

Bibliographic Note

These additional works were also helpful.

On Chrétien: A. M. Colby, *The Portrait in Twelfth Century French Literature: An Example of the Stylistic Originality of Chrétien de Troyes* (Genève: Droz, 1965); A. Fierz-Monnier, *Initiation und Wandlung: zur Geschichte des altfranzösischen Romans im zwölften Jahrhundert* (Zürich: Schwarzenbach, 1951); J. Frappier, *Le roman breton, Chrétien de Troyes, Cligès* (Paris: Centre de Documentation Universitaire, 1951); J. Frappier, *Le roman breton, Yvain ou le Chevalier au lion* (Paris: CDU, 1953); J. Frappier, *Le roman breton, Perceval ou le Conte du graal* (Paris: CDU, 1953); J. Frappier, *Chrétien de Troyes, l'homme et l'oeuvre* (Paris: Hatier-Boivin, 1957).

On Hartmann: Hugo Kuhn, "Hartmann von Aue als Dichter," *Deutschunterricht* 2 (1953): 11–27; P. Wapnewski, *Hartmann von Aue* (Stuttgart: Metzler, 1962); H. B. Willson, "Love and Charity in Hartmann's 'Iwein'," *MLR* 57 (1962): 216–227; H. B. Willson, "*Amor inordinata* in Hartmann's 'Gregorius'," *Speculum* 41 (1966): 86–104; H. B. Willson, "Kalogrenant's Curiosity in Hartmann's 'Iwein'," *GL&L* 21 (1968): 287–296; H. B. Willson, "Sin and Redemption in Hartmann's 'Erec'," *GR* 33 (1958): 5–14.

On Wolfram: J. Bumke, *Wolfram von Eschenbach* (Stuttgart: Metzler, 1964); D. M. Blamires, *Characterization and Individuality in Wolfram's Parzival* (Cambridge: Cambridge University Press, 1966); J. Fourquet, *Wolfram d'Eschenbach et le Conte del Graal* (Strasbourg: Publication de la Faculté des lettres de Strasbourg, 1938); M. F. Richey, *Studies of Wolfram von Eschenbach* (Edinburgh: Oliver and Boyd, 1957); H. D. Sacker, *An Introduction to Wolfram's Parzival* (Cambridge: Cambridge University Press, 1963).

On the Tristan material: W. T. H. Jackson, *The Anatomy of Love* (New York: Columbia University Press, 1971); W. T. H. Jackson, "The Artist in Gottfried's Poem," *PMLA* 77 (1962): 364–372; P. Jonin, *Les personnages féminins dans les romans français de Tristan au XII*[e] *siècle* (Gap: Ophrys, 1958); B. Mergell, *Tristan und Isolde* (Meinz/Rhein: Kirchheim, 1949); J. Schwietering, *Der Tristan Gottfrieds von Strassburg und die Bernhardische Mystik*, Abhandlungen der Preussischen Akademie der Wissenschaften, phil.-hist. Klasse (1943), no. 5; J. Schwietering, *Die deutsche Dichtung des Mittelalters* (Darmstadt: Wissenschaftliche Buchgesellschaft, 1957); G. Weber and W. Hoffman, *Gottfried von Strassburg* (Stuttgart: J. B. Metzler, 1962).

On Malory: R. M. Lumiansky, ed. *Malory's Originality; a Critical Study of Le Morte Darthur* (Baltimore: Johns Hopkins, 1964).

CHAPTER V

Beyond Courtly Love: Religious Elements in Tristan *and* La Queste del Saint Graal

Esther C. Quinn

The religious aspect of courtly love is, of course, an enormous subject. From its first expression in the lyrics of Guillem IX to the final working out of its effects in the Arthurian world of Malory's *Morte Darthur* one finds a continuous interplay between the erotic impulse and courtly and religious ideals. In the context of the present study it might be of value to consider in detail two late romances, each illustrating a different response to courtly love and a different development in the interaction between religious and secular attitudes. The two traditions of secular love reflected in the medieval romance were sensual love as a destructive force and devotion to a lady as ennobling. It will be our purpose here to explore more fully, especially in terms of the religious influences and implications, the way in which these two views are altered, combined, reasserted, and rejected in Gottfried von Strassburg's *Tristan* and in *La Queste del Saint Graal.* In Gottfried's poem it is shared sensual love, not service to the lady which is presented as ennobling (its destructiveness is a subordinate theme); in the *Queste,* both sensual love and devotion to woman are condemned, and the only truly ennobling love is represented as the love of God (within this scheme fraternal love is accepted as good and reproductive love as permissible).

These works, at first glance almost wholly different, upon analysis can be seen to resemble each other in a number of ways.

Both reject courtly love with the utmost seriousness, and both represent a sustained imaginative effort to present an alternate ideal. Both are built upon already established story patterns, reflect the general Christian culture as well as the specific influence of Bernardine mysticism, and make extensive use of symbolism and allegory. The resemblance between the two works is attributable not to direct influence but to the use of common traditions.

It has been observed that Gottfried brings God and the church into his poem more frequently perhaps than any of his contemporaries,[1] but there has been little agreement among scholars as to his precise intention and the final effect of his religious references. Although it is generally recognized that he sets up a religion of love which draws heavily upon Christian sources, it is less clear whether this structure exists merely apart from Christianity or in opposition to it.[2]

For his use of religious language to express sensual love, Gottfried had ancient and well-established precedents. Among the most notable and influential examples of the interrelationship between erotic love and religious devotion are the Song of Songs, the Epithalamium whose exalted language assured it a place in the canonical scriptures; and in a somewhat different spirit, Ovid, who uses religious terms to describe amorous games. Both patterns—the elevation of sensuous love and a mock-religion of love—can be found in the lyrics of the troubadours and in the early romances. For the most part, however, the intention and effects are different from those which Gottfried achieves. His *Tristan* represents the most serious and systematic use, not only of Christian forms, but of Christian mysticism to exalt the physical love of man and woman.

Gottfried's most explicit exaltation of the love of Tristan and Isot occurs in the prologue where both the bliss and pain of love are stressed; in the narrative itself, however, love proves not only blissful and painful but disruptive.

From the beginning of the story, in the prefigurative love of Tristan's parents, Riwalin and Blanscheflur, the darker side of sensual love is recognized. Riwalin is ensnared, powerless to escape, and Love, the tyrant, has entered Blanscheflur's soul.[3] But like the love of Tristan and Isot, their love is mutual and like them too, "they would not have given up this life of theirs for any other heavenly kingdom" (11. 1371–72). Although strongly resembling the love of Tristan and Isot, the differences are noteworthy: the relationship is not adulterous; they do marry "in church," "according to the Christian practice" (11. 1630–34), though belatedly and at the insistence of Rual, and Blanscheflur dies, not like Isot out of sheer love,[4] but in giving birth to a child.

Not only is Gottfried's view of love established early, but so is his attitude toward the role which God is to play in his narrative. In the episode in which young Tristan is taken to sea by Norwegian sailors, Gottfried reveals both a strong sense of God the creator of all things and Lord of a Universe in which Tristan is the center. The tempest which arose at His will and command serves as a prick to the conscience of the sailors, who dutifully free the young hero and set him down in Cornwall to pursue his destiny.

Early in his narrative Gottfried creates a strong sympathy for Tristan; he is a forlorn and homeless boy, who prays earnestly to God. His prayer, however, is that of any terrified lad who has been taught to pray in times of stress, and typically, his piety does not prevent him, when the two old pilgrims appear, from exercising his extraordinary talent for deception (1. 2692). For all his remarkable accomplishments in languages and music, he is a self-centered boy, skilled in the use of deceit. This quality, which is strong in the early versions of the Tristan story,[5] Gottfried not only retains but stresses, implying that such behavior is appropriate in a strange and hostile world. In the early part of the story, Tristan deceives everyone except Rual, who is a paragon of selfless devotion. Not only is Rual wholly devoted to Tristan, but, as Gottfried says, the affection which Rual and Tristan bore each other was evenly matched (11. 4523 ff.). Before Tristan's love for Isot, his most genuine affection seems to have been for Rual, his foster father.

There are many religious references in connection with Rual and throughout the work, especially in the episode of Tristan's battle with Morolt. Here a conception of the Deity is revealed which resembles that found in the Old Testament and in the *chansons de geste*. For instance, as the bloody fight goes on, Gottfried remarks, God himself would have been glad to see it (1. 6865). The episode is cast in the mold of the judicial combat with many references to Cornwall as right and Ireland as wrong, and Tristan as God's champion. Like Beowulf defeating Grendel and ridding Denmark of the terror, Tristan delivers Cornwall from the enemy. Like David, in his combat with Goliath, Tristan is young and innocent and the instrument of God's will against the huge and evil oppressor. As has been pointed out, the *judicium dei* or judgment of God, the putting of the case in God's hands, does not necessarily imply piety and religious faith, but might be regarded as an attempt to force God to render judgment, to force Him to serve man's ends, not His own.[6] It may be, as has been suggested, that Gottfried's handling of the battle with Morolt, as well as the combat with the dragon, are intended as mock heroic.[7]

Significantly, in his encounter with Morolt, Tristan wears a helmet which has the appearance of crystal, and on it is a dart which foretokens love. In this youthful battle he follows the pattern of the traditional hero who delivers his country from evil; but the wound he receives leads him toward his true destiny, which is love. In the narrative itself, up to the point at which the wounded Tristan arrives in Ireland, the religious references are generally conventional. But the encounter with the Chaplain may be more revealing than its minor part in the story suggests. Gottfried's attitude toward the Church is complex, as befits a complicated man and artist, but its basic outlines can be seen at this point in the story. When Tristan first arrives in Ireland, wounded, playing his harp, the court chaplain appears. He feels pity and admiration for Tristan's musical skill, which he recognizes as superior to his own. It was this chaplain who had taught Isot all that she knew of books and music, and it is he who recommends Tristan to the Queen as a tutor whose ability surpasses his own.[8] The relationship between Tristan and the Chaplain is entirely amicable: the Chaplain provided Isot's basic instruction, and Tristan, who is acknowledged as superior, begins his work where the priest left off. It is not too farfetched to see reflected here Gottfried's basic attitude toward the Church, however that attitude may vary in tone: he acknowledged the vast resources of the medieval church—its music, sculpture, architecture, and theology. But as Tristan the artist-lover builds with superior skill upon the foundation which the Chaplain provided, so Gottfried the artist-lover constructs a new vision of love upon the doctrines of the medieval church. The analysis of the *Minnegrotte* and the Prologue will make this point clear, but we should consider first the relationship which develops before the *Minnetrank*.

As the young Tristan, restored to health by the Queen, begins to teach the young Isot, they share a state of innocence. He teaches her not only music and languages but *moraliteit;* its teaching, remarks Gottfried, enables one "to please God and the world" (l. 8013). As the gifted Tristan shares his accomplishments with Isot, however, something else grows, which the later drinking of the potion unleashes, a force which makes it impossible to please both God and the world.

The love potion is one of the oldest features of the story, and like so many of the others, it is derived from Celtic mythology. It belongs to a world in which magic is not illusion or a symbol but a controlling force. In Celtic lore this force is controlled by a female figure, the fairy-mistress; in the Tristan story, by Queen Isot. Gottfried not only retains this feature, but emphasizes it.

Strictly speaking, the potion either is or is not responsible for their irresistible passion. If we accept, for the purposes of the story, its magic potency, then the lovers are pathetic victims of a cruel fate from which they derive some very real pleasure. If, however, the potion merely symbolizes the power of their love, then they do become responsible for their actions. Gottfried weaves his story between the two positions, now veering to the power of the potion, now toward their great mutual love. It is his art which creates the illusion that Tristan and Isot, while compelled to love by the potion, have nevertheless the dignity of beings who have chosen each other and that their love elevates them above the social, moral, and religious code of their time.

With the drinking of the potion, the relationship between the lovers is altered; their original innocence is lost. It is comparable to Adam and Eve's eating of the apple, with the important difference that there has been no explicit prohibition against the drink. As the potion takes its effect, Tristan struggles to resist, aware that to succumb to this love would be a violation of loyalty and honor, and Isot, aware of modesty, also struggles, but both succumb: *deist liebe reht, deist minnen e,* "that is love's right, that is love's law" (l. 11858).

The imagery which Gottfried uses reveals the nature of the new love and is reminiscent of that used in connection with

Riwalin and Blanscheflur: Love has overcome them; their hearts are bowed beneath her yoke; Tristan is a captive; he is in a snare. They are Love's huntsmen: they lay nets and snares for one another. Tristan complains that this passion robs him of his reason, that he has gone astray, and admits to Brangaene that they have both gone mad.[9]

As Gottfried relates the story, following Thomas, he interrupts his narrative from time to time to reflect upon the action. When he says, however, "We cultivate love/ . . . with deceit and cunning" (11. 12237–39), he is not referring to the deceit of Tristan and Isot in their relationship to Mark, but is contrasting their love, which he is celebrating, with the debased love of his own time. In this passage, Gottfried makes clear his ideal of love: fidelity of the lovers to each other. As he resumes his narrative, it becomes increasingly apparent that fidelity does not extend beyond the enchanted circle of the two lovers; on the contrary, their fidelity to each other involves them in guile and deceit in their relations with others.

Although Gottfried's sympathy for the lovers is unmistakable throughout the work, there are in the earliest versions of the story—and Gottfried retains them—episodes which illustrate the destructive consequences of sensual love. As Isot plots to substitute Brangaene in Mark's bed, Gottfried observes: "Love teaches/ pure minds/ to engage in deceptive thinking" (11. 12447–49). One finds here, as in so many works of medieval literature, the sensual, destructive aspect of the Love goddess. Perhaps the most striking episode illustrating this aspect of *Minne* is Isot's turning upon the faithful Brangaene, who has sacrificed her maidenhood to protect the Queen's secret, and ordering her death. As Isot plots the murder of Brangaene, Gottfried remarks: "The troubled queen/ showed by these actions/ that people dread scandal and mockery/ more than they fear God" (11. 12709–12). In Isot's plan to have her faithful servant murdered, Gottfried shows the extreme lengths to which one may be driven in an effort to preserve both love and reputation. He reveals Isot as capable not only of deceitfulness, but ingratitude, betrayal, and the will to murder. She serves her will, and had her will been done, Brangaene would have lost her life as well as her maidenhead to save the "honor" of the Queen. In Brangaene's willingness to be sacrificed, in her moving account of the two girls and their white garments, and her forgiveness of the Queen, she emerges, in this scene at least, as the more noble. It is only Isot's remorse for her part in the intended murder which saves her. Significantly, this is the only time that Gottfried's Isot has any sense of wrongdoing; she never feels she wrongs Mark.

Among the more powerful passages in which Gottfried reveals his sense that an outrage is being perpetrated is the dream in which a boar tosses the King's bed and fouls the royal linens with his foam. True, the dream is Marjodoc's and conveys his sense of things, but this is part of the total truth of the situation which Gottfried is imparting.

As we have seen, it is characteristic of lyric poets to speak a great deal of the enemies of the lover; in the lyric, these enemies are a projection of the lover's own carnality, as the lady is an aspect of his ideality. In Gottfried's romance, the lady is real and so are the enemies: they are malicious and spy and plot. But like the enemies of the courtly lover they have their point and place: though they are ugly, they speak the truth— at least from the world's point of view.

The sympathy of Gottfried for the lovers is constant, and Melot, the spying dwarf who would inform the king, Gottfried says is "cursed," "a tool of the Devil" (11. 14510–12), and "full of deceit" (11. 14522–26). Although Tristan and Isot are equally deceitful, their deceit is practised in the protection of their love, whereas the dwarf and Marjodoc (*Der nidege Marjodo,* 1. 13637) Gottfried condemns because they are malicious. Throughout, the poet presents Tristan's skill in deception as inevitable in view of the world's hostility. As the love relationship develops, Tristan combines deception with prayer. In the episode in the orchard, Tristan, no longer the innocent boy who first came to Cornwall, prays in the same naive way: "Almighty God . . . protect Isot and me" (11. 14637 ff.). Interestingly enough, he prays not only for himself but for his beloved.

Isot also prays, expressing a special concern that the Lord help them preserve their "honor" (11. 14706–9). When one reflects that their "honor" is lost and only deceit can protect their reputation, one gets the feeling that it is not all for love and the world well lost, but the attempt to enjoy simultaneously an adulterous relationship and the status of respectability. Isot's skill in deceitfulness is revealed when she swears, knowing Mark and Melot to be concealed, that before God she never conceived a liking for any man but him who had her maidenhead (11. 14760 ff.)—literally true but false in spirit. This episode clearly prefigures the more spectacular ordeal of the hot iron.

Gottfried's handling of the trial by ordeal reveals both his strong sympathy for the lovers and considerable daring in the use of religious ideas. He says of Isot, she confided her cares "to Christ, the Merciful,/ who is helpful when one is in trouble" (11. 15545–46). Christ is here made to play the role which, in the popular miracles of Our Lady, was assigned to his mother, the one who could provide at once the access to Divine power and the human heart which sinners never failed to move to pity. Isot's ruse, even Gottfried admits, presumed "very far upon her Maker's courtesy" (1. 15552). In the hope that He might overlook her very real trespass and restore her to her honor, she gives away her gold, silver, and jewelry. Like many another rich lady in a tight spot, Isot combines her skill in deceit with a supreme sense of self-confidence and an ostentatious display of "charity." As the Queen swears the oath, technically true but false in spirit, and succeeds in bearing the hot iron, Gottfried remarks, thus it was confirmed "that the mighty Christ/ is windblown like a sleeve" (11. 15735–36). In this statement, which has been variously interpreted, it seems that Gottfried is doing two things. First, he is registering his disapproval of the part which the bishops and prelates, as representatives of Christ's church, played in this barbarous practice of trial for adultery by ordeal. The presence of such a trial in the Old Testament (Numbers 5:12–31) gave it sanction in the Christian Middle Ages, although many theologians were opposed to the practice.[10] But the aspect of the ordeal which troubled theologians, that it was an attempt to force God to render a judgment whether or not He was ready to do so, was probably not the basis of Gottfried's objections. More likely, since innocent women often suffered the effects of the ordeal, Gottfried found a "rightness" in permitting the guilty woman to be saved by her guile. It is noteworthy that at the Fourth Lateran Council in 1215, Pope Innocent III forbade the clergy from performing any religious ceremony in connection with ordeals.[11]

Gottfried, however, has another objective: not only do the enemies of the barbarous custom rejoice, but also those who would excuse the deception and the adultery because the love of Tristan and Isot is beyond human judgment. Gottfried presents the exoneration of Isot before the highest tribunal by the direct intervention of the Deity. This is, of course, a fictitious Deity, indifferent to His own laws, but it is a daring stroke on Gottfried's part—to involve the Lord Himself in the web of deceptions which the subtle Queen weaves—to present Him as deceived or as willing to aid her in deceiving. Gottfried has responded to the presumptuous attempt to force God to signify Isot's guilt by presuming to make God proclaim her innocence.

This stage in the life of the lovers—their precarious practice of love at Mark's court, aided by Brangaene, but spied on and plotted against by Melot—comes to an end when Mark bids them leave his court and country. The next stage—the forest retreat—is one of the oldest features of the Tristan story, being derived from the old Irish *aitheda,* or elopment of the young lovers to the wilderness where they make their home.[12] In the versions of Béroul and Eilhart, the forest idyll of early Irish story is altered to stress the physical and emotional hardship of their life, and the whole episode takes on a penitential cast.[13] Gottfried, following Thomas, preserves the forest idyll and eliminates all trace of suffering. There is not, as in Béroul and Eilhart, any encounter between the lovers and the hermit; nor is there any awareness of sin.

Their life in the wilderness is, in a sense, an exile; they have sinned against the king and been driven from his court. But ironically they go, not like Adam and Eve from Paradise into the imperfect world, but on the contrary: they leave the imperfect world of the court, and their exile becomes a state of bliss, an earthly paradise. Here a new stage in the development of their love is achieved in blissful isolation, ironically reminiscent of that enjoyed by Adam and Eve before the Fall. Gottfried describes an innocent, even exalted sensuality, not unlike that of Milton's primeval pair, with the significant difference that in the garden of Tristan and Isot there is no prohibition. Neither are there any hymns of praise to God the creator; in the paradise of the lovers, the goddess *Minne* rules, and they devote themselves wholly to her. The songs they sing are for each other, and they are songs of lovers. It is here in the *Minnegrotte* that Gottfried fully develops his religion of love.[14]

In the ideal setting, the love of Tristan and Isot reaches a new high level of mutual devotion, but their falseness in dealing with Mark persists and penetrates their life in the sanctuary: they send Curvenal back to court to report that they had returned to Ireland to proclaim their innocence. Ironically, this lie may reflect their wish to recapture the state of innocence which, in fact, they shared when they left Ireland.

The first details Gottfried provides of the *Minnegrotte* reveal its primitive aspects: it is a cavern, in a savage mountainside, that had been hewn out of rock in heathen times, when giants ruled. The door, however, is of bronze and bears the inscription, "the cave of lovers"; through it Tristan and Isot enter not a rocky cavern, but a handsome edifice with a bed at the center made of crystal, and engraved and dedicated to *Minne.* Although the cavern itself dates from heathen times and is dedicated to the goddess of Love, the round edifice with its smooth white walls, green marble pavement and high windows suggests the sanctuary of a Christian Church. In constructing his chamber of love to conform to ecclesiastical architecture, Gottfried sets the stage for his ritual enactment of the *hieros gamos,* the sacred marriage. Outside the door of bronze is the garden of delight, the ideal landscape: three linden trees, a spring, flowers and green grass, and singing birds. But beyond the mountain with its cave and garden there is a wasteland.

Part of the extraordinary effect which Gottfried creates in the *Minnegrotte* episode depends on the juxtaposition of primitive elements against a background permeated with the most sacred associations. Throughout the episode he is drawing on a number of religious sources, among the most important being the Song of Songs and the mystical interpretations, especially those of Saint Bernard of Clairvaux.[15] First in *De diligendo Deo* (1125–35) and later, more fully in *Sermones in Cantica Canticorum* (1135–53), Bernard develops his conception of love as a mystical marriage, in which the ardor of the Bridegroom is interpreted as the tender and faithful love of Christ for His Bride, the Church. Here Gottfried finds a ready-made vision of perfect mystical love. Even the choice of the rocky cavern as the place of the lovers' retreat was probably determined by a reference in Canticles 2:14 to "the clefts of the rock,"[16] where in Bernard's commentary, the Bridegroom enjoys his happiness, and where there are treasures laid up and a great variety of sweetness.[17] Like Saint Bernard's Bridegroom and His Bride, Tristan and Isot hasten to a Paradise which is "a safer dwelling place, a sweeter pasturage, a richer, more fruitful field, a land where they may dwell without fear and have abundance that cannot be exhausted."[18]

Central to Saint Bernard's conception of love is his eighty-third sermon on the Canticles,[19] in which a number of passages seem especially appropriate to Gottfried's lovers: "Though a soul be an alien on the earth, in which it finds so many enemies, yet it may dare to aspire to the heavenly nuptials and to bear the sweet yoke of love." Bernard goes on to refer to a relationship which "is more than a contract, it is a communion," concluding, "Love is the great reality, and very precious." Particularly applicable to Tristan and Isot is Bernard's sense of the reciprocal nature of love, of love as a mystical marriage, an embrace, not a contract.[20] In speaking of the Bride and Bridegroom, he stresses their mutual love and their oneness: one inheritance, one dwelling place, one table, one bed, one flesh.[21] But, when Bernard goes on to remind his readers that love belongs exclusively to a wedded pair, and that it must keep in continual relation with Him who is its origin, then the differences between Gottfried and Bernard become apparent: Tristan and Isot serve the goddess *Minne,* whose only condition is total surrender of the lovers to one another.

The garden which Gottfried creates for his lovers is, as in the Canticles, a real garden, an ideal landscape, and a metaphor. In the Canticles (4:12) the lover says, "my spouse is a garden . . . a fountain." Gottfried, following Bernard, allegorizes the metaphor: the conception of the beloved as a garden, a fountain, fuses with the lovers' enjoyment of an idyllic life. In the morning they stroll to the meadow; and when the sun reaches high noon, they seek the shade of the linden tree and tell tales of love. When they tire of stories, they slip into their retreat, the cave dedicated to the goddess *Minne,* and play the harp and sing amorous lays. Now says Gottfried, "The cave's true mistress/ gives herself to/ her sport in earnest" (ll. 17229–31). In the Canticles the lovers have their bed in the garden: "Our bed is flourishing. The beams of our house are of cedar, our rafters of cypress" (1:15–16). It is there that they enjoy their love: "My beloved is gone down into his garden . . . I to my beloved, and my beloved to me . . ." (6:1–2; 5:1).

Gottfried, however, alters the bed of boughs in the garden: the bed of Tristan and Isot is of crystal and set apart in the inner grotto. He separates the mystical rite of love celebrated upon the altarlike bed at the center of the sanctuary from the preliminary strolling and telling of love stories in the garden. This separation of the garden and cave marks the distinction between the preparation for love which takes place in the garden and ecstasy comparable to the mystic vision which is reserved for the inner sanctum. Like the place where Saint Bernard's Celestial Bridegroom visits His Bride, the cave is the chamber of the heart, the inner chamber, the bed chamber; it is lofty and secret, the place of rewards.[22]

Building upon the sense that what the lovers enjoy in the cave is a state of being, Gottfried proceeds to identify its architectural features with the qualities of perfect love, constructing his own allegory on the patterns of ecclesiastical allegories, according to which the architecture of the church signifies the dimensions of God's love.[23] When Gottfried says, "the roundness is the simplicity of Love" (11. 16931–32), he is following the commentators who refer to the circular structure of the church as symbolic of the love which God has extended throughout the circle of the world. When he says, "the breadth is the power of Love" (1. 16937), he is echoing ecclesiastical commentators who state that the breadth of the church signifies charity. When he tells us, "the height is its lofty spirit" (1. 16939), he follows the commentators who say that the summit of the church—round and of great height—signifies perfect faith. As the crown at the vault is borrowed from ecclesiastical architecture, so Gottfried's allegorical interpretation of it as the Crown of Virtues is derived from the commentaries which identify it as the Crown of Eternity.

Gottfried uses the colors white and green and their allegorical significance in ecclesiastical tradition to create his vision of perfect love. The walls of the churchlike edifice are white, which according to commentators symbolizes chastity, innocence, God's own perfection, or the integrity of man's relationship to God; for Gottfried, white represents the integrity of the lovers' relationship to each other. In the greenness of the marble floor, which Gottfried informs us betokens constancy, is combined the perennial greenness of vegetation and the permanence of marble. It is from this green marble foundation of constancy that the crystal bed of pure love arises.

The churchlike inner grotto is reached through the bronze door which separates the garden world from the inner sanctum. In representing the door as bronze, Gottfried is probably drawing on several religious traditions. In the Old Testament bronze is used lavishly, especially in the books dealing with Solomon (in 2 Chronicles 4:9 Solomon's court has bronze doors). Also, in the Middle Ages church doors were often made of bronze. In the allegories of the church, the door represents obedience, the obedience of Jesus to His Father, His willingness to become flesh; in Gottfried, the door is the obedience of the lovers to each other's pleasure. On the inside are two seals of love turned toward each other, one of cedar, the other of ivory; both seals and the substances of which they are made seem to be drawn from the Canticles.[24] The allegorical meanings which Gottfried assigns to cedar and ivory—knowledge and purity—are reminiscent of the qualities which Bernard assigns to cedar and cypress—strength, steadfastness, hope, patience, right faith, and pure life.[25] The symbolism of the latch and lever, working together to open love's door, is transparently erotic: the lever of tin, which indicates willingness, fits into the latch of gold, which signifies success. If a man set his thoughts on *Minne,* this lever will carry him to the tender transports of love. In the bronze door, Gottfried has created a highly elaborate allegory appropriate both to his exaltation of love and to its erotic nature.

The three little windows, a standard feature of Gothic architecture, which in the allegorization of the church symbolize the Trinity, become in Gottfried, kindness, humility, and courtliness, the qualities of perfect love. Thus the allegorical interpretation of the cave establishes it as a state of virtuous love, exalted and ennobling.

It is, of course, in the crystal bed at the center of the grotto that the ritual act of love, the sacred marriage is consummated. In his conception of the bed as crystal, Gottfried leaves behind the world of bronze, gold, and tin, and the green world of the garden, associated with Solomon and the Old Testament, and draws upon two different traditions: the Celtic Otherworld[26] and the Apocalypse, where crystal is used to suggest the incandescence of the heavenly city.[27] Gottfried refers to crystal earlier in the *Tristan:* when the young hero is about to do battle with Morolt, he is armed with a helmet like crystal, and on it is a dart, foreteller of Love. Also it was from a glass vessel that Tristan and Isot drank the love potion. Gottfried seems to be linking through his use of crystal and glass the earlier episode to this culminating vision of perfect love.

He includes in his allegorical interpretation of the *Minnegrotte* the remark that he has been there—has found the lever and seen the latch, even pressed himself to the bed of crystal, but never enjoyed repose on it. This passage, with its humor and pathos, is usually taken to be a personal revelation, but this too has its parallel and probable source in Bernard, who wrote, "that is a chamber into which entrance has sometimes been granted to me, but alas, how rarely that has happened and for how short a time it has lasted."[28]

Early in his description of the *Minnegrotte,* Gottfried raises the question of how the lovers nourished themselves, and he answers that they enjoyed the best nutriment, pure devotion:

> They looked at one another,
> they nourished themselves on that;
> the fruit which their eyes bore,
> that was their nourishment.
>
> [11, 16815–18]

The full implications of this passage can only be realized in several contexts: the Tristan story itself, the religious tradition, and Gottfried's own intention. In the early Celtic versions, the lovers enjoy pastries and wine brought by Tristan's page;[29] in Béroul and Eilhart they suffer hunger.[30] Gottfried, in insisting that the lovers need no nourishment but love, is making two points: he is suggesting a spiritual, mystic love, such as that of Christ for His Church; but he is also suggesting that love is the most delicious of foods, its full enjoyment gratifies the whole being, and the abundance of love's delicacies is a feast. Every day is a feast day for Tristan and Isot, and the high feasts of love which they enjoy are contrasted with those at court: King Arthur never held a high feast that gave keener pleasure. The sense of erotic love as the most delicious of foods is expressed early and exquisitely in the Canticles: "thy lips . . . are as dropping honeycomb, honey and milk are under thy tongue . . ." (4:11), "thy throat [is] like the best wine" (7:9), and "thy breasts are better than wine" (1:1). In suggesting that the lovers need no earthly food, Gottfried is relating them to the Chosen People of the Old Testament who are nourished by the manna of Heaven and to the Saints in medieval tradition who lived on the Eucharist. But Gottfried's pair, Tristan and Isot, surpass the holy ones: as pure spirits they need no earthly food, only love. In going beyond the religious tradition, Gottfried at once mocks the ascetic view and uses it to assert his own view: what one really needs to live is love. They hunt, says Gottfried, not for food but for pleasure.

This idyll, in which the hunt is an erotic game, is shattered by the real sound of the horns and hounds of Mark, chasing a strange hart. As these sounds penetrate their sanctuary, Tristan's skill in deception is again brought into play. On the bed between himself and Isot he places his naked sword, using this time-honored symbol of chastity to convey the impression of innocence.[31] As intended, Mark is willing to accept the sword as evidence of their chastity. In resuming the motif of Tristan the master trickster, Gottfried is, of course, following Thomas, who in turn is following the primitive story pattern.[32] But the intrusion of the trickster motif into the *Minnegrotte,* set off by the appearance of Mark, disturbs the mystical serenity and points toward a return to the world of intrigue.

With Mark's appearance at the little windows (one of which betokens kindness), we have again a striking resemblance to a passage in the Canticles: "He looketh forth at the windows" (2:9). When Mark sees the lovers, lying high on their crystal bed with the naked sword between them, he is inclined to think them innocent. Love, the Reconciler, says Gottfried, stole to the scene; over her white face was the gold paint of deception (11. 17536 ff.). According to Bernard's interpretation, he who looks through the windows is the Bridegroom in the *flesh* (italics added); and if one makes confession of his sins, throws open the window of the heart, he who is *kind* (italics added) who stands behind our wall, will look benignantly upon us.[33] Mark is very much a man of *flesh* and *kind;* without receiving a confession of sin but rather newly deceived and self-deceiving, he forgives her.

Gottfried has also borrowed Bernard's sense of how one moves from carnal or natural love, *amor,* a love of self for one's own sake, through the love of others and of God to the highest form of love. According to Bernard, the final degree is to be inebriated with Divine love, forgetful of self, to pass over into God and become one spirit with Him. It is only for the holy to experience such a state in this life and only at rare intervals or once, and only for a moment. It is a chaste love, and the soul will obtain this supreme degree when no enticement of the flesh will draw her back. Bernard establishes as the condition of this degree the aligning of one's will with God's and thinks of this state chiefly in terms of the holy martyrs.[34] It is part of the supreme audacity of Gottfried that he represents Tristan and Isot as having achieved in the *Minnegrotte* a state of bliss resembling this final degree of love. Actually each has passed beyond self-love but not beyond physical love. Their relationship exists for the sake of each other; it is *Minne* they serve, not the Christian God.

There are a number of paradoxes involved in the interrelation between the Canticles, Bernard's mystical interpretation and Gottfried's use of them: that one of the most sensuous of all love songs should become part of the holy scriptures; that these love songs should be interpreted by a celibate addressing his fellow monks as a marriage, even a mystical marriage; and that this marriage of Christ and His Church should be so glowingly described that its spirit and imagery should be borrowed to exalt a love which defies conventional, contractual marriage; and finally, that Gottfried in celebrating an erotic love, should use not the sensuous language of the Canticles, but Bernard's allegorization of the rich similes and metaphors.

To Gottfried, as to Bernard, love is the dominating power of the universe.[35] But the conception each has of love is different. The fact that they seem similar rests upon Gottfried's having adopted the language of the mystic without altering his conception of love. In Bernardine mysticism and in Christian thought generally, Christ represents love and mercy, but the sinner he came to save must repent (Mark 2:17). One of the noteworthy features of Gottfried's Tristan and Isot is that they assume their love to be entirely justifiable and never think of themselves as sinners. They feel they can do no wrong and so God must surely protect them from their enemies, that is, those who out of malice and jealousy spy on them and would reveal their relationship to the king.

The *Minnegrotte* is at once Gottfried's supreme creation and the best illustration of his technique of using religious images and ideas. It represents the highest stage of love achieved by Tristan and Isot, a vision of love's perfection largely based on the vision of Saint Bernard. The central conception—the mystical marriage—is drawn from the Canticles and Bernard's allegorical interpretation. Ironically, since the love of Tristan and Isot is celebrated not only outside of marriage but in defiance of marriage, it must be condemned by the very tradition which nourished it. The *Minnegrotte* is neither the Earthly Paradise nor the Heavenly City, though it derives features from each; it is an interval and a prefiguration of the lovers' ultimate bliss. For its construction Gottfried has drawn materials from many sources—from the ancient and sensuous Canticles and from the mystical interpretations of it; from the churches of Christendom and the ingenious allegorizations of its structure; from the scriptures, Old and New Testaments, and from the vision of the Holy City. Gottfried, the artist, has selected carefully from among the richest and noblest works and skillfully blended the borrowed elements into his own vision of ideal love.

In describing a love which is physical in spiritual terms, Gottfried establishes the essential paradox of Tristan-love: it cannot survive in the real world of Mark's court; it must create a court apart from the courts of this world; yet it cannot survive in the Otherworld. In his conception of a court away from court, Gottfried seems moved by the psalmist's words: "How lovely are thy tabernacles, O Lord," "my soul longeth and fainteth for the courts of the Lord," and "a day in thy courts is better than a thousand."[36] The lovers are human beings, however, and they need not only physical and mystical love but a society beyond each other. They had their court, but their loyal servitors were the green linden trees, and their service was the song of the birds (11. 16879–87); they cannot be satisfied by this game of playing court. They have their own honor (11. 17068–70), but it is not the world's honor, and they are led back to court, mistakenly thinking it will be possible to enjoy both.

After the lovers leave the *Minnegrotte* and resume their practice of love at the court of Mark, Gottfried, in one of his revealing asides, takes up the question of Mark's lack of honor. It is Gottfried's view that neither Tristan nor Isot deceived Mark. Gottfried blames the king himself, stating that he is guilty of lust. To the reader who is aware that Tristan and Isot have in fact deceived Mark and are themselves possessed by a powerful mutual lust, this comment seems strange. As Gottfried continues to discuss the many husbands who are blind with lust, one begins to understand his preoccupation with a type, but in the narrative Mark is a much abused husband, who permits himself to be deceived. In the passage on surveillance (ll. 17844 ff.), Gottfried establishes both the general nature of surveillance (cf. his own earlier comments—l. 12196 ff.) and its specific consequences in the story. He makes clear how the ill will of those who engage in surveillance and the oppressive atmosphere which it creates precipitate, especially in susceptible women like Isot, the very behavior it was intended to prevent. The passage thus serves ironically to shift to Mark the responsibility for the resurgence of sensuality in the lovers, following their return to the real world. The bed which Isot prepares in the orchard is not the crystal bed of the Otherworld, nor is there a naked sword to suggest innocence. The violation is clear; exile for Tristan is unavoidable.

Following the discovery in the orchard, Gottfried, faithful to his story, relates a new phase in Tristan's love—how in grief and confusion he deceives Isot of the White Hands by singing to her a song of the other Isot: "Isot my mistress, Isot my beloved, in you my death, in you my life" (ll. 19213–14). The relationship with the second Isot is marked by deception and self-deception and the agony of separation from Isot, the Queen. It is at this point for reasons unknown that Gottfried leaves his story unfinished.

Our interest in the Thomas version is minimal; it lacks the special quality of Gottfried's genius, but supplies the episodes which bring the story to its completion. In marrying Ysolt of the White Hands, whom he does not love and with whom he refuses to consummate his marriage, the Tristan of Thomas reveals a perversity which never emerges in Gottfried's Tristan. Turning from the living wife beside him, he escapes to a cavern and there embraces a statue of Queen Ysolt.[37]

Thomas's Hall of Statues, *Salle aux Images,* is second only to Gottfried's *Minnegrotte* as an instance of the religion of love. The Hall is, like the Grotto, set apart from the real world, separated from it by a perilous water barrier. Like Gottfried's cave, the rocky isle of Thomas is strongly associated with pagans and giants, but the Hall itself lacks the lofty splendor of Gottfried's church-like edifice. And at the center, in place of the crystal bed with its multiple associations of Celtic Otherworld and Mystical Marriage, is the statue of Ysolt, an exact replica of the living woman. As Tristran embraces and speaks to the wooden image, one gets a powerful graphic sense of the idolatry of courtly love, the worship of the image. The statue itself, the beautiful woman crowned, dressed in regal splendor and treading her enemy, the weeping dwarf, underfoot, resembles not only Ysolt, but the Church as the Bride of Christ or Mary the Virgin Queen.[38] In addition to the awe one must feel for the lifelike replica of Ysolt is our wonder as a sweet odor issues from her lips. The sense of mystery is dispelled, however, as we learn how the ingenious workmen placed a canister of herbs in the hollow bosom of the statue, with gold pipes leading to the mouth. The idea comes, as so many of Gottfried's did, from Bernard's Commentary on the Canticles. But one has only to read Bernard's sermon to feel to what unworthy uses it has been put. Bernard, seeking to interpret the Canticles as the mystical love of Christ for His Church, begins with the sensuous reference in the opening verse to the "breasts which are better than wine." As he struggles to uplift the minds and hearts of his celibate listeners, the breasts become the source of virtue, and the sweet smelling ointments of the next verse become the perfumes of piety and charity, "worthy of the bosom of the Bride, agreeable to the senses of the Bridegroom."[39]

It is impossible to know what Gottfried would have done with Thomas's Hall of Statues had he continued. But after the *Minnegrotte,* after the mystic vision of a perfect mutual love, Gottfried must have contemplated with melancholy the remaining incidents—the marriage of Tristan, the continued intrigue, and the idolatry of the Hall of Statues. Only in their death can one imagine Gottfried responding again with full sympathy to his theme. Although Thomas is not the great artist that Gottfried is, it is impossible to read Thomas's last lines without being profoundly moved. Finding her lover dead, Ysolt drinks of the same cup from which Tristran has drunk and joins him in death. In her willingness to die she becomes love's martyr.

It is in Gottfried's Prologue, even more than in the *Minnegrotte,* that his religion of love finds its most exalted and daring expression. It is here that he draws together and elevates all the parts of the story.

In addressing his Prologue to the *edele herzen,* "the noble hearts,"[40] Gottfried resembles the courtly poets who write for a small, select circle, but the religious and mystical overtones suggest a pattern of exclusiveness which is more religious than courtly. The *edele herzen* are like the Chosen People, the Remnant, the Elect. In John especially, one finds a strong emphasis on "the brethren," a feeling of intimacy and exclusiveness, a little circle of believers who enjoy Christ's special love.[41] In his First Epistle, for instance, he says, "They are of the world." "We are of God" (4:5,6.). The feeling of exclusiveness one finds in John is reflected in Bernard, who conveys a strong sense in several of his sermons on the Canticles of the brethren, a special group to whom he can speak of "other truths than to those persons who are of the world."[42] As Saint Bernard addresses the Cistercian monks in his religious community, those united by their devotion to Jesus, Gottfried addresses the *edele herzen* in his Prologue. As Bernard speaks of the joys and sorrows of Christ's love for His Bride, the Church, Gottfried tells of the joy and sorrow of Tristan and Isot. As Bernard seeks to edify the brethren, so Gottfried intends to reinforce the constancy of true lovers.

It is at the end of the Prologue, however, when Gottfried offers up for the spiritual nourishment of his noble hearts the bread, which is the tale of the loving life and death of Tristan and Isot that he approaches most closely the example of Bernard, who offers to share the bread of the Canticles with his brethren. Here Gottfried echoes not only Bernard but the liturgy of the Mass. As the priest offers the host to the faithful, he does so in imitation of Jesus, who the day before He suffered death, took bread and offered it to his disciples. Now the Canon of the Mass includes the offering of bread and wine. As Jesus offered wine to his disciples to drink, the priest in a symbolic gesture, holds up the chalice.[43] Gottfried has separated the elements of his ritual: in the Prologue the bread is offered; the cup which symbolizes the passion and death of Tristan and Isot was drunk on board the ship bound for Cornwall. Tristan and Isot, drinking the potion which involves their passion and death, parallel Jesus, who drinks the cup of his passion and death; Gottfried, however, presents Tristan and Isot as drinking without knowing what is in store for them, whereas Jesus knowingly drinks the cup of his death, and through his willing acceptance, it becomes the chalice of salvation. In the Sacrament of the Eucharist, as the offering of bread and wine takes its meaning from the crucifixion, in Gottfried, the *Minnetrank* and the ritual offering of the bread lead to the *Minnegrotte*. The central act on which Gottfried's religion is based, analogous to Christ's passion and death on the cross, is the *hieros gamos,* which takes place on the crystal bed in the churchlike grotto. The lovers, having drunk the potion, become Love's agonized and joyous victims.

In telling the story of their love, their persecution, and death and in offering it as the bread to the *edele herzen,* Gottfried follows the theological pattern almost exactly: as the word which was God and was with God became flesh, so the words of Thomas are with Gottfried; he gives them flesh in the living tale; as Jesus and his life of joy and suffering and death became the words of the holy gospel which became the words of the Mass—the ritual offering which sustains the Faithful in their efforts to be at one with God, so the life of Tristan, his love, suffering and death become the words of Gottfried's story—the bread he offers to sustain the lovers in their quest for perfect love. As Jesus died and the faithful keep alive his sweet name through the celebration of the Eucharist, so Tristan and Isot are dead, says Gottfried, but "their sweet name lives on" (1. 223). In the retelling of their story, their lives are renewed for the noble hearts. The reenactment of their life and death becomes the bread, the Eucharist which nourishes the lovers who live. How one responds to what Gottfried is doing will vary, but his intention is clear: the tale of sensual love is being celebrated with the reverence which Christians associate with the Mass, the ritual reenactment of the Last Supper which prefigured Christ's sacrificial death.

The strong emphasis Gottfried places on the willingness of the lovers to suffer, to endure all trials for love, seems to have gained some of its intensity from the emphasis placed on the exaltation of suffering in Christian thought. The persistent stress on the inextricable relationship between joy and sorrow seems related to the pattern of joy and sorrow in Christian theology, where both were raised to a new pitch of intensity: the joy at the Incarnation, sorrow at the Crucifixion, joy at the Resurrection. The exalted suffering of Tristan and Isot is intimately related to the Christian context, in which the cultural as well as religious center was the love and willing death of Jesus.

In Gottfried's poem there are two different conceptions of God. There is the God of this world, of society, of conventional morals, of the rights of husbands, of worldly reputation, of Mark's court and of the Church hierarchy. Those who espouse the God of this world are the enemies, and they persecute the lovers. There is also the God of the Tristan-world, who favors and protects them. Although guilty by the conventional moral standards of adultery and deceit, in the eyes of this God they are exalted by their love for each other; they are "innocent." Neither God is the Christian God who reveals Himself in the scriptures, in the scriptural commentaries, and in the Church. Although Gottfried's references attest to his knowledge of the Bible and Church tradition, yet he seems not to be attuned to this God: a God of love, but not adultery; a God of love but also of truth; He is a God who loves sinners, but only if they repent, who insists that His will, not man's, be done.

As for Gottfried's attitude toward the Church, it is important to bear in mind that we are dealing with a work of art, the imaginative retelling of an ancient tale. There is no question of heresy, which involves the denial of doctrines, a public and official expression of dissent; nor is there blasphemy—Gottfried does not revile or reproach what is sacred, but borrows it to describe what he feels is of highest value, and so implicitly he acknowledges the excellence of the sacred. At most, there is irreverence, impiety, a mock-solemnity.[44] He is not expressing any new ideas, but using an old story to reflect his intense interest in love, an interest which permeates the literature of the period. He has no thought of reforming the social order; his lovers adjust to the enmities of Mark's court by evasion and deceit, which he sanctions; in a base world, the lovers create their own world, for a time enjoy it, only to return to the real world which demands their separation and death.

Tristan-love essentially functions outside the realm of Christianity, yet the continuous use of Christian expressions and patterns creates a certain tension and demands that we formulate an explanation. But ironically, what the work demands, it also denies: Gottfried created a poem, not a treatise, and the mystery and subtlety of his art defies neat formulas or pat explanations.

The paradox of courtly love conceived as service did not disappear when love became mutual as in *Tristan;* it just assumed a somewhat different shape. When love is reciprocal, although the lady is no longer merciless, she can no longer be venerated. It is *Minne* herself, rather than the lady, who is idolized. Involved in the paradox of Gottfried's treatment of Tristan-love is his glorifying an adulterous love, which the Church condemns, and to exalt this love he uses not only conventional religious references, but the pattern exemplified by Christ of the persecution of the innocent by the evil forces of this world. And as Gottfried shapes Tristan-love to resemble Jesus-love—the joy and sorrow, the passion and death—the differences stand out in sharper relief: Jesus, obedient to the Father's will, devoted to truth, celibate; Tristan, disobeying God's commandments, evading the will of his uncle and king, and of truth itself, absorbed in the love of a woman flawed like himself. Part of the paradox of Tristan-Isot love is that their spiritual marriage must also be physical; moreover it cannot be a contractual marriage; it can only exist outside of, and in defiance of, ordinary marriage. Another crucial aspect of the paradox is that their true love for each other involves them in a web of lies and deception. However one articulates or explains the paradoxical love of Tristan and Isot or the paradoxical treatment of it by Gottfried, the *Tristan* remains the supreme example of the religion of love; it represents the most elaborate and sustained use of religious doctrines, imagery and sentiment to exalt the mutual and physical love of man and woman.

The ultimate development in the opposite direction, love as it is subordinated to religion appears in *La Queste del Saint Graal,* a work which rejects both carnal and courtly love and reaffirms the need to devote one's energies to God, the source and end of love. Gottfried's unfinished masterpiece in which adulterous love is celebrated with religious fervor is counterbalanced by the *Queste* in which adultery is strongly condemned and the love of God is presented as the highest adventure.

Gottfried had chosen the Tristan and Isot story to represent the supreme instance of mutual love between man and woman, but the author of the *Queste,* while creating a new hero to embody his ideal, uses as his point of departure the waning love of Lancelot for the aging Guinevere. Their relationship was as culpable in his eyes as that of Tristan and Isot, but it contained certain redeeming aspects; it was Lancelot's passion for the Queen which led to the conception of the son who was to surpass all his predecessors. Here, as elsewhere in the *Queste,* the value of carnal love is confined to the production of offspring or repentance. There is throughout the work a deep and persistent adherence to the pattern of orthodox Christianity: sin, from the original sin of Adam to the adultery of Lancelot, must be followed by repentance. It is at this point that the *Queste* represents the sharpest divergence from the *Tristan.* The God of the *Queste,* unlike the God of *Tristan,* is a God of the Old and New Testaments, of the medieval church and of Cistercian mysticism. He is the Creator and Redeemer whose Commandments are to be obeyed, or if they are broken, the sinner must repent and confess.

Unlike Gottfried's account of the inevitable love of young Tristan and Isot, the *Queste* narrative begins when Lancelot's love for the Queen has been in progress for some twenty-four years. In the actual course of the story they never enjoy each other's love; there is not a kiss, a glance, or any expression of love on the part of Lancelot. Guinevere is never the object of adoration, but from the start is on the sidelines, an observer, and finally she disappears entirely from the story. The females who play roles, as Guinevere fades into insignificance, are damsels who serve as messengers, abbesses who give good advice, biblical women like Eve and Solomon's wife, and finally Perceval's virgin sister. Although Elayn does not figure in the narrative, the fact that her relationship with Lancelot—which was the antithesis of both courtly and mutual love—led to the birth of a son who is to replace his father as the Best Knight is sufficient to establish her importance.

More significant, however, than the elimination of Guinevere is the humiliation of Lancelot, the paragon of courtly lovers. From the first page of the *Queste,* when he follows the damsel to the abbey of nuns, leaving the court and Queen behind, to his twenty-four day trance at Corbenyc, his downfall is painfully and relentlessly depicted. Lancelot, like Tristan, suffers, but his suffering is not that of the lover separated from his lady but of the sinner who recognizes that because of his love for her he has lost his chance to take part in the highest of adventures.

The first episode which marks Lancelot's recognition that he is to be supplanted is Galahad's successfully drawing the sword from the stone and passing the test of the Perilous Seat. As Guinevere and other members of the court observe the ascendancy of Galahad, the public humiliation of Lancelot is spelled out by a damsel who announces that he no longer is the best knight.

Associated with the arrival of Galahad is the appearance of the grail, with its power to provide every man with whatever food he most desires. The presence of the grail and the virgin knight marks the shift in values from courtly love, with the lady as the center of attention, to the quest for a more ennobling love. Actually the fellowship of the Round Table is presented as good, albeit a limited good, as though Arthur had prepared the way for the creation of a higher fellowship. As he says before the knights depart, he has raised them up and advanced them to the utmost of his power and has always loved them like sons and brothers. The gloom of Arthur, the sorrow of the ladies when they learn that the quest excludes them, and especially the grief of Guinevere at the departure of Lancelot, all signify the end of courtly life and its values. It is worth noting that on the eve of their departure Galahad sleeps in King Arthur's bed, and Lancelot sleeps with Gawain. Next morning when Lancelot leaves the Queen, her powerlessness is evident as she insists that he would not go if she could prevent him, and in referring to his departure as betrayal, she reveals the deep cleavage in values which has been established. The weakness of King Arthur himself is apparent: he is permitted to accompany the grail knights only until they reach a cross, and then he must return to Camelot.

After the first important chapter, which establishes the new hero and new set of values, succeeding chapters describe adventures which illustrate the unfolding of Galahad's perfection, the testing of the near-perfect virtue of Perceval and Bors, and the inferiority of all other members of Arthur's court.

Of Arthur's knights it is Lancelot, the paragon of courtly lovers, who is made to suffer most keenly. His humiliation is depicted in episodes interspersed throughout the work. In the section which begins significantly in the Waste Forest, Lancelot encounters Galahad, fails to recognize him, charges him, and is toppled. Subsequently, in a ruined chapel, he sees a vision of a suffering knight healed by the grail, but he cannot stir because of his sin. This trance of Lancelot is no longer a sign of devotion to his lady but of a condition of spiritual inadequacy; it prefigures a later, longer, and in its consequences, more devastating trance. A voice describes his soul as "harder than stone, more bitter than wood, more barren than the fig-tree."[45] As Lancelot ponders the meaning of these words, one senses the ironic contrast; what had seemed to be the softness and sweetness of his love is now interpreted as a hardness and bitterness of soul. In using the word *barren,* the author has touched on a very crucial issue. Barren is intended to suggest the lack of good deeds; but one of courtly love's chief boasts was that for the love of his lady the knight would perform extraordinary acts of prowess. In using the image of the barren fig tree to describe the condition of Lancelot's soul, the Cistercian author is suggesting the barrenness of courtly lovers: in caring only for each other they serve neither nature nor society.

The image of the barren tree, used here to represent the unproductive nature of Lancelot's dependence on Guinevere, appears again later in the *Queste* when a hermit addresses the following words to Gawain: "You are an old tree, bare now of leaves and fruit" (P.161, M.175). These images of barren trees contrast interestingly with the two lilies of chastity which occur in the same dream; from these, says the abbot, will grow trees which will bear fruit (P. 171, 186, M. 184, 198).

As the sun shines and the birds sing—the perfect setting for love—Lancelot is presented as lamenting his surrender to lustfulness through which he has lost all his joy and great strength. Up to this point, Lancelot has not admitted his relations with the Queen to anyone. Like Tristan and all good courtly lovers, he has preserved the secrecy of his affair. But as he arrives at the hermitage and kneels before the hermit, he is urged to confess. The hermit speaks of God the Creator, who has given Lancelot great gifts with which to serve Him, not His enemy, the devil. He continues by speaking of God's love—of Jesus who stretched out His arms on the cross as if to draw all men to Him. As Lancelot is urged to confess, he hesitates. But his tongue is loosed at last and he confesses to having sinned in loving Queen Guinevere. Lancelot is brought to repent by being promised that if he will abjure the sinful commerce with the Queen, the Lord will love him again.

Subsequently, he encounters a squire who rebukes him, insisting he has lost the joy of heaven and all honor here below, that he has drained the cup of shame to the dregs. Highly susceptible to these charges and deeply penitent, Lancelot seeks a priest, who proceeds to describe how the devil entered Queen Guinevere and as she gazed at Lancelot the devil smote him with one of his darts. No longer was Lancelot a servant of God or even the Queen, but of the devil. Erotic love has become not the evil Venus but the devil himself.

Not only is adulterous love strongly condemned in the *Queste,* but there is an attempt to substitute for the adoration of the lady a higher type of devotion. To qualify for this special state, one serves Jesus, and to enter fully into His service means the rejection of adulterous love and of all sexual relationships, including marriage itself. The Cistercian author does not speak of marriage or married love any more than Gottfried, but it is chastity, not adultery, which is presented as the ideal state. Of the three who achieve the quest, Galahad and Perceval are virgins and Bors is chaste, having succumbed but once. Not only is there an absence of any attachment to any woman, physical or emotional, but there is a strong emphasis on the joy of male companionship.

The avoidance of carnal love is shown not so much as good in itself as it is a sign of one's capacity for true love, spiritual love—the only kind of love one can have for God. From the beginning, the nature of Galahad's devotion is established: he kneels before the relics; he is the servant of Jesus Christ, and the nature of the quest is clearly spelled out:

> For this is no search for earthly things but a seeking out of the mysteries and hidden delights of Our Lord, and the divine secrets which the most high Master will disclose to that blessed knight whom He has chosen for His servant [P. 19, M. 47].

Galahad, although destined for the ultimate vision, must pass through successive stages of active engagement and initiation; he must free the Maidens, understand the message of Solomon's ship, as well as heal the Maimed King before he can lie on the bed of Solomon.

So strong is the rejection of sexual love in the *Queste* that, not only Guinevere, but any beautiful and amorous damsel is apt to be the devil. This pattern of woman as temptress is especially clear in the episode in which Perceval is alone on an island. Here he is to be tested to determine if he is Our Lord's faithful servant. Highly susceptible when confronted by the beautiful damsel, he promises to do her bidding. He drinks deeply of the cup which she offers and woos her openly; like the courtly lady, she holds him off to increase his ardor, while a beautiful and luxurious bed is prepared. It is only the sign of the cross which prevents his succumbing. When he succeeds in resisting her, she accuses him, as Guinevere had accused Lancelot, of betrayal.

Significantly, in his prayer, he uses many of the expressions in addressing the Lord God that the courtly lover uses in addressing his lady: he is "thy servant," "unworthy"; he asks for "mercy" and wishes to "never leave thy service" and be a "good and trusty champion" (P. 95–6, M. 116). These expressions, which correspond exactly to those of the courtly lover, are used by Perceval not to win the lady but to gain the power to resist her. Unlike the courtly lover who threatens to do himself injury if his lady will not love him, Perceval, because he almost yields to her, actually slashes himself. In his willingness to suffer to atone for his sin, he resembles Lancelot, but in his willingness to shed his blood he goes beyond Lancelot and comes to resemble his saintly sister, who offers her blood to save the life of another.

As Perceval's repugnance for carnal love grows, so does his affection for his grail companions. The prospect of joining Bors and Galahad fills him with "the greatest joy any man could feel" (P. 115, M. 133). Thus Perceval, by preserving his virginity and strengthening his fraternal attachments, proves himself fit to join his companions in the pursuit of the grail.

In the adventure of Bors, one sees the second of Galahad's companions put through a series of tests to prove his fitness to participate in the later stages of the grail quest. Bors represents the man who had experienced carnal love once but has henceforth remained chaste. Like Perceval, he is virtuous but not perfect, and so must be tested to prove his worth. He is prepared for his ordeal by the advice of a priest, who warns him specifically against adultery, fornication, and murder. Urged to eat only bread and water, he consents "for the love [*amor*] of Him who was crucified" (P. 166, M. 179). Having been fortified with good advice, he is placed in a difficult predicament: he must choose between saving his brother Lionel from what seems certain death or a maiden from equally certain rape. His decision to save the maiden is presented as the right choice: in coming to her rescue, he saves not one virgin but two, whereas his brother cannot be saved because he is intent on evil. Later in an agonizing scene, Bors is forced to fight against his brother—to kill him or be killed. When two other men—a hermit and Calogrenant—give up their lives to rescue Bors from his brother, one sees emerging a different kind of brotherly love—one based not on blood, but on a spiritual kinship between those who give their primary allegiance to God.

Somewhat like Galahad in the Castle of Maidens episode, Bors is presented as a defender of the damsel in distress. He not only saves the virgin from rape, but in another episode defends a lady against her evil oppressor. In each case he is not interested in winning her love but in protecting her or restoring her to her rightful place. In the allegorical interpretation which follows, the Cistercian abbot explains to Bors that this damsel whom he defended is Holy Church, and *li rois Amanz,* "King Love," who granted her dominion over lands and men, is Jesus (P. 169, cf. 184; M. 182, 197).

Having defended women, Bors, like Perceval, must prove that he is immune to their charms. The episode in which a damsel tempts Bors differs from the simple sensuous temptation of Perceval and is appropriately complicated by the damsel's threat of suicide if he will not yield. But Bors remains impervious, even though the damsel and twelve of her maidens threaten to leap to their doom.

The kind of love which the Cistercian author is primarily concerned with is revealed in Bors's dream of the great bird who pierces its breast to revive its young. The bird is later identified as Jesus, who out of love shed his blood for the salvation of man; the dry tree in which the bird rests is identified with the cross (P. 167–68, 184; M. 181, 196). This vision, which prefigures the actual sacrifice of Perceval's sister, prepares Bors for his part in the last stages of the grail quest. Having emerged from an excruciating series of tests as a loyal servant of Jesus, Bors is summoned by a voice to join Perceval.

The idea of love as sacrifice is best exemplified in the narrative by Perceval's sister. She first appears at the beginning of the Solomon's ship episode to summon Galahad, insisting that she has a "great need of him" (P. 198, M. 209). Her need is not love, however, and when Galahad says, "I will follow you anywhere," he seems to understand perfectly that she is not so much a damsel as a link in the divine chain which is leading him to the grail. She is, like Galahad, a virgin, and except for her superior knowledge, is much like the other grail companions, her brother and Bors. One of her most important functions is to bring them together and lead them to Solomon's ship, where they learn the remarkable story of its origin, with its bed, sword, crown, and spindles.[46]

The three colors of the spindles—white, green, and red—are used throughout the *Queste* to represent the kinds of love which the Cistercian author values most highly. White is important from the beginning of the story—a man robed in white leads Galahad to Camelot, and monks, hermits, and holy men garbed in white reappear throughout. To some extent white is also Galahad's color, but more often it is red. When he first appears at Pentecost, he is wearing red armor, and red tunic and mantle lined with white. Here, as elsewhere, red corresponds to the flame of the Holy Spirit. In the Solomon's ship episode and more often throughout the text, however, red is associated with Galahad, not so much because it suggests the flaming love of the Holy Spirit, but because it represents the blood of Christ. Galahad's white shield has a red cross made of the blood of Josephus.

The ship which brings the grail companions to Solomon's ship and the great ship itself are covered with white samite, but on board the ship, red represents sacrifice. Both the red spindle and the scabbard of the sword (called "memory of blood") were made of the tree which became red when Abel's blood was shed (P. 219, 224, 227; M. 229, 233, 237). Red as a symbol of sacrifice is important also when Bors sees the great bird, when Perceval's sister gives her blood to heal the leprous lady, and finally, when Galahad heals the Maimed King with the red blood from the lance.

Although the chief colors of the *Queste* are white and red, symbolizing virginity and sacrifice, green also appears with considerable frequency. Sometimes green symbolizes the virtue of long suffering, which like the emerald gleams with a constant light. Green is often associated with grass, sometimes in dreams—as in Gawain's dream of a meadow of greenest grass. Later, this is interpreted as humility and patience, the virtues on which the grail fellowship was founded, the fraternal love which binds its members, but which to Gawain remains an unattainable dream. In contrast, both Bors and Galahad actually sleep on fresh grass. The symbolic sense of the green grass emerges with the reference to the path of Jesus, which quickens with life and greenness. Two interesting passages connect greenness and blood: the grass grows especially green on the graves of the twelve maidens whose blood was shed for the leprous lady, and Easter, which follows Jesus' sacrificial death, is referred to as the season which clothes all things in green.

Color symbolism occurs throughout the *Queste,* whereas, in the *Tristan* Gottfried concentrates his use of color in the *Minnegrotte.* The love which the Cistercian author envisions in the three colors is very different from either courtly love or Tristan-love. White symbolizes celibacy, not pure sexual love; green represents constancy in following God's will, not the lover's; and red, significantly absent from the *Minnegrotte,* symbolizes sacrificial love, on which he places the highest value.

In the relationship between Galahad and Perceval's sister, virgins both, we have erotic love, purified and sublimated. When she arms Galahad, he says, "this makes me your knight forever." She, feeling her mission is completed, says only, "it matters no more to me when death shall take me" (P. 228, M. 237).

In the episode following the departure of Perceval's sister and the grail companions from Solomon's ship, she is seized, like all virgins, to fulfill "the custom of the castle"—to give her blood for the cure of the lady who is afflicted with leprosy. The grail companions oppose the barbarous custom and fight to defend her. She, however, agrees to give her blood in order to prevent further fighting and to cure the lady. Before her death she gives her last command to the grail companions; it is however, "His command to you through me," and her last words are, "such is the Master's will" (P. 241, M. 249).

In the willing sacrifice of her blood, Perceval's sister becomes a virgin martyr. Out of love for her Lord, she imitates His redemptive death; she surrenders herself for the healing of another. In this she is the antithesis of the courtly lady, who demands that her lover sacrifice himself for her. In their willingness to die for their love, Perceval's sister and Ysolt resemble each other; for Perceval's sister, it is sacrifice as the culmination of a chaste life, devoted to the will of God; for Ysolt, it is the willingness to share Tristran's death, as she shared his life and love.

In the *Queste* the voluntary giving of one's life represents the highest form of love; it is patterned on Christ's redemption of man from the blight of original sin by His supreme act of love. Galahad's healing the Maimed King with Christ's blood and later lying on the bed on Solomon's ship in symbolic crucifixion relates him to Christ in His central redemptive act. The fact that it is Perceval's sister who actually gives her blood to heal another, who is also female, suggests that this sacrifice is intended to redeem woman. Perceval's sister is, moreover, an aspect of Galahad himself, and submits as part of the total surrender. Galahad's love of God is expressed as perfect devotion; he progresses through successive stages of understanding His nature and doing His will: freeing the oppressed and healing the suffering. Galahad and Perceval's sister reflect God's own love; together with Bors and Perceval they represent the fellowship of the love of God.

More important perhaps than the relationship between Perceval's sister and Galahad is his relationship to Perceval, the brother. After spending the night in a chapel they face the prospect of parting. The setting is "the edge of the forest known . . . by the name of Aube [dawn]." In the following passage one perceives the Cistercian author's version of the lover's parting at dawn: Galahad and Perceval "embraced on parting, for the love that they bore one another ran deep, as was well proven in their death, for the one did not survive the other long" (P. 246, M. 253). Although Aube is an actual place, its use in so symbolic a work can scarcely be attributed to chance.

While Galahad and Perceval exchange a fraternal embrace at dawn, Lancelot obeys an order to enter the boat in which the corpse of Perceval's sister has been placed. He kneels before the dead virgin, and the air he breathes is so sweet he knows not whether he is on earth or in the Earthly Paradise. His thoughts turn not to Guinevere but to Galahad, and the reward for the repentant Lancelot is the sight of his son who has surpassed him. Father and son embrace and kiss with a jubilation that defies description. As Galahad leaves his father, he commends him to

Jesus in these words: "may He keep you ever in His service," and Lancelot replies, "beseech the Master . . . not to let me quit His service, but to keep me His servant . . ." (P. 252, M. 259). Later when Lancelot is rebuked by a voice, he accepts with the same humility that he had shown when Guinevere had rebuked him in the *Charette;* now, however, he adores Jesus and begs to be His Servant.

When Lancelot arrives at Corbenyc, his ultimate unworthiness is established: as he approaches the grail, he is struck down and falls into a trance. This is the Cistercian author's version of the love trance: Lancelot is reduced to insensibility for twenty-four days to correspond to the twenty-four years he served Guinevere.

In a work in which the supreme act of love is sacrifice, in which chastity is the ideal and sexuality is acceptable only if it leads to offspring, the barren Queen is no longer an ideal. The former center of adoration, she is now ignored. Unlike the other women, she plays no part in the redemptive story, but is cast in the role of enemy; she deceives Lancelot, causes him to misspend his life.

The theme of deception, so pervasive in Gottfried's *Tristan,* appears in the *Queste,* but is treated somewhat differently. Whereas Tristan and Isot are equally deceptive and Gottfried seems to condone their behavior, in the *Queste* it is the deception of woman which is stressed. In most instances there are redeeming features: Eve deceived Adam into eating the forbidden fruit, but she is repentant and from their union came the lineage which was to culminate in the grail knight. Solomon's wife was deceitful, but it was she, not Solomon, who was responsible for the ship called Solomon's. Lancelot had been deceived into a union with Elayn, but from this union came Galahad. Guinevere, it seems, is the worst deceiver; she deceived Lancelot into squandering his life. For her, he has lost his honor and jeopardized his chance of enjoying the ultimate reward of Heaven. It is not so much women who are condemned in the *Queste,* but courtly women like Guinevere who are deceptive and barren.

Among the numerous resemblances between these very different works, perhaps the most striking is to be found in Solomon's ship and the *Minnegrotte.* As Tristan and Isot journeyed a great distance to the *Minnegrotte,* Galahad and Perceval's sister likewise journey a great distance to Solomon's ship; they are, however, joined by their companions, Bors and Perceval. For Tristan and Isot, the *Minnegrotte* is the experience of wholly knowing each other; for the grail companions, Solomon's ship is an introduction to their part in God's redemptive plan. In each, entrance is limited to the elect; there is the same sense of exclusiveness, whether the condition be true love or true faith (P. 201, M. 212-13).[47]

The *Minnegrotte* is a vision of love's perfection; it had been prefigured by Tristan and Isot's first experience of love following the drinking of the love potion on board the ship bound for Cornwall; it, in turn, prefigured their final union in death. It becomes the lovers' retreat to the Otherworld where they can enjoy their love unmolested by the world of the court. That they go together marks their perfect mutual love; that their retreat is a cave, rather than a ship or an island, is appropriate in terms of their clandestine love.

Solomon's ship has also this otherworld quality, but the choice of a ship rather than a cave makes possible a wider range of reference both in time and space—from the Earthly Paradise where man's redemptive history began to the distant holy city of Sarras, where Galahad experiences his final mystic vision. Galahad is brought to Solomon's ship by Perceval's sister, who is neither lover nor would-be lover, but a virgin priestess instructing the initiate in the divine mysteries. Galahad and Perceval's sister play their roles in this high adventure, bound together only by ties of mutual willingness to do the will of God. The love they have for each other is wholly subordinate to their fulfillment of their part in God's redemptive plan. Theirs is the perfectly sublimated love.

Both retreats are churchlike, with strong erotic associations: in both, the bed in the center symbolizes the kind of love which is being celebrated. Both beds have their ultimate origin in the bed of Solomon in the Canticles, and have been interpreted as a symbol of the mystic vision.[48] But the crystal bed on which Tristan and Isot enjoy their love differs from the elaborate bed of the *Queste* with its ancient trappings—crown of Solomon, sword of David, and the three colored spindles from the tree of knowledge. Although constructed in the days of Solomon, this bed is no nuptial couch. It is more closely related to the cross. In lying on it, Galahad experiences not so much the mystic vision, as a symbolic reenactment of the crucifixion. Although the origin and ultimate meaning of the beds on Solomon's ship and in the *Minnegrotte* may be similar, one is struck by the ironic contrast between Tristan and Isot, who share their passion on the crystal bed, and Galahad, who stretches himself on the ancient bed in a lonely ritual gesture, reminiscent of Christ's passion and death.[49] But each represents its creator's sense of the highest form of love.

Likewise, in both *Tristan* and the *Queste,* the supernatural source of sustenance is linked to the kind of love which the work celebrates. In the *Minnegrotte,* Tristan and Isot live on their love for each other; in the *Queste* the Grail, which symbolizes the gift of God's love, provides food and drink for the grail companions. It resembles not only the magical dish of Welsh legend, but the manna which sustained the Israelites in the desert, Christ's multiplication of the loaves and the fishes, His forty days in the wilderness, and the Last Supper.[50] It also reminds one of Saint Bernard's idea that the Divine Presence pleases the soul's palate in different ways.[51]

Closely related to the idea of the grail as the source of sustenance is the idea that the word nourishes. During Perceval's island sojourn, he is visited by a priest who speaks to him and whose words are so delightful that he has no wish for meat and drink.[52] In Gottfried's Prologue, the words of his story become bread for true lovers. In the *Queste,* the true knights who have served Jesus, who have suffered for His sake, who have attained the spiritual life while still in the flesh, arrive at Corbenyc and receive "the highest reward," the Word which became Flesh, of which they partake in the form of the Eucharist (P. 269, M. 275).

The wound-cure motif, which figures strongly in the *Tristan,* also appears in the *Queste,* although much modified. In Gottfried it is the lover himself, Tristan, who is wounded—in the beginning he is wounded through the thigh, fighting for a just cause. He is cured by his enemy's sister, the Queen of Ireland. Later, he receives a second wound in slaying the dragon, and the Queen again cures him; as before, the wound is a physical one. It is also the Queen—the enemy/benefactor—who brews the magic potion, which results in a deeper wound, one that neither she nor her daughter can heal.[53] Here the physical wounds become associated with the image of the wound and cure of love so well-established in the courtly love tradition, in Provençal and German lyrics. The death of Tristran is caused by a wound which Ysolt is too late to heal and which has come to symbolize their fatal love.

In the *Queste*, there are many instances of wounding and healing, and the cure of the Maimed King is the central episode of the work.[54] Here the wounded, including the Maimed King, are sinners—men who are punished for their presumption: King Bademagus, who is wounded for seizing a shield which was destined for Galahad; Melias, wounded for seizing a crown; King Mordrain, deprived of sight and strength for drawing too near the grail; Lancelot, struck unconscious for twenty-four days because he presumed to cross the threshold where the grail rests; and Perceval, who wounds himself after nearly succumbing to temptation. The Maimed King himself had been wounded for presuming to draw the sword of David, which was destined for Galahad. In the *Queste* sinners are wounded and holy men heal them. Melias is taken to an abbey to be healed by the monks; Perceval reports that since the arrival of the priest, he feels as though he had never been wounded; and finally Galahad, the Christ figure, heals the Maimed King. Perceval's sister, the virgin who cures the leprous lady, is the only female in the *Queste* who has curative powers. However, she most resembles Jesus, who through His wounds made possible the healing which was necessitated by the Fall. There is in the *Queste* a clear attempt to suggest the association, not of wounds and love as in courtly poetry and the *Tristan*, but of wounds and sin; and not of healing with the granting of a lady's favor, but with the gift of God's redemptive love.

Tristan and Galahad, for all their differences, resemble each other in that each represents the ultimate development in virtually the opposite direction. Like most heroes of romance, each has a unique destiny to fulfill; but whereas Tristan's destiny is his tragic love for the woman whom he won for his uncle, Galahad's destiny is an unfolding of his special mission—to redeem Arthur's court with a new kind of love, by being their Messiah. He too dies and his death comes as the fulfillment of this destiny

—union with Him whom he served. In each case it is the hero himself who is all important. The person or persons who share his fate are mirror images of himself. Isot is the image of Tristan; Perceval's sister, Perceval, and Bors are reflections of Galahad. These mirror images reflect the kind of love which the hero represents: Tristan and Isot—the mutual love of man and woman and their achievement of a spiritual union through physical love; Galahad and his companions—fellowship in Christ and the achievement of spiritual love through denial of the physical. The undying love of Galahad and his companions is symbolized by the grail.

Galahad represents the sharpest possible contrast both to Tristan and the courtly lover: he has never shown any interest in any lady; his deeds of prowess, which surpass theirs, are undertaken in the service of the Lord; and his reward, his great joy and bliss, is found not in the arms or in the image of any lady but in the mystical contemplation of the Lord, in whom he finds the true source of all nourishment and all healing. As Saint Paul writes (1 Cor. 2:9, quoting Isa. 64:4), "Eye hath not seen nor ear heard, neither hath it entered into the heart of man, what things God hath prepared for them that love Him."

The *Quest,* a religious allegory built upon the patterns of courtly romance, thus provides an interesting commentary on Gottfried's *Tristan,* a romantic tragedy elevated to religious heights.

Notes

1. A. T. Hatto, trans., *Tristan* of Gottfried von Strassburg (Baltimore, Maryland: Penguin Books, 1960), p. 13. See also, W. T. H. Jackson, *The Anatomy of Love* (New York: Columbia University Press, 1971), pp. 32, 55–57, 62.
2. Joan Ferrante, *The Conflict of Love and Honor: The Medieval Tristan Legend in France, Germany and Italy* (The Hague: Mouton, 1973), p. 20; and Jackson, *Anatomy,* p. 56.
3. Gottfried von Strassburg, *Tristan und Isold,* ed. Friedrich Ranke

(Berlin: Weidmann, 1930), ll. 813 ff.; 961 ff. All quotations of the poem are from this edition. The Hatto translation was used throughout, but in some instances a more literal translation has been provided. Here Gottfried uses the word *minne* for love; in the passage quoted below, he uses both *minne* and *liebe*. As Jackson points out, *Anatomy*, p. 242, "the distinction between the two words is not so precise as some critics have tried to show."

4. In the Thomas version, Gottfried's source. For texts and translations, see nn. 29 and 37.
5. On the early versions of the Tristan story see Gertrude Schoepperle Loomis, *Tristan and Isolt*, 2d ed. (New York: Burt Franklin, 1960); Helaine Newstead and Frederick Whitehead in *Arthurian Literature in the Middle Ages*, ed. Roger S. Loomis (London: Oxford University Press, 1959), pp. 122–33, 134–43.
6. Morton Bloomfield, "Beowulf, Byrhtnoth, and the Judgment of God: Trial by Combat in Anglo-Saxon England," *Speculum* 44 (1969): 545 ff.
7. John S. Anson, "The Hunt of Love: Gottfried von Strassburg's *Tristan* as Tragedy," *Speculum* 45 (1970): 605.
8. W. T. H. Jackson, "The Artist in Gottfried's Poem," *PMLA* 77 (1962): 367.
9. See especially ll. 11711–15, 52–55, 84, 11930–34, 12016–22, 12107–9, and Anson, "The Hunt of Love," pp. 600 ff.
10. Bloomfield, "Beowulf, Byrhtnoth, and the Judgment of God," pp. 549, also 547, 548.
11. Ibid., p. 555.
12. Loomis, *Tristan* II, 392 ff.
13. Ferrante, *The Conflict*, pp. 131–2; Frederick Whitehead, "Tristan and Isolde in the Forest of Morrois," in *Studies in French Language and Medieval Literature* (Manchester University Press, 1939), pp. 393–94.
14. W. T. H. Jackson, *The Literature of the Middle Ages* (New York: Columbia University Press, 1960), p. 149.
15. J. Schwietering, *Der Tristan Gottfrieds von Strassburg und die Bernhardische Mystik*, Abhandlungen der Preussischen Akademie der Wissenschaften, phil.-hist. Klasse, 5 (Berlin, 1943); also *GR* 29 (1954): 5–17.
16. All biblical quotations are from the Vulgate or Douay versions.
17. Saint Bernard, *Sermones in Cantica Canticorum*, Sermo 61.2, 5, PL, 183, col. 1071, 1075; trans. Samuel J. Eales, *Works of Saint Bernard* (London: John Hodges, 1896), vol. 4.
18. Saint Bernard, *Sermones*, Sermo 33.2, 4.
19. Etienne Gilson, *The Mystical Theology of Saint Bernard*, trans. A. H. C. Downes (New York: Sheed and Ward, 1940), pp. 140–41; Saint Bernard, *Sermones*, Sermo 83. 1, 3, 4, 5, 6.
20. Gilson, *Mystical Theology*, pp. 9–12. According to Gilson, Bernard often uses the words *redamare, consensio*, and *benevolentia*, which appear in Cicero's *De amicitia*, 6.14.
21. Saint Bernard, *Sermones*, Sermo 7.2.

22. *De diligendo Deo,* 3.8; ed. and trans. Edmund Gardner (New York: E. P. Dutton and Co., n.d.). Saint Bernard, *Sermones,* Sermo 23.3, 11, 17; cf. 10.9.
23. Jackson, *Literature of Middle Ages,* p. 150, n. 17; *PMLA* 77 (1962): 371; *PMLA* 85 (1970): 1000; Jackson, *Anatomy,* pp. 126–7; F. Ranke, *Die Allegorie der Minnegrotte in Gottfrieds Tristan,* Schriften der Königsberger Gelehrten Gesellschaft, Geisteswissenschaftliche Klasse, ii, no. 2 (1925), 21–39. Gulielmus Durantis, *Rationale Divinorum Officiorum,* 1.15, 16, 17, 23, 3.18; trans. John Mason Neale and Benjamin Webb, *The Symbolism of Churches and Church Ornaments,* 3d ed. (London: Gibbings and Co., 1906).
24. Seals in Cant. 8:6; cedar in Cant. 1:16, 8:9; and ivory in Cant. 5:14, 7:4.
25. Saint Bernard, *Sermones,* Sermo 46.3, 28.
26. In early Celtic literature, objects of crystal often appear in Otherworld journeys; see Stith Thompson, *Motif-Index of Folk Literature,* rev. ed. (Bloomington: Indiana University Press, 1955), F 162.0.1. There are crystal boats, F 157.1; chambers, F 165.3.1.1; bowers, F 165.3.5.1; castles, F 771.1.6; islands, F 731.2; and bridges, F 842.1.1; see also Tom Peete Cross, *Motif-Index of Early Irish Literature* (Bloomington: Indiana University Press, 1952).
27. Apoc. 21:11.
28. Saint Bernard, *Sermones,* Sermo 23.15.
29. Roger S. Loomis, trans., *The Romance of Tristram and Ysolt,* rev. ed. (New York: Columbia University Press, 1951), pp. xxi. ff.
30. See n. 13.
31. It is instructive to recall that in the 9th century Irish *aithed* or elopement of Diarmaid and Grainne, the hero in fleeing the amorous queen placed a stone between them to prevent intimacy and to indicate to his uncle that their relationship was chaste. See Newstead in *Arthurian Literature,* p. 127, and "Isolt of the White Hands and Tristan's Marriage," *RPh* 19.2 (1965): 158.
32. Loomis, *The Romance of Tristram and Ysolt,* pp. xxi ff.
33. Saint Bernard, *Sermones,* Sermo 56.1, 7.
34. *De diligendo,* 8.23, 25; 9.26; 10.27, 28, 29. In his Sermons on the Canticles, Bernard refers to three stages in the progress of the soul in its love for Christ: the kiss upon the Feet, the Hand, and finally the holy kiss upon the Divine Lips; Saint Bernard, *Sermones,* Sermo 3, 4.
35. W. T. H. Jackson, "Gottfried von Strassburg," in *Arthurian Literature,* p. 155.
36. Psalm 83:2–3; quoted by Bernard in *Sermones,* Sermo 33.4. For Abelard's hymn based on Psalm 83, see Helen Waddell, *Mediaeval Latin Lyrics,* 5th ed. (London: Constable, 1948), pp. 162–65.
37. For this section on Thomas, the author is especially indebted to Frederick Whitehead in *Arthurian Literature,* pp. 134–43 and Ferrante *Conflict,* p. 139. The editions used were J. Bédier, *Tristan,* SATF (Paris, 1902), I; and B. H. Wind, *Les Fragments*

du Tristan (Leiden: E. J. Brill, 1950); the translations of Hatto, *Tristan,* pp. 301–53; and Loomis, *Tristram and Ysolt.*

38. Whitehead, in *Arthurian Literature,* p. 143.
39. Saint Bernard, *Sermones,* Sermo 12.1, 10.
40. As Hatto, *Tristan,* points out, Gottfried is the first to use the expression in German; p. 15.
41. Anders Nygren, *Eros and Agape,* trans. Philip S. Watson (London, SPCK, 1953), p. 154.
42. Saint Bernard, *Sermones,* Sermo 1.1, also 1.12 and 3.1.
43. *The Roman Missal* (New York: P. J. Kenedy and Sons, n.d.), pp. 49–51.
44. F. P. Pickering, *Literature and Art in the Middle Ages* (Coral Gables, Florida: University of Miami, 1970), pp. 145–46.
45. Albert Pauphilet, ed., *La Queste del Saint Graal,* SATF (Paris, 1923), p. 61. All quotations are from this edition, cited in text as P. Translation, P. M. Matarasso, *The Quest of the Holy Grail* (Baltimore, Maryland: Penguin Books, 1969), p. 85, cited in text as M.
46. E. Quinn, "The Quest of Seth, Solomon's Ship, and the Grail," *Traditio* 21 (1965): 185–222.
47. Matarasso, *The Quest,* p. 296, n. 56.
48. Ibid., pp. 303–4, n. 85.
49. Quinn, "The Quest of Seth," 199, n. 50.
50. Matarasso, *The Quest,* p. 288, n. 21; p. 290, n. 29; on the Welsh origins see H. Newstead, *Bran the Blessed in Arthurian Romance* (New York: Columbia University Press, 1939).
51. Matarasso, *The Quest,* p. 286, n. 8.
52. For a more detailed treatment of this idea, see W. Boletta, "Earthly and Spiritual Sustenance in *La Queste del Saint Graal,*" RN 10 (1968–69): 384–88.
53. The relationship between potion and poison has been pointed out by Hatto, *Tristan,* p. 7.
54. The origin of the wound-cure motif in the grail stories is the wound in the foot which the Welsh Bran received from a poisoned dart; in Chrétien's *Perceval* the Fisher King's wound is in the thigh. See Newstead, *Bran,* pp. 15, 19, 65.

Esther C. Quinn

Bibliographic Note

In addition to the works cited in the notes, the following studies provide interesting or important discussions of the interrelationship between religion and courtly love:

Erich Auerbach, "Passio als Leidenschaft," *PMLA* 56 (1941): 1179–96; and *Literary Language and Its Public,* trans. Ralph Manheim. Bollingen Series, 74 (New York: Pantheon, 1965), pp. 67–81.

A. J. Denomy, a series of essays appearing in *Medieval Studies:* "An Inquiry into the Origins of Courtly Love" 6 (1944): 175–260; "*Fin' Amors:* the Pure Love of the Troubadours, Its Amorality, and Possible Source" 7 (1945): 139–207; "The *De Amore* of Andreas Capellanus and the Condemnation of 1277" 8 (1946): 107–149; *The Heresy of Courtly Love* (New York: D. X. McMullen Co., 1947); and "Courtly Love and Courtliness," *Speculum* 28 (1953): 44–63.

Denis De Rougemont, *Love in the Western World,* trans. Montgomery Belgion, 2d ed. (Garden City, N.Y.: Doubleday Anchor, 1957).

C. S. Lewis, *The Allegory of Love* (New York: Oxford University Press, 1936).

Charles Muscatine, *Chaucer and the French Tradition* (Berkeley, University of California Press, 1964), especially pp. 14–16, 41.

F. X. Newman, ed., *The Meaning of Courtly Love* (Albany: State University of New York Press, 1968) and review by Charles Muscatine, *Speculum* 46 (1971): 747–50.

CHAPTER VI

The Comic Rejection of Courtly Love

Saul N. Brody

The literature of courtly love springs from the perception of man's dual nature, of his conflicting impulses toward transcendent love and carnal love. The awareness in the courtly poets of this conflict prompted them to consider whether the courtly ideal could be operative in the impure world of sensual men and women. Their poetry, with its acute consciousness of human moral inadequacy, can be read as the record of their struggle to preserve the ideal from destruction. On the other hand, there were some poets who wrote about courtly love without recognizing the tension between man's spiritual and corporeal nature. These writers did not have the redeeming perspective of the more sophisticated poets: their poetry is derivative and naive. It imitates the elegant rules of the earlier poetry, the codified and ritualized behavior, but it is written without an awareness of the serious element of play in the earlier poetry. Consequently, it becomes laughable—and especially laughable in that it celebrates perfect courtliness at a time when the courtly world is crumbling.

We encounter such a poem in a lyric by Burkhart von Hohenfels (fl. 1200–1250), "Min herze hât mînen sin,"[1] a lyric in which the interplay between the fictional playground and the outer world does not exist. The situation reflected in Burkhart's poem is classic: he courts a beautiful woman who does not reward him, and so he poses the question: *Wie wirt mir daz stolze wilt?*

"How shall I make the proud quarry mine?" (l. 11). The poet/hunter faces a practical, tactical problem. The quarry is elusive, and he must find a way to trap it. The technique is to be absolutely loyal, for *Minne* befriends only the loyal man, and it is *Minne* who "wants to bring forth what he desires" and who, at the very least, by means of thoughts, "can draw the image of his pleasure upon his senses" (ll. 45–49). The sense of the lyric seems to be that if the lover is loyal, he can experience *Minne,* and if he can't have the woman in bed, at least he can have her in mind.

The subject is a familiar one, and so is the language used to describe it: the heart pictured as the hunter, the eyes of the woman compared to a lure, the willingness of the lover to serve, his captivity by *Minne,* the strength of the lion, the cunning of the fox—these are conventional images. They are clichés, and the fact that the poem is so carelessly full of them suggests that the poet is engaged in the performance of a ritual, and because he does not understand its meaning, his poetry is both hackneyed and confused. The poet takes the traditions of the courtly love lyric seriously; therefore he uses conventional language. But he has lost the perspective of the earlier poets, and in particular, the awareness of his own position—the redemptive consciousness.

Stylistically, this is reflected both in the clichés and in the poem's horrendous accumulation of mixed metaphors. The first strophe announces the hunt his heart has organized: his thoughts lead the way, and they are followed by his feeling, *sin,* and his spirit, *muot.* The quarry "lies in the covert where the lady dwells"—and he stands ready to serve her, but in order to capture what he seeks, he needs the cunning of a fox. Thus, in the opening strophe, we encounter a hunter who needs to be like an animal to capture his prey, whose servant he hopes to be.

The second strophe informs us that her inner qualities overcome his; but he adds that her beauty, a quality of body, not of mind, has made a fool of him before. And accordingly, in strophe three, he grieves. His heart, which earlier organized the hunt, is now the ocean floor in which grief is anchored while joy sails away. On the other hand, his spirit seals fast the image of the woman; earlier a hunter, it is now like the sun which encloses the sun's splendor. At the end of the strophe, the image shifts again: the griffin's claws could not break apart the bonds between his spirit and her image. In strophe four, the poet considers the lady's eyes, greeting, and beauty, which brings bliss and honor. The joy which before sailed away is now cast forth by the look in her eyes like a lure. Her beauty is now the hunter his heart was in strophe one, and it sets traps for his thoughts (which led the hunt in strophe one). But if his thoughts are captured and educated, they are at the same time like a bird which soars toward *Minne,* and *Minne* captures it; consequently, thought, a captured bird, must pay a toll. Strophe five provides no resolution of these confused images: *Minne* becomes a friendly hunter on a strange track, looking for Loyalty and rewarding the man who has gained it.

The poet's mixing of similes and metaphors does not speak for a clear conception of his subject. He examines what it is like to love a beautiful woman who does not return his love, but the poetry produced is mannered, overly ingenious, unintentionally ludicrous, and finally unrevealing. The poet seems to believe in the seriousness of courtly love, but he does not see that it is at the same time a game, a matter of play. He has no perspective, and so he takes himself seriously. There is no self-mockery, no laughter at his own pretensions—for he does not know that they are pretensions. His own view of the matter is that he is refined: his thoughts have been taught the ways of courtly breeding, he tells us, although we have reason to doubt him.

He tells us that the lady's swift thought, wisdom, and strength of spirit are sufficient to overcome his thoughts, his sense, and his spirit: his mind cannot deal with hers. But in an amazing and unconsciously significant *non sequitur,* we learn that it is not actually her mind which defeats him, but her beauty—which has made a fool of him before (1. 20), and which lays the trap that is set to catch thoughts (11. 34–35). And what thoughts he must have, for they need refinement: they must be taught "the ways of courtly breeding" (11. 36–37). He is, it turns out, a sensual man, and remains one to the end. He insists he wants to serve her, but *Minne* becomes his assistant, devoted to providing him with the "good comfort" unknown to him in his grief. In fact, because he serves only himself, his service is neither real nor legitimate; his interests are in *his* joys, *his* desires, *his* sensual pleasures (11. 44–48). This is the good comfort he deserves as a man of courtly breeding and loyalty. Burkhart's self-absorption is epitomized by his hope to "make the proud quarry mine," a hope which does not square with his assertion of servitude.

Burkhart, it emerges, is a common, everyday man, but—apart from talent—what separates him from the Reinmars of this world is that he does not know that he is. There are various possible explanations for his lack of self-awareness—it might be a matter of personality, or it might be the loss of a courtly audience with which he could enter into a dialogue. However it was, the crux of the matter is that striving for courtliness is absent from the poem: what Burkhart seeks is not *zuht,* "courtliness," which he believes he has attained, but the woman herself.

It is in poets like Burkhart that the old courtly tradition dies, because its perspective dies. There is no magic circle for him, no play area separate from the ordinary world, no special territory in which refined and impossible ideals can find existence. Consequently, the only dilemma that exists is how to satisfy sensual desires, and the only absurdity apparent is refusal by the woman. For the great courtly poets, the dilemma is how to preserve a love which cannot be sustained if satisfied, and the absurdity is for such coarse and common men to seek such a refined love. The true courtly poets, the ones who distinguish the ordinary world from the play world, know what they are and what they might be—if they could live within that playground. But a Burkhart knows no play, no absurd striving, no self-mockery; therefore he deserves to be mocked and parodied. If the courtly tradition dies in writers like Burkhart, it only needs other poets to bury it.

Ulrich von Lichtenstein was one of those poets who participated in the burial of courtly love. In *Frauendienst* (after 1257), written about a writer of poems, about a Burkhart, he gives us an autobiography, but its subject does not have the consciousness of the Ulrich who actually writes it. That is, there are two Ulrichs. One of them is the writer who asked himself, "Suppose an ordinary man who is also a poet tried to actually live the life of a courtly lover. Suppose he were to really serve women and not only write lyrics about it. And suppose he were to keep a record of this attempt to love extraordinarily in an ordinary world. What would that record be like?" The other is the fictional Ulrich, the poet's persona, who tries to be a courtly lover in a world of real time and real space. And he does not in the beginning know enough either about that world or himself to be self-mocking. Like Burkhart, he takes himself seriously, and so we laugh at him.

Ulrich-the-poet does not parody the conscious courtly lover, the man who can distinguish a game from reality. He parodies the lover who is blind to that distinction and who therefore deals with himself and his world as if they were actually courtly. The rules, as he understands them, are aristocratic and refined and civilized. As a small boy, Ulrich-the-lover reads and is told by wise men that the man who serves women loyally will surely have lofty reward.[2] What he is given to understand is that on this earth, there is poetic justice: true lovers are rewarded. Ulrich-the-lover, begins where Burkhart does: he takes the poetry seriously and it is not a game to him. As a child, he rides a hobby horse, presumably in imitation of true knights, and he dedicates himself to the ideal of truly serving women. At the age of twelve, he begins to travel about in order to learn about worthy women, and decides to go to the one who is praised as perfect in virtue by the best in every land, to the one who embodies the courtly society's idea of perfection in a woman. For more than four years, he is her page, and he resolves that she is the one whom he ought to serve. As he dedicates himself to her, he quotes one of Gottfried's lines. In his prologue, Gottfried writes:[3]

dem lebene si min leben ergeben
der werlt wil ich gewerldet werden,
mit ir verderben oder genesen.

[64–66]

Let my life be dedicated to this life,
let me be part of this world,
to be destroyed or saved with it.

Ulrich-the-lover thinks to himself:

wol mich, sol sî daz sîn,
diu werde süeze vrowe mîn,
bî der ich immer mêr muoz wesen,
bî ir verderben oder genesen

[21.5–8]

Happy I, if it should occur
that that sweet lady become mine
with whom I must dwell forever more,
to be destroyed or saved with her.

That he should quote Gottfried suggests that he hopes to have in this world what Gottfried reserves for another world distinct from the ordinary one: *ein ander werlt die meine ich,* "I mean another world" (1. 58), than the one in which men wish only to revel in bliss. Ulrich thinks he sets his goal to become one of the *edele herzen,* but a crucial difference exists between his object and Gottfried's. Gottfried devotes himself to a life and to a world, while Ulrich devotes himself to a woman: the courtly poet consecrates himself not merely to a woman but also to the ideal he locates in her, whereas Ulrich-the-lover, dedicates himself to a particular female with whom he must dwell. What Ulrich seeks is not "courtliness," *zuht,* but the woman herself.

Ulrich-the-lover is thus blind to his own common inner nature. He imagines that by living his life according to courtly forms, by performing a ritual, he can be courtly. In his naiveté, he believes further that women actually exist who embody the ideal he has encountered in poetry. He does not yet know that the realm of courtly ideality is not the world, but the playground—a separate territory.

Ulrich's complete dedication to the woman is a function of his inability to distinguish between ordinary reality and the idealizations of his own making. He tells how a small thing could heighten his joy—such as coming to the place where his lady washes her hands (25. 1–4). His lady may be doing a perfectly banal thing, but he is a witness as if to a holy act. The wash water is sacred to him;[4] he carries it away secretly and drinks it (25. 5–7). Ulrich thus transfigures reality; he makes the woman a saint and the things she touches sacred. In his mind, the common things of this world lose their usual qualities; he loses touch with reality, as his comment on the effect of the drink reveals: his sadness became ill (25. 8). Where we would expect an upset stomach, we find love sickness cured.

In this extravagant fashion, Ulrich continues to serve the lady as her page. When his father finally takes him out of her service, his heart remains behind. He enters the service of a margrave, who gives him instructions on how to deal with women, an activity which greatly depends on appearances and style. The whole scene is reminiscent of Parzival's instruction under Gurnemanz, but the margrave's teaching is entirely superficial. He tells

Ulrich that for a man to win a woman, he must do two things: use sweet words to them and perform true chivalric deeds (33–34).

After a time, Ulrich's father dies, and the margrave gives the boy permission to leave, "because all his virtues seemed to be complete in me" (36. 2–3). Ulrich-the-poet uses the word "seemed," *schein,* advisedly, for Ulrich-the-lover's perfection is truly a matter of appearance.

Ulrich writes that in order to serve his lady he must be a knight, and so—in the style of a squire, *knechtes wis* (39. 1)—he enters tournaments, and after three years is given the name of a knight. *Do wart ich ritter,* he says, without elaboration. As in Gottfried's *Tristan,* the crucial event passes without description, but where Gottfried deemphasizes the ritual in order to establish Tristan's separation from ordinary knighthood, his perfection as an artist, Ulrich-the-poet points to a defect in his lover. The implication is that for Ulrich-the-lover, there is not much difference between acting like a knight and being one, between playing a role and being the thing played; in his mind, style and inner truth are hardly distinguishable.

Not long after his knighting, he sees his lady again, but he has no way of approaching her until he meets his cousin, his *niftel,* his Brangaene, who becomes his messenger. However, the *niftel* has a surer grasp of reality than Ulrich, as becomes clear during their conversation. The girl is dismayed to learn that Ulrich has the presumption to love a noble lady. *Si ist ze hohe dir geborn,* "she is too highly born for you," she says, and warns him that the lady will have nothing to do with him. The *niftel* speaks of class distinctions, of the snobbism which defines the distance between classes—she speaks of fundamental social realities, but Ulrich, whose sense of reality comes from the poets and the margrave, believes that sweet words will gain his reward. Accordingly, he composes a lyric for the lady,[5] which he has the *niftel* communicate for him. Having thus informed the lady of his desire, he is filled with *hoher muot* (68. 1).

The story of the courtship is a story of courtly perseverance, and if it were not acted out in the world of ordinary men and women, it would surely be in the classic courtly tradition—for that is what the lover wants it to be. The pattern of the wooing is painfully familiar: Ulrich pleads with the lady to requite his love, and the lady refuses him; the lover pledges undying loyalty to the lady, and because of his fidelity and his service, she should accede to him—but she doesn't; he perseveres in pleading, she perseveres in refusing. Ulrich knows his role, and he plays it to the hilt. When the *niftel* brings back the lady's answer, she brings back a denial. His service cannot please her because she is more noble than he, and consequently he ought to realize that there is no hope of reward. Her last word is the deepest insult of all, for it is an attack on the very thing he relies so much on: his uncouth mouth, *sin ungefüige stênter munt* (80. 6), which must be a source of pain to a woman. The lady passes judgement on Ulrich's words, but the lover—who has a harelip—takes the remark as a comment on his physical condition. He thinks she cannot love him because of his mouth, and accordingly he resolves to have an operation performed on it. He tells this to the page of the lady Ulrich worships, that is, to a common page in an ordinary court, who is naturally astounded at what he hears. *Got weiz wol, ir sît sinne blôz,* he says, "God knows, you are mad." The page goes to watch the operation performed, and comments that if he had ridden from Ulrich without seeing it in person and told the lady, she would not have believed him. Ulrich, judged by the standards of ordinary people, is a madman. He is an exaggerated imitation of the courtly lover, and as such he emphasizes the *tumpheit* of a person who would actually try to live by courtly standards. What heightens the foolishness of such an ambition is the essential grossness of the man, which is slowly made clear.

By engaging in tourneys, he places his body at the service of the woman. The action is potentially heroic, but details of real life keep undermining romantic possibilities. At the end of one tournament, financial problems rise to the surface: the captives have lost their horses, and in order to regain them, they must borrow from the Jews by giving valuable pledges. The money problem deflates the exalted quality of the contests. In another tournament, Ulrich wounds his finger, and the wound causes him pain, but it is only a finger. Perhaps, in order to make the wound a hero's wound, Ulrich sends a messenger to the lady to tell her that he has lost his finger—when in truth at most he has lost the use of the finger. He also continues to write lyrics to the lady, but she remains untouched. She accuses him of flattery and lying—the very faults the margrave warned him against. And what is the lie? His finger was not really cut off, so that Ulrich must now act to redeem himself, and to prove his constancy he has the finger cut off and sent to the lady. The lady is astounded: no man in his right mind would do such a thing to himself (448).

And she is right. Ulrich is not quite sane, for as with a madman, his reality is the creation of his own mind. The world may be a place where fingers grow dark and crooked, where knights go into debt, but Ulrich can transcend all that. He can be anything he chooses—even Venus; hence, he puts on a Venus disguise and goes through the world arranging tournaments and distributing rewards. *Minne* has lodged itself in his heart, and therefore he is *Minne,* but others may not know this and so he must dress like *Minne* and act like *Minne*—and be *Minne.*

However, he fools no one but himself. His disguise is not successful as he is frequently taken for a man. Nonetheless, there are many who enter into the game he establishes, with the consequence that *Minne* is debased. Those who participate in Ulrich's play know it is only that, and their attitude toward it seems different from Ulrich's. He becomes Venus, the goddess of love, to show that *Minne* can live in a man. The disguise proclaims: "I am a true lover." Ulrich makes himself into the very thing his "sweet words," his poems, assert him to be and becomes not merely a lover but—as a man in whom Love has lodged itself—he becomes Love itself. Nevertheless, those who see Ulrich as Venus are unable to accept such abstractions; they know reality when they see it, and they can distinguish the game from the truth. In this episode, Ulrich-the-poet gives us a model of why courtly love poetry had to fall into decline. The audience for such poetry no longer contained *edele herzen,* "noble hearts," but was now limited to *die valschen* and *die nideren,* "the vulgar" and "the hypocrites" —the enemies. These hypocrites can pretend to be devotees of *Minne,* but they don't believe in her, for they know that beneath the disguise is the body of a man. The uncourtly audience denies the poet his poetry, since it ridicules the game; it allows no place for courtliness, even as a fiction. Accordingly, the allegory which Ulrich-the-lover undertakes has a meaning he would rather not recognize: no matter how a man dresses up his love, no matter how he intellectualizes and refines his activity, the ultimate truth about him which is operative in this world is the unavoidable physical truth: he has the body of a man.

The next disguise assumed by Ulrich makes the same point

even more forcefully. In response to one of the lyrics (XI) in which he asks requital of his lady, she sends Ulrich instructions to come to her disguised as a leper.[6] However, she makes it plain that although she will grant him an audience, she will not grant him her body. The lady knows him for what he is and what he wants. He is a lecher and wants to get into bed with her, and so she has him come wearing a disguise which announces and mocks his lechery, and she denies him the thing he seeks. Leprosy was thought to be a venereal disease in the Middle Ages, and lepers were described as driven by lust.[7] In having Ulrich associate himself with the lepers outside the castle, the lady causes him to assume a role which perfectly mirrors his internal condition. The lepers' physical corruption corresponds to Ulrich's sensuality, and just as the lepers are forced to abase themselves as they beg, so is Ulrich whenever he seeks requital.

Ulrich arrives at the lady's castle, but she does not immediately receive him, and he is forced to endure a rainy and cold night outdoors, where he is bitten by worms, vermin and insects. He deserves better, he thinks—he would like to be an Ereck in the arms of Enite (1169. 6–8). During the next day he is once more refused admission, and with the coming of night he hides in a ditch beneath a balcony. The head steward of the castle pauses on the balcony while making his rounds and urinates directly on Ulrich. Thus, by design as well as by chance, Ulrich's exalted notion of himself is grossly deflated.

Nevertheless, the time for him to be raised to the balcony comes; he is taken up by means of linen cloths and given a change of clothes and brought before the lady, who is surrounded by eight women—too many, in Ulrich's view (1203. 5–8). Needless to say, he would rather be alone with her than in the company of these ladies, for what he wants is best given in private. But Ulrich does not hesitate to publicly say what he wants: to lie with her (1206. 2–4). The lady naturally denies him; in view of God and her honor, she will not commit adultery, though if she wanted to, there would be nothing her husband could do to prevent it (1210. 6–8). Her remark is important, for however much Ulrich may idealize *diu reine, süeze, guot,* "the pure, sweet, good one" (1207. 1), she is very much a woman of this world. However, it takes time for Ulrich to learn that about her; in this scene he still believes her to be like the lady of some poet's lyric. Accordingly, when the *niftel* tells him that if he wants his requital, he ought to kneel before her and ask her grace, he follows the suggestion. He asks for grace, but ever hopeful, he cannot refrain from asking for more; he tells her he wants to get into bed with her (1222. 4–8). In typical fashion, Ulrich cannot accept the realities which constantly confront him, not even the obvious reality that the lady is a woman who will not grant him her body. In spite of the lady's denials, Ulrich is obstinate in his hope that she will reward his service, so much so that the lady finally must hit on a plan to get rid of him. She tells him that she will let him down from the balcony and then raise him up again and fulfill his desire (1265. 6–8). He fears she will not raise him again; she tells him to hold her hand. In this fashion, he is lowered a short distance down the balcony. The lady remarks that God knows she never saw or knew such a dear knight as the one who holds her hand. She tells him that he is welcome, and taking him by the chin, an action with traditional sexual implications,[8] she says, *friunt, nu kusse mich!* "Friend, now kiss me!" Joyously, he lets go her hand—and is dropped to the ground. His first impulse is to drown himself, and he is barely prevented from doing so.

The episode epitomizes Ulrich's relationship with the lady. His hopes are raised, then crushed, and he falls into despair. But out of the conviction that true service must be rewarded, he continues in his devotion. For example, he receives a message that the woman will reward him with her body if he will make a pilgrimage, a journey over the sea; she will tell him when to go. He passes the winter in winter activities—writing poetry and observing women—and when summer comes he engages in the summer activity of tourneying. Thus, Ulrich patterns his life after the dictum of the margrave: in winter he uses sweet words and in summer he performs chivalric deeds. And finally, incredibly, the lady he worships is so moved by his extraordinary devotion that she decides to requite his service (1348. 6–8). The long-awaited moment arrives, and Ulrich describes what happened and how he felt about it:

> diu reine, süeze tugentrîch
> sach in dem lande gerne mich;
> dá von vil hôchgemuot was ich:
> mîn senlîch trûren ende nam.
>
> [1350.4–7]

The pure, sweet, virtuous one
gladly saw me in the realm,
I was exalted from that:
my yearning sorrow came to an end.

In only four lines the lover describes the experience he has been striving for for years. And why? It cannot be that Ulrich-the-lover, who assails us with every detail of the wooing, refrains from detailing the requital out of a sense of propriety, for he has little of that. Rather, the story of his triumph is glossed over simply because it turns out not to be a triumph, for the lady who takes him to bed turns out not to be a lady at all. At the moment she makes herself accessible, she can no longer be idealized; she becomes all too real, too common, and accordingly, the relationship cannot be sustained. Still, the lover tries to keep up appearances. In the lyric which he presents to us immediately after the requital, he reveals that he is not a fully joyous man, for his lady kills his joy (XV. 8–9). Moreover, there are some who shame him by pointing out that he is not as joyous as he once was (10–12). These, the enemies, accuse him of having had no more than any man can get from any woman—the absence of joy confirms that—and their mockery of him challenges his claim to courtliness. His solution is to separate his body from his heart. The first will be satisfied, and he will keep up the appearance of happiness in order to disarm those who would mock him (19–21). His heart, however, will continue to yearn: *daz herze mîn/ kan sehnen niht gesparn* (22–23). It is only through longing and through service that the lover can be courtly. Still, not even Ulrich can avoid the reality of the woman who grants him her body. After only a year goes by, the woman does something that causes him grief (1361. 7–8), and he alludes to her *ungüete,* "her ignobility" (XX. 28). A lyric he sends her (XX) does not succeed in changing her; she persists in her *untât,* "misdeed" (1365. 1); her *lôn,* "reward," and her *habedanc,* "thanks, acknowledgement," are so sick that it does both of them harm (XXI. 27–30). Her misdeed, Ulrich finally says, is that she is guilty of *wandel,* "inconstancy" (1368, 4)—she has fallen from her former perfection. Nevertheless, we feel sure that she is the same as she ever was; it is only the lover's perception of her which has changed.

Ulrich-the-poet thus assumes a cynical view of Ulrich-the-lover. The lover is a sensual man, different from other men only in his pretension to refinement and in his blindness to the fact that women are not creatures to be exalted. The purity, beauty and goodness he locates in a woman are qualities he creates in her, and this is brought home to him when he gets into bed with her. Before the sexual act, he could keep her reality from infringing upon his notion of her perfection, but after the consummation—when her commonness can no longer be denied—he must surrender the ideal notion of her. He discovers that her sensuality matches his; she becomes a mirror in which he sees his own grossness, and therefore, since his pretension to refinement is offended, he must reject her. At the same time, he must regain his courtly identity, and to do so he must once again love a woman. This time, though, the woman will be different: it will be possible for her to reward her lover and still embody the ideal of perfection. Ulrich accomplishes this by creating a fantasy almost pornographic in nature. In this fantasy, the lady he loves can be perfectly sensual, but her sensuality is no longer a threat because it is isolated from the ethical context. Formerly, when Ulrich loved, he chose not to deny the carnality of his woman; now, he exalts her carnality, denying it in yet another way by fantasizing its perfection. In this way, he escapes the despair which reality engenders, and preserves his courtliness.

Ulrich-the-lover is nothing if not in love; and he knows it, because to not serve a woman is to be uncourtly (1388. 2–3). He decides that he must find someone to love, and he sets his mind on someone he knows. Once more, Ulrich creates the woman in his mind and seeks her out in his thoughts (1390. 7–8).

> Ich gedâhte dort, ich gedâhte hie,
> ich gedâht an dise, ich gedâht an die:
> swaz mir dô frowen was bekant,
> an der decheiner ich niht vant
> tugende mêre dann an ir.
> ir sült für wâr gelauben mir:
> si was gar alles wandels frî,
> ir was guot wîplîch güete bî.
>
> [1392]

> I thought there, I thought here,
> I thought about these ladies, I thought about this one:
> wherever women were then known to me,
> I could not find in one
> more virtues than in her.

> You should in truth believe me:
> she was completely free from inconstancy,
> and she was noble womanly goodness.

The repetition of the verb *denken,* "to think," emphasizes how much the idealization of the lady is independent of her reality. It is not that the woman is not in fact this exemplar of perfection; it is just that she need not be in reality what Ulrich wills her to be. Ulrich needs a woman who will not disappoint him as the first one did; he needs a woman "completely free from inconstancy." In short, he needs not a woman, but the image of perfect womanhood, and accordingly he takes not a woman, but the image of perfection into his heart, for it is only in his heart that her ideality can be preserved. By this device, he succeeds in having both the woman and the idealization: the woman can give him her body, and he can take it without tarnishing her image.

Of course, this avoidance of the contradiction between the idea of the woman and the woman herself is workable only so long as the dissociation between the idea and the reality remains clear. Ulrich's idea of courtliness can retain its validity only insofar as the courtly ideal can be separated from practical realities. However, Ulrich is not a lover who can easily maintain such a separation, for his courtly identity depends upon public acknowledgement not simply of his courtliness,[9] but of the idea of courtliness. Thus, the man who once determined to ride out as Venus, the embodiment of what his poetry proclaimed him to be, now determines to ride out in the guise of *künic Artûs,* "King Arthur," in the guise of knighthood personified. He enacts another allegory, a kind of play in which he becomes at one with the idealized image. He challenges knights to serve their ladies by fighting him, and those who prove themselves by breaking three spears with him are given a place at the Round Table. Erchengêr of Landesêr becomes Ywân (1436–1437), Alber of Arnsteine is made Segremors (1439–1445), Nycolâ von Lebenberc takes the place of Tristram (1454), but everyone, including Ulrich, knows that the pretense is laughable. He promises to bestow castles, people and lands on the Prince of Austria; and he remarks that in so doing he will not diminish his wealth (1459–1460). The speech caused laughter, he observes, *Der rede wart vil gelachet dâ* (1461. 1). When men encounter him, they know him to be Ulrich-the-lover playing at being King Arthur. Hence, when Schenk Heinrich von Habechspach greets him, he says: *got willekomen, künec Artûs!* "Welcome, King Arthur!" and he recalls that at their last meeting Ulrich sang a new lyric about how his heart leaped in his breast. "Everyone laughs," *der rede man lachen dô began* (1468–1469).

Ulrich's open acknowledgement that he is playing a game sets the Arthur episode apart from the earlier Venus episode, when, dressed as Venus, he believed he would not be openly recognized (463). In this last section of the book, there is a heightened consciousness of reality on the lover's part, and its reality operates as a constant reminder that the courtly ideal is only an illusion. The reality intrudes in the form of men such as Râpot von Valkenberc, a knight in the retinue of Prince Friderîch, but a knight of whom good is seldom spoken: "He was an evil, angry man . . . much involved with plunder" (1491. 5–7). Reality intrudes again when Friderîch himself tells King Arthur not to go to Bêheim; the king there is his enemy, he says, and if he captures any of Arthur's men, Friderîch will have to get up the money to ransom them, and he doesn't want to have to (1605–1608).

At a later point in the book, Ulrich receives notice that Friderîch was overrun in a battle and killed—hardly a romantic death, and certainly not a heroic one, for during the fighting he lay unnoticed and dying. After the carnage, his body—with wounds in the cheeks and with a leg "blackened by a horse's tread"—was discovered by a scribe (1670). Friderîch's fatal wounds stand in stark contrast to the bruises suffered by Arthur's men during their jousting, bruises which do not prevent them from jousting again (1562. 6–8; 1563. 1–3). It is, after all, only jousting, only a game and not the real thing, not a battle in which a prince is unheroically killed. The result of Friderîch's death is as uncourtly as the death itself, for men rob the lands night and day, and the noble rich oppress the poor (1678–1679). The lover observes pathetically that such behavior will deprive them of grace before God and women (1679. 4–5), as if that were a consideration relevant to their concerns. The lover can find no other way of giving a context to the actions of the plundering noblemen than by applying the standards of courtly love and Christian salvation. By judging the plunderers according to those ethical codes, he protects his own increasingly vulnerable ethical sense, his courtliness. For the lover, Christian salvation and courtly love are both forms of protective withdrawal from the world's crudity; naturally, in this world, he will be a man, but a man unlike others: he will be a perfectly courtly man, one who has the good fortune to receive joy from a pure, good woman (1686–1688). When he thinks about her, he is happy, for then the uncourtliness of the world is forgotten.

However, the uncourtly world cannot be eliminated; its gross realities force themselves on Ulrich persistently. After he writes a lyric (XLVI) to be sung only by one who is happy, he is taken prisoner by his own *erepman,* his own servant, and imprisoned in his own tower with his son, while his wife is driven away with the rest of the children. When Ulrich's friends come to rescue him, his captors threaten to hang him unless he sends them away. Thus, there seems to be no escape for Ulrich, and his days are spent in chains. While imprisoned, he writes a lyric in which he calls for the help of women, without whom his exalted spirit, his *hochgemüete,* will perish. The narrative goes on to suggest that he would have perished had not Graf Meinhart von Görz rescued him after more than a year of imprisonment. He decides not to spend any detail on how his two sons and daughters—given as pledges—were rescued; he would rather speak about women. It is hard to imagine a more concerted denial of this world than the lover's. His moral world is crumbling about him. Friderîch is dead, his life and the lives of his family have been threatened, yet he would rather speak about women. He says that nothing makes him as happy as thinking about his lady, particularly when he is alone in bed. He writes a lyric (XLVIII) which celebrates his lady's beauty and virtue and her smile but points out that the lyric was sung during the time of the plundering in Steir and Austria (1738. 1–3). Indeed, it becomes clear that what goes on in the world, its insistent uncourtliness, is a constant challenge to the lover. His poetry takes up moral considerations—he writes of the necessity for women to avoid unseemly men (1739 ff.), and an accompanying lyric (XLIX) takes up the same theme. The comedy all but vanishes from the book at this point: Ulrich is a man disillusioned with the world; for him to be courtly in this world is virtually impossible, but, in spite of it, he will be courtly:

swaz si tâten, ich was vrô, "Whatever the evil ones did, I was happy" (1752. 1).

It is clearly a happiness of his own making; it does not even depend upon the presence of the woman. For instance, the lover writes a lyric (LVII) which begins with the assertion that he does not grieve because his spirit is high through wishing, which gives him pleasurable joy. He lay alone and wished that his lady were beside him—and a miracle happened: he saw her with his heart's eyes. What follows is the record of a sexual fantasy. He imagines her to be close to him, and his body thinks of joys with her. *Minne* unites them, he says, *minne flihtet arme und bein,* "Love intertwined arms and legs" (LVII. 22). The poetry seems to be recounting an actual, that is, a physical, sexual experience, but in fact it is all imagined. This lyric is one of the last in Ulrich's book.

Frauendienst comes to its conclusion in a moral fashion. Ulrich warns women against deceivers, he lists the important things which please a man—pure women, food and wine, fine horses and clothing, knightly accoutrements—and he lists the four things for which men strive: the grace of God, earthly honor, comfort, ("*gemach*"), and possessions. He admits that he foolishly strove for all four objectives and that he cannot renounce three of them in order to gain one. He wagers his soul in the service of a woman, and hopes that God will take his loyalty to her into account (1824–1840).

The passage is strangely moving, as confessions can be, and pathetic as well, for it is the document of a bourgeois courtly lover who finds his fulfillment in fantasies, apart from real women and the real world. Ordinary reality has no place for true courtliness because it depends not only on pure women, but also on food and wine and possessions. Indeed, to the trinity of divine grace, worldly honor, and possessions enunciated by Walther, the lover adds *gemach,* "comfort."[10] He is no courtly exemplar, nor could he be. There is no possibility of courtly perfection in his world because there is no true aristocracy; there are instead rich and powerful men who use and abuse power; courtly ideality as defined by the poets is none of their concern. Thus, Ulrich-the-lover is driven to his fantasies by the coarse realities of women, the world, and himself. His courtly fulfillment cannot be obtained anywhere but in his imagination.

Ulrich's blending of the comic and pathetic in *Frauendienst* sets his work apart from most parodies of courtly love poetry. The mixture of styles gives his poem an uncommon seriousness, for as Ulrich laughs at pretensions to courtliness in an uncourtly setting, he at the same time laments the sordid realities which confront him. In contrast, most of the writers of courtly love parodies find no sadness in the condition of the world, but simply a comic affirmation of its unexalted nature. The *fabliau,* the ribald story, is perhaps the best-known instance of this kind of response to the courtly ideal.

The tale *De Guillaume au Faucon,* "William and the Falcon," provides a convenient illustration of the genre.[11] Guillaume is a handsome and debonair squire who has been in the service of a castellan for seven years, and in all this time he has not been made a knight, nor does he wish to become one. The reason for this unusual lack of ambition is that he has fallen in love with the castellan's wife and does not want to be separated from her. The squire thus plays the role of the classic courtly lover: he loves another man's wife and loves her profoundly. True to the form, he is separated from his lady, and he can have no hope of closing the distance between them—she knows nothing of his extraordinary passion for her, and even if she did, she would not pay him any heed. This disdain for him would also be very much in the tradition: the lady is conventionally above her lover in rank and moral perfection. However, the *fabliau* departs from the convention at this point: not only is the castellan's wife not the embodiment of some courtly ideal, she is indistinguishable from women generally. She is simply one of that class of women who delight in tormenting true lovers: when they know a man is overcome by love, rather than speak to him they play with a broken-down vagabond (11. 30–38). Accordingly, this lady is not chaste perfection. On the other hand, she is—in the best courtly tradition—exceedingly beautiful. The poet must restrain himself in describing her; he must speak of her, he says, *par soutill guise,* "in a delicate manner" (1.66). He begins decorously enough as he describes first her clothing and then her hair and face. In her robes she is more charming, elegant, gracious than a falcon, sparrow hawk, or parrot. Everything about her is conventionally perfect: her hair is gold, her forehead, shinning and smooth, eyebrows, brown, eyes, wide-spaced, nose, fine and straight, cheeks, rose-colored, mouth, like a flower, and throat and bosom, clear and bright. When the poet turns his attention to her breasts, the culmination of the description is reached:

Et desus le piz de devant
Li poignoient .II. mameletes
Auteles comme .II. pommettes.
[108–110]

and on her chest
were hung two little breasts
like little apples.

They are, presumably, good for nibbling. The lady, then, though not marked by moral perfection, has an extraordinary body, and the poet emphasizes this by ending his description of her with a cliché: "Nature in making this lady had brought all her powers to work . . . so that for a long time afterward she was left impoverished" (11. 115–118). The poet's description of the castellan's wife accordingly juxtaposes courtly commonplaces—which imply the conventional awe which such beauty produces—and the clearly sensual response which implies little of humble reverence. The simultaneous awe and sexual desire are also what characterize the squire's feeling for the lady; the God of Love, we are told, makes his life a martyrdom (11. 52–53).

In his suffering, Guillaume realizes that he cannot go on without hope of requital. He concludes that it is madness not to tell her of his love, for in his present state he might as well love *Totes les femes d'outre mer,* "all the ladies beyond the seas" (1. 152). Guillaume, who has been able to love at a distance for seven years, now finds that he can no longer live as a martyr; if he were to be satisfied with unending separation from his lady, he might as well be separated from all those ladies the lyric poets love in exile. The two aspects of his feeling for her, the awe and desire, are in conflict, but desire gains the upper hand and he goes to her chamber, where he finds her alone. She seems glad to see him, and they talk idly until he asks her advice about a problem. Is a man wise or foolish to conceal his love from a lady for seven years? The lady gives a very practical answer, or at any rate an answer which does not imply much sympathy with the ideas of loving from a distance and being content with unrequited love: if a man gets the chance, he ought to tell the woman he loves her:

if she refuses him, he would be foolish to suffer for her (ll. 231–237). Her judgement prompts Guillaume to announce that he loves her. His declaration is very nearly a catalogue of courtly-love commonplaces. He yields himself to her; asks that she cure his wound; tells her that he was, is, and will be hers; complains of his suffering; and asks that she grant him the gift of her love. She listens closely, but holds his declaration in contempt (ll. 276–279), and grows angry and insulted. She will not play Guillaume's game. "I understand nothing of what love means nor of what you ask of me," she tells him (ll. 290–291). She promises to reveal Guillaume's stupid, mad passion to her husband, and sends Guillaume on his way. As he leaves, he promises to go on a hunger strike (ll. 325–328). It will be a long fast, she replies, and he goes to his chamber and takes to bed. He does fast and suffer, and he has erotic visions of embracing his lady in bed, but eventually the visions fade. *Fols est qui chace la folie,* "He is mad who pursues madness" remarks the narrator (l. 364).

We come to understand Guillaume from three points of view. First, there is his own, that of a true and faithful courtly lover—a man who will die of his love, if need be. The lady's view is that Guillaume is a fool who both loves without hope and is disloyal to his master; he may die, but it will either be of starvation or at the hands of the castellan. The narrator seems willing to judge Guillaume mad, but that decision hinges on the outcome of Guillaume's pursuit of the lady.

When the castellan, who has been away from his court, returns home, he inquires after Guillaume, and his wife tells him that the squire suffers from an incurable malady. They go to Guillaume's room, and the lady tells Guillaume to give over his illness or else it will be too late. The squire throws himself on her mercy, but she nevertheless threatens to tell her husband what the truth is. She gives Guillaume one last chance to eat, but he refuses, saying that he will not have food unless the pain in his heart is first assuaged (ll. 558–559). And suddenly the woman takes pity on him. She explains that Guillaume has been fasting because he wants one of his castellan's falcons; the castellan gives the falcon to the squire, and the lady—who has fallen in love—indicates that she is willing to accept him as her lover.

Guillaume having thus achieved his goal, the narrator is ready to draw the moral that in order to win a lady, her lover must persist until she accepts him. The lesson is thus one of tactics, and Guillaume emerges as a model of the successful lover. He plays a dangerous game, but wins it, and that is what matters.

The delight this kind of story provides grows, in part, out of the humorous opposition between what Guillaume imagines himself to be and what he actually is. Guillaume believes that a refined and aristocratic style will win him his lady; the lady reminds us that however courtly the role Guillaume chooses to play his only goal is to commit adultery by taking his castellan's wife to bed. Another part of our delight, of course, follows from the outrageous and unlikely success which Guillaume has. The tale thus holds up for admiration neither the courtly ideal nor conventional morality; it has no illusions either about love providing moral exaltation, or moral standards operating in a world whose goal in not salvation but sex.

Parodies of courtly love typically create situations in which lovers use the language and style of courtly love, but the lovers reveal themselves not to be so much courtly as commonplace. In *fabliaux,* the would-be courtly lover is often a *vilain* with courtly pretensions,[12] though as *De Guillaume au Faucon* illustrates, he can also be an aristocrat. What both approaches suggest is that courtliness is little more than a style, a tactic. The view of aristocratic refinement which the parodies take is blatantly cynical. Hence, the parodies adapt the settings made familiar in the literature of courtly love and populate them with sensual lovers who cloak their lust in courtly refinement. The lovers in the Provençal *Roman de Flamenca* are just such a couple. They play the involved and familiar game in which the lady is married to a jealous and cruel husband who keeps a close watch over her. The lover is thus forced to adore at a distance, and his courtship of the lady is fraught with danger and difficulty. Still, he finds a way to ask for requital, and she grants him her love. We are in well-known territory when we enter *Flamenca:* the lady is exceedingly beautiful, the husband exceedingly cruel, the lover exceedingly in love. These are conventions of courtly love, and *Flamenca* abuses them in the fashion of a *fabliau.*[13]

The setting of *Flamenca* is preeminently aristocratic, a point emphasized by frequent descriptions of the elaborate settings, ceremonies, and costumes of the nobility. Nonetheless, the elegance and style of the courtly setting barely disguise its crude sexuality. When Archimbaut arrives for his wedding three days early, he sees Flamenca for the first time and immediately falls in love with her. He so burns with desire that he does not sleep for the three nights preceding the ceremony, and during the wedding his impatience can hardly be contained; the ceremony is too long for him, as is the feasting which follows. His burning desire focuses only on the sexual consummation.

The opposition between refined manners and unrefined lust is suggested again and again in the poem. Archimbaut's court at Bourbon is even more elaborate than his father-in-law's, and seemingly perfect in style and refinement, but it is uncomfortably aware of how sexual intrigues are a basic part of its activities. When the Queen sees that her husband has a lady's sleeve tied to the end of his lance, she is immediately jealous, and makes it known to Archimbaut that she suspects an affair between the king and Flamenca. Archimbaut becomes inflamed by jealousy, and when he sees the king and his wife together, he believes his worst suspicions to be confirmed. The king is courtly and elegant, and so is his retinue, but as they leave the services, the king shatters any illlusion of true refinement; leading Flamenca out, he puts his hand on her breast, as if with intimate familiarity (11. 937–940). Archimbaut is consequently driven to anguish by his suspicion of his wife. He imagines Flamenca to be unfaithful, and suspects every man of evil intentions toward her. Convinced that she will take every opportunity to cuckold him, he decides to guard her from the enemy, from some "vagrant who might sham courtly love" (11. 1197–1199).

But, of course, there can be no safety from such a one, and the vagrant arrives on the scene soon enough. His name is Guillem de Nivers, and he comes from Paris. The poet describes him lavishly and glowingly. He is a knight made perfect by Nature (11. 1564–1567), a veritable paragon of beauty. But it is comic beauty, for Guillem, a man seven feet tall and with slim hips, is an awkward combination of masculine and feminine features, a synthesis of the epic hero and the courtly heroine. What is more, Guillem—this marvel of a man—has had no experience in love (11. 1762–1763). What he knows about love he has learned from reading authors who describe the way lovers act. Book knowledge is not enough, however, and he decides that he must experience love personally by falling in love. His resolution is very reminiscent of Ulrich-the-lover's. Both men conclude it would be appropriate for them to be in love, and both then select women to love by determining who is thought to be the best woman around. Guillem is told Flamenca is the best, the most beautiful, and the most courtly, and it is on the basis of her reputation that *en cor li venc que l'amaria,* "he resolved in his heart to love her" (1781). Guillem's being in love is thus an act of will—since he ought to be a lover, he will be a lover. What is needed is for him to find someone to love, and so he does.

It is natural that a man who derives his view of love from books should seek to behave the way lovers in them do. In modeling himself after those lovers, Guillem becomes an actor, a man who plays a role. In fact, Guillem is adept at playing roles. To make his presence in Bourbon seem legitimate, he plays at being sick when he arrives at the baths, and in order to approach Flamenca—who only appears in public when she attends church, and then is veiled and guarded closely—he plays at being a canon. Like a good actor, he must present the right appearance; he has the priest cut his hair into a tonsure, and has him provide a gown. Guillem knows the priestly office, yet he rehearses the lines (3769–3771), and we are reminded that he is a serious performer of a role. But of all the parts Guillem plays, the part of a courtly lover is the one he plays most intensely. He decides to be in love with a woman he does not know and who does not know him—and the very thought of a sexual consummation causes him to nearly swoon. His squire puts him to bed, and the poet remarks that no man was ever so quickly overcome by love as Guillem (11. 2144–2145). It is a case of love before first sight.

As he lies in bed, Guillem dreams erotic dreams and enjoys *plazer esperital,* "spiritual pleasure" (1. 2164)—though as the narrator comments, that sort of pleasure is only a shadow of the real thing. Given his separation from Flamenca, however, it is the best Guillem can do, and he does it elaborately. Guillem's dreams serve to grant him in fantasy what he does not have in fact, and the fantasies, though of erotic and not spiritual fulfillment, are always exalted by courtliness. When Guillem begs mercy of Flamenca in his dream (11. 2802–2961), he does what courtly lovers regularly do: he affects humility, declares that merely to be in her presence would be enough, and asserts that if she denies him he will surrender his life. She responds in terms equally refined, telling him that she is moved to pity by his prayer, that she will fulfill his desire because he is brave, strong, courtly, and noble. Guillem has read books and learned the language of courtly love, a language remote from the objective nature of his experience. At one point, Guillem considers that if Flamenca could see him in all his distress she would extend him grace, though of course she might not, for women can be merciless, *so dison cil c'o an proat,* "so say those who have experienced that" (2753). All he knows about love he knows through books and hearsay, but he has learned enough to play at being courtly, much as he has learned to play at being a canon.

Guillem involves himself in a game whose main characteristic is to transfigure reality by causing it to abide by rules. Guillem acts like a courtly lover, and since the books suggest that courtly lovers worship their women, Guillem worships his, in a church. The first time he sees her there, she is only gradually revealed to him. He catches a glimpse of her from a distance; then he sees the part in her hair as the priest sprinkles her with holy water; when she crosses herself, he sees her hand and he becomes virtually transfixed by the sight; next he brings her the Peace, and when she kisses the breviary he carries, he sees her mouth. At that moment *fin'Amors* tells him that he has arrived at a very good port (ll. 2565–2568). Guillem has still barely seen the woman, but he knows that he ought to be overwhelmed by her, and so he is. Guillem is a player, and he plays so seriously that he does not know how to distinguish between the game and cold reality.

What makes it particularly easy for him to assume the role of courtly lover is Flamenca herself, who quickly becomes an eager participant in his game. She also knows how to play a role. Like Guillem she can feign being sick in order to make use of the baths; she is able, by her acting, to convince her husband that she will die unless she can have the healing waters. When she is unsure whether Guillem was able to hear her whispered words in church, she plays the whole scene over again with her maids. Alis takes the role of Guillem, and offers the Peace—the prop for the breviary is, appropriately, a courtly romance about Blancaflor—while Flamenca repeats the words to her. Flamenca and her maids may giggle as they perform the little routine, but they play the scene easily. They also have experience with books, and have learned the language of courtly love.

Given the literary orientation of Guillem, Flamenca, and the maids, it seems natural that the courtship presents an essentially literary problem to them. Once Guillem decides that his chance to proposition Flamenca can only come in church as he offers her the Peace, what remains is for him to find the right words, a problem complicated by the fact that he can speak only a word or two at a time when there. Accordingly, each remark that he utters is carefully thought out in advance, and each is subjected to careful interpretation by Flamenca and her maids, who compose their responses with great deliberation. Perhaps in order to emphasize the literary nature of the exchange, the *Flamenca* poet takes the opening of it directly from a lyric by Peire Rogier,[14] but his description of the thought which goes into each utterance of the interpretations which follow alone establishes the point.

Guillem and Flamenca are thus a perfectly matched couple: both are accomplished actors, both are dedicated to the play of courtly love, and both are familiar with the rules that govern such play. Their game is, as games should be, highly ritualistic, a characteristic emphasized by the fact that the courtship is enacted in church on Sundays and holidays. Of central importance to the ritual is the language which is used—for it is largely by language that the lovers make their essentially banal affair seem sublime. Guillem is a man intent on one thing—having intercourse with Flamenca—but he says that he dies (l. 4505) of love (l. 4880) for Flamenca (l. 4970), and must be cured (l. 5098). Hearing such declarations, the ladies decide that he is *sener de cortesia,* "lord of courtliness" (l. 5012), and when Flamenca finally is alone with Guillem, she tells him that he has long had her heart, in *fin' amor* (ll. 5866–5869).

If saying that something is so could make it so, then the affair of Guillem and Flamenca could be a matter of *fin'amor.* However, the affair never attains such heights, and the distance between the lovers' view of it and ours is what makes that apparent and comic. Repeatedly the poet reminds us that they are a merely sensual couple in an unrefined world, that is, in the ordinary world inhabited by ordinary people. The poem is set in a real place, and many of the characters in the work have names which suggest that they might be identified with historical figures. Customs are pictured in minute detail, foods are listed, songs are named, clothing is described. Even the baths are set forth in detail—the way the hot water is mixed with cold, the unpleasant odor of the waters. Lovers may say they seek spiritual exaltation, but they are merely carnal, as their erotic fantasies and sexual activities so graphically confirm. Flamenca may compliment Guillem for his *fin' amor,* but in the next breath she gets to the point and offers him her body (5870–5871), which he happily takes. And for all of Guillem's timidity, once the preliminaries are out of the way he shows no awe of the woman; he even asks her to arrange for her maids to take his two cousins as lovers. She gladly accedes, as do the maids (11. 6453–6492), who immediately take the squires to chambers in the baths *per deportar,* "for amusement" (1. 6473).

Flamenca, through its central characters and through its careful depiction of their society, mocks elaborate pretensions to refinement. The truth about the world of *Flamenca* is discovered openly in what its inhabitants do, not in what they wear or say, for the clothing and the food and the speech generally conceal an inner crudity. It is a world aristocratic only in style, and the comedy of the poem functions to expose its dissembling.

Like Ulrich and the writer of *De Guillaume au Faucon* and the *Flamenca* poet, Geoffrey Chaucer is also amused by the pseudocourtly sensual man—the man so unaware of the banality of his desires that he can believe himself to be a second Tristan. In his lyric, "To Rosemounde,"[15] the speaker says what Ulrich-the-lover might, or Guillaume, or Guillem:

> Nas never pyk walwed in galauntyne
> As I in love am walwed and ywounde,
> For which ful ofte I of myself devyne
> That I am trewe Tristam the secounde.
>
> [17–20]

The speaker holds himself to be an expert at courtly behavior. He knows all the ritual, including the ritual of how to suffer and how to tell a woman that he suffers. His head is full of clichés. The sight of his lady dancing, her cheeks like rubies, is an ointment to his wound, even though she affords him no *daliaunce.* And therefore he weeps a cask full of tears, and he goes courteously, bound in love, burning in *amorous plesaunce,* "amorous happiness," and promising to be her thrall forever. He signs the poem *Tregentil. Chaucer.*, "Very noble. Chaucer."

The man parodied here is one who has learned the forms of courtly behavior but not the essence of courtly awareness. He knows the ritual, but its meaning is lost to him. He does not seek to heighten his nobility, for he is already noble, nor does he seek to deserve the woman but he looks for *daliaunce,* a sexual toying. He is a superficial lover: his woe does not perturb his heart, *Yet may that wo myn herte nat confounde* (10), and the effect of the wound of love is no more serious than to cause him to *brenne ay in an amorous plesaunce* (22). We recognize the voice which speaks in "To Rosemounde" as self-satisfied, and we are amused by the complacency. Whether the voice is actually that of a sophisticated lover who knows that he is playing a role in order to charm his lady, or whether it belongs to a man who is unaware of how foolish he sounds, the poet is surely parodying the courtly lover, in whom he regularly discovers enormous comic possibilities. A courtly lover pursues a sublime goal, and though he could be presented as facing a tragic dilemma, as he is in *Troilus and Criseyde,* Chaucer nearly always characterizes him as comic or ludicrous, for the poet was hard put to take courtly love altogether seriously. The idea of it regularly inspired him to laugh, and his laughter, which was and is infectious, helped place the courtly ideal in perspective.

The *Parlement of Foules* gives some insight into the philosophical basis for Chaucer's comic rejection of courtly love. The *Parlement* turns over the problem of how a man ought to love. Macrobius offers Chaucer an ascetic view of this *lytel erthe,* a world whose delights should be scorned in order that salvation be obtained (PF. 64–66). Macrobius's counsel is otherworldly; it seems to deny the validity of love which draws a man to this world. In the dream he has following his reading of Macrobius, the narrator comes to consider two varieties of worldly love. The dreamer finds himself in a beautiful garden, and in the garden he moves into two areas, Venus's temple and Nature's parliament. In the Temple of Venus, he encounters the shameful Venus, the goddess who is wanton, erotic, and lascivious.[16] She is worshipped by the *likerous folk* Chaucer reads about in Macrobius (74–84), those who recognize none of God's claims on them and practice love with but one goal in mind: sexual satisfaction.

Their love is concupiscent and profane, and in direct opposition to the kind of love which Macrobius counsels.

But there is an alternative to the loves associated with Macrobius and the shameful Venus, and the dreamer encounters this third possibility—what Jean de Meun calls "natural love"—when he comes to Nature's parliament. It is St. Valentine's day, and the birds have gathered to choose their mates. The occasion is thus fully sexual and worldly, but it is legitimate, for it operates under the guidance of God's deputy, Nature. To be sure, the entire setting reflects God's plan, both in its plenitude and its hierarchical organization, and the birds have assembled to fulfill their obligation to replenish life on earth.[17] In keeping with divine principles, Nature stipulates that the selection of mates proceed according to rank and with the understanding that no bird can be compelled to accept a mate. All that is needed to insure that God's program be carried out is that the participants accept the rules and go about their business.

The participants, however, are birds in form only; in all else they are human, and the natural consequence of their humanity is that they have difficulty in following Nature's direction. Since she proceeds according to hierarchy, Nature starts with the aristocrats—the courtly birds who love according to courtly ideals—and in their pursuit of those ideals the *gentil* birds threaten to overturn Nature's plan.

It is clear that the aristocratic tercels are involved in playing the game of courtly love. They woo a perfect, conventionally modest, distant female by asserting their devotion, humility, and readiness to die for her. These birds live their lives according to special rules—according to an ideal which is not identifiable with Macrobius's asceticism, Venus's lasciviousness, or Nature's program for the replenishment of the species.

Their love, in all its nobility and refinement, is extraordinary, and to all the ordinary birds who hear them declare it at such length, it is beyond understanding. How can the tercels sacrifice themselves for the sake of a mere female? If she won't accept one of them as her lover, let him find someone else; she is, after all, not the only bird on the wing. The common birds are impatient and want to go about their mating, but the cuckoo cynically gives voice to their need: he doesn't care how long the tercels debate—let them live singly all their lives!—as long as he can have his mate

(603–607). Of the commoners, only the turtledove, speaking for the seedfowl, shows a refined outlook, for only turtledove endorses absolute fidelity to a woman (577–588). Refined sentiments are not the exclusive property of the nobility, but neither are they generally found among the lower classes.

The relationship of the tercels to the audience before whom they plead their cases is thus a paradigm of the courtly lover in his relationship with those who hear him announce his love. There are some who have gentle hearts and others who don't. The gentle hearts can understand how it is possible to love at a distance, to beg for mercy, to serve without hope of reward, to seek reward on the basis of aristocratic refinement, whereas ordinary hearts simply don't understand. For them, one female is as good as another, and in any case the point is not to serve her but to *swyve* her. The approach to love taken by most of the lower-class birds may be direct and unrefined and even unprincipled—the duck and the goose and the cuckoo seem to serve themselves principally and Nature unwittingly—but it is assuredly productive and real, and that is its essential justification. Alongside duck love, the vulnerability of courtly love is exposed. As practiced by the tercels and the formel, it involves neither withdrawal from the world nor participation in it, whether for worship of Venus or God. It avoids the three realities defined by Macrobius, Venus, and Nature; neither ascetic, nor lascivious, nor productive, it insists upon its own unreality, and thereby opens itself to ridicule.

Palamon and Arcite in the Knight's Tale, first cousins to the *Parlement*'s three tercels, are faced with the tercels' dilemma. Like the eagles, the two young knights are aristocrats who compete for the hand of the same aloof female. Like the birds, each believes he is most deserving of the girl, and to decide who shall have her, they are willing to engage in judicial battle. And, where the eagles are able to love from a distance and without hope of reward, so too are Palamon and Arcite; whether imprisoned or exiled, they are able to love unswervingly. Separation from Emily in time and space is a severe hardship for her lovers, but it is no obstacle to their love.

And who is the object of all this devotion? A girl who is committed to remaining chaste and who in any case knows nothing of their love—an irony that is not lost on Theseus (*CT* A 1806–1810). It is of course Theseus who expresses the ridicule that Palamon and Arcite deserve. Having been a lover himself, his mockery is gentle, but directly on target. They might have lived royally in Thebes, in no danger.

> And yet hath love, maugree hir eyen two,
> Broght hem hyder bothe for to dye.
> Now looketh, is nat that an heigh folye?
> Who may been a fool, but if he love?
>
> [*CT* A 1796–1799]

For Theseus, the humor in the situation lies in the great folly of two young men who are willing to sacrifice themselves over the love of a girl who does not return their love. That kind of love is unreal and unproductive, and so Theseus sets out to find a solution which will remedy those defects. What he finally obtains is a love that is nothing if not practical and productive. It brings about a political alliance, and significantly the couple is brought together through Theseus's suggestion that the marriage can align them with God's creative scheme.[18] Through its final resolution, the Knight's Tale legitimizes the courtly love ideal by transforming it into an ideal which serves something outside itself; he gives it a transcendent aim, a metaphysical cause which brings it to serve the world and God.

In offering this high purpose to an audience of *sondry folk,* the Knight attempts something similar to what Nature does in the *Parlement,* and the chance of his bringing them all to accept his philosophy is about as likely as Nature's. Predictably, of all the pilgrims, the *gentils* are most sympathetic to what they have heard (3109–3113), and equally predictably, the rejection of the Knight's principles comes from a *cherl* who speaks "out of the donghil." The eagle may speak with eloquent voice, but the duck will also have his say.

The Miller has heard what love is all about in Athens and Thebes, and he thrusts himself forward to explain what it is all about in Oxford. His tale, which consciously answers the one the Knight has told (3126–3127), uses the same situation met in the Knight's Tale: two lovers compete for the same girl, and some of the things they say and do are reminiscent of things said and done by Palamon and Arcite. Palamon and Arcite, noble young men, speak nobly; Nicholas and Absolon, educated bourgeois young men, also speak nobly, or try to. Absolon serenades Alisoun in language reminiscent of the Song of Songs,[19] and both he and

Nicholas speak in the language of popular romance.[20] Nicholas says he will die of love, as do Palamon and Arcite and most conventional courtly lovers (cf. *CT* A 1118–1122, 1567–1568, 1733–1738, 3280). Like the lovers in the Knight's Tale, and especially Arcite (1355–1379), Abolson suffers physically for his love (3701–3707), and like them he has need of his lady's pity (cf. Theseus's appeal to Emily, 3083–3089; and Absolon, 3362), just as Nicholas does. In short, Nicholas and Absolon affect courtly refinement and imitate the ritualistic language and behavior of courtly lovers—but when used by them the patterns of courtly behavior are emptied of significance. In a proper aristocratic lover —a "kynges brother sone," for example—courtly ritual and service may express the virtue of the inner man, his drive for perfection, and his humility before his lady. However, the courtly forms used by Nicholas and Absolon are merely a cover for their purely carnal impulses.[21] Alisoun is a beautiful girl.

> She was a prymerole, a piggesnye,
> For any lord to leggen in his bedde,
> Or yet for any good yeman to wedde,
>
> [A 3268–3270]

and like any lord or any good yeoman,[22] Nicholas and Absolon want her, and they want her now. Their whole hope is for satisfaction, both immediate and physical.

The lady herself is not different from her lovers in her drive for sexual gratification. Although she may speak in the manner of a proper courtly heroine, as if she were *daungerous,* she is by no means committed to chasity. When Nicholas grabs her, she only threatens to call for help, and it is not long before she agrees to be his lover. The selection of Nicholas over Absolon is made on practical ground: where she might have chosen him for his cleverness and wit, and rejected Absolon because of his vanity and pomposity, the actual reason is that she wants a lover and wants him to be convenient. Therefore, because Nicholas is *hende,* near at hand,[23] he is chosen. Considerations of service, of rank, of suffering are of no consequence.

The Miller's Tale parodies and ridicules courtly pretensions to refinement. It proposes that love between the sexes depends upon sexual, not spiritual, intercourse; that noble bearing and fine emotions are nothing more than covers for the sensual drives which motivate all human beings, whether aristocratic or not; and that love is about something other than spiritual exaltation. The Miller, if he is at all aware of the implications of his tale, may agree with the Knight that courtly lovers make fools of themselves, but he utterly rejects the idea that the way around the foolishness is to substitute divine principles for courtly ones. In any event, Chaucer seems to imply not that divine or courtly principles are themselves foolish, but that being elevated they cannot be followed by men, who are essentially carnal. In Chaucer, the truth about comic courtly lovers is that for all their inflation and posturing, they are basically self-seeking, gross and sexual.

The Merchant's Tale is about three courtly people—*a worthy knight, a gentil womman, a gentil squier*—who try to elevate their lust by acting the parts of refined lovers, but they are driven by an unexalted desire for sexual pleasure.[24] Similarly, the tercel who woos the courtly falcon in the Squire's Tale—even though he can go down "on his knees" and behave "so lyk a gentil lovere of manere" (F 544–546)—is no perfect lover, for he soon tires of the falcon and deserts her for a kite. What motivates the tercel is his own sexual pleasure, and she ought to have seen that. Another zealous courtly lover appears in the Franklin's Tale, where the squire Aurelius threatens to die if the wife does not show him the pity she should. Aurelius is one more in Chaucer's train of young courtly men who follow a pattern in their wooing: they all plead for pity and they all say that they are dying of love—the conventional assertions of the lover in service to a lady—but the poet will not allow us to take these young men altogether seriously. Sometimes they are aware of how extravagantly they behave and sometimes not, but we are always prompted to see the humor in what they say and do. It is the extravagant style of these lovers which causes laughter, or more exactly, the disparity between their style and the sensuality which it masks.

It is sometimes tempting to disregard that kind of irony in Chaucer. For example, the Squire would have us sympathize with the falcon's weeping and regrets (as Canacee does), but in order to do so we would have to accept the romantic and improbable world the Squire describes. And what prevents us from doing that is the unromantic presence of the tercel, who is more of this world—or, more accurately, of the world of the *fabliau*—than of the world envisioned by the Squire.

A second instance of a tale which invites a response without viewing the irony is the Franklin's. Dorigen and Arveragus are an exemplary courtly couple; in their marriage, they seem to have adapted conventional courtly love to acceptable patterns of social behavior. Accordingly, there is a neat twist when the threat to their marriage comes from a perfectly typical courtly lover, Aurelius. The problem is not the *Tristan* problem of whether their courtly love can endure against society's conventional demands, but whether their accommodation to society's conventions can survive the attack of Aurelius's courtly passion. As far as the Franklin is concerned it can, because Dorigen and Arveragus are exemplary. They are willing to sacrifice themselves for a principle, and they bring others to emulate their idealism; they are so perfect in their *gentilesse* and *trouthe* that they can quench both Aurelius's courtly lust and a magician's need for gold. As in the Knight's Tale, courtly love is at its best when it is able to serve a transcendent ideal.

The Franklin asks us to take a high-minded view of the action, but we may feel compelled to simultaneously take an ironic view—and if so it is partly because of Aurelius, who calls to mind the amoral world of the *fabliau,* just as the tercel does in the Squire's Tale. Interpreted cynically, the Franklin's Tale can be said to give a bourgeois and superficial view of courtly love and courtliness. Each of the characters in the tale is supposed to illustrate courtly *gentilesse* through his generosity, but it can be argued that no one gives up anything he has a right to hold.[25] Indeed, it has been pointed out that if "worldly attitudes" are put into play in judging the characters, each emerges as a fool.[26] In short, when the tale is subjected to an analysis which seeks out irony, the moral vision developed by the Franklin fades. And I think Chaucer wants us to see the irony, just as he wants us to see the characters' perfection. It is natural to point out that the characters seem foolish not to have insisted upon what they had every opportunity to insist upon (for example, Dorigen could have insisted that she did not mean her oath to be taken literally), for people don't ordinarily behave the way the Franklin's creations do. It seems that Chaucer wished to remind us that those characters are fictional, that they are undoubtedly exemplary, but that they do more than we ought to expect of human beings. He asks us to see two sides to courtly love, as he does whenever he deals with it, and to recognize the great value of courtly love as an abstract conception, as well as to recognize that humanity is not as perfect as the ideals it holds. He has the sophisticated perspective of the early poets, but for all that he is not the same as they are, for where those poets defend the courtly ideal, Chaucer must finally reject it. He rejects it not because it is in itself unworthy but because it has no place in the world he knows.

Chaucer's world was not the world of those early lyric poets, and consequently his position in it could not be the same as theirs. The lyric poets who first wrote about courtly love wrote for an audience which had a fine sense of its rank. It was separate, and intended to keep it that way; its intention was to maintain the status quo, to preserve the integrity of the courtly class. Therefore, it sought to educate its children aristocratically, to develop in them a sense of tradition, a sense of rank, a sense of their own exclusiveness from the lower classes. This select group of people —with its education and its sophistication—was receptive to what the lyric poets were doing. Because they could respond to the complex perspectives in the poetry, they made it possible for that poetry to exist. The courtly poet spoke to them and for them, and because they understood his game, they made it possible for him to play it. Being aristocrats, they could sympathize with his call to ideality and perfection, and they could laugh at his posture without being threatened by the laughter; they were, after all, participants in an elaborate and refined game played by elaborate and refined people.

The special position held by the courtly audience could not long endure. The pressure of the lower classes to be admitted to their closed precincts was too great, and in time men of more humble origins came to hold wealth and power and titles. They brought with them values different from the old aristocracy's— values consistent with their frequently middle-class origins. The old feudal nobility was being undermined by these changes. It tried to hold on to the traditional patterns of life, but these were hard to preserve, and they came to seem artificial and out of touch with reality. The feudal economy was being replaced by a money economy, and the political power of feudal nobility was giving way to central government. In France, England, and Germany the old feudal nobility were finding that the changing money system was operating to rob them of their wealth, and with the loss of wealth there naturally followed a loss of status and power. The nobility did what it could to maintain its position—the sumptuary laws are one expression of its attempt to keep the new and wealthy merchant class in its place—but that position was inevitably eroded. A burgher would purchase an estate, and live on it and play the part of a nobleman; he would see to it that his children married profitably and properly, and in general he would insure his family its place among the upper class.[27]

With this change in the composition of the nobility, starting at the end of the thirteenth century and accelerating during the fourteenth and fifteenth centuries, there naturally came a change in the audience for courtly poetry. The style of life described in the courtly lyrics and romances must have seemed archaic and even absurd to a part of this new audience, though to other parts of it the behavior in the literature may, in fact, have seemed exemplary. The courtly rituals were, after all, elegant and refined, and the ambition of new entrants into the nobility was to be as elegant and refined as the old aristocracy. These bourgeois noblemen would seek to perform the old rituals, but they could never have the perspective on them of the feudal aristocracy—the inner significance of the rituals was lost to the new arrivals. In other words, the ludic aspect of the literature was dissolving, and with the loss of the play element there came a loss of perspective, and with the loss of perspective, the loss of the old courtly ideal.

The poetry of Chaucer and Ulrich and the other poets considered here reflects these changes in the courtly audience and the courtly world. The Franklin who defends the courtly ideal in his tale is a bourgeois man, and his characters mirror his bourgeois ideals; the Knight and Squire in the Merchant's Tale, aristocrats though they may be, are hardly exalted through their devotion to the lady. The *fabliaux* generally point their ridicule at bourgeois types who seek to behave like noblemen, but as *De Guillaume au Faucon* and *Flamenca* reveal, noblemen with empty pretensions to true aristocracy were also subjected to mockery. Of all these works, it is probably Ulrich's which most forcefully describes the loss of a courtly setting; it is in Ulrich that the change of knights from *Ritter* to *Raubritter* becomes obvious.

The poems examined here were written independently of each other in Germany, the north and south of France, and England. No direct lines of influence can be established among them—Chaucer, for example, seems to have known nothing of Ulrich, *De*

Guillaume au Faucon, or *Flamenca*. If any generalizations can be drawn from these poems, it is not because they are the work of a school of poets, but rather because they are the expression of an attitude characteristic of the waning Middle Ages. It is true that the rejection of courtly love seen in these poems matches views of courtly love seen at the outset: the notions that no man can be as refined as the lovers say they can, that no woman can be as perfect as her lover says she is, that no man ever really dies of love. But what separates the poems examined here from the earlier material is their insistence upon the absurdity of refined aristocratic love in an increasingly unrefined and uncourtly world. Ulrich's lover moves toward disillusionment in a crumbling Germany, the lady Guillaume courts in the *fabliau* is hardly virtue herself, the lovers in *Flamenca* do what they do, not in the court, but in the odorous baths of Bourbon, and Chaucer's courtly lovers are similarly manifestations of an uncourtly world.

The insufficiency of the courtly ideal in such a world was difficult to deny, and the writers who parody and burlesque that ideal were addressing themselves not finally to a literary convention but to a social reality, to the hard fact that the old aristocratic culture was rapidly decaying. Its forms were becoming empty rituals like those practiced by the burghers of Tournai, who in 1330 organized a society of the Round Table.[28] Those who held onto the decaying forms were manifestly seeking to preserve an obsolete style of life. There is always something laughable in that kind of attempt, and writers like Ulrich and Chaucer and the others sought to heal such human folly through laughter. The laughter is sometimes at the expense of contemptible men, like Chaucer's January; sometimes it is appreciative, for we can be amused by the unlikely success of a Guillaume; and sometimes it is purgative, as when we see ourselves in those who amuse us. In truth, the would-be courtly lovers mirror the vanities of all pretentious men; there is reason to think that the laughter they generated was often intended to expose the folly, not only of the lovers, but also of their audience.

Still, there is another side to the matter, for laughter is not the only possible response to those characters. Ulrich's lover is a fool, but he is also pathetic and in his quest for perfection even admirable. Guillaume is a silly young man, but his willingness to surrender his life, rather than his love, is in one light creditable.

The lovers in the Franklin's Tale can also produce a dual response, for they are simultaneously foolish and exemplary. The would-be courtly lover can be Quixotic, and his experience can reveal the ridiculous alongside the sublime aspect of the human condition.

The writers who dismiss courtly love through their comedy often reflect the essential paradox which underlies all the literature of courtly love. For better or for worse, carnality and spirituality are qualities inherent in men. The comic writers simply remind us that though we may worship the legitimate Venus, it is the sinful Venus who usually rules.

Notes

1. Carl von Kraus, ed., *Deutsche Liederdichter des 13. Jahrhunderts,* I (Tübingen: Max Niemeyer, 1952), 41. The translation is by Frederick Goldin, *German and Italian Lyrics of the Middle Ages: An Anthology and a History* (New York: Doubleday, 1973), pp. 193, 195.
2. Ulrich von Lichtenstein, *Frauendienst,* ed. Reinhold Bechstein, 2 vols. (Leipzig: F. A. Brockhaus, 1888), pp. 8–9. (References to *Frauendienst* are given by strophe and line number—e.g., 8. 4–8 or by lyric and line number—e.g., XIV. 6–10.)
3. Gottfried von Strassburg, *Tristan und Isold,* ed. Friedrich Ranke, 7th ed. (Berlin: Weidmannsche Verlagsbuchhandlung, 1963), 11. 63–65.
4. There are analogous episodes in saints' lives; for example, St. Gerald of Aurillac's wash water is said to have cured the sick. See St. Odo of Cluny, "The Life of St. Gerald of Aurillac," in *St. Odo of Cluny,* ed. and trans. Dom Gerard Sitwell (London and New York: Sheed and Ward, 1958), p. 141.
5. Even in this there is an irony. Ulrich-the-lover is a poet who can neither read nor write (see 169. 1–5). What is ironically true for Wolfram—who by insisting upon his illiteracy asserts backwardly that he is in fact what the poets strive to be—is the literal truth for Ulrich.
6. A similar episode occurs in the versions of the Tristan story by Thomas and Eilhart, and with much the same point. See Thomas, *Les fragments du Roman de Tristan,* ed. Bartina H. Wind (Genève: Droz, 1960), Douce 1. 501 ff.; and Franz Lichtenstein, ed.,

Eilhart von Oberge, QFSK, Vol. XIX (Strassburg and London, 1877), 11. 7026–7048. The numerous echoes of episodes and motifs from the romances is an important characteristic of *Frauendienst,* which is intent upon "testing the adequacy of the courtly ideal to the demands of actual life." See Chapter Four, "Ulrich von Lichtenstein and the Mirror of the Actual World," in Frederick Goldin's *The Mirror of Narcissus in the Courtly Love Lyric* (Ithaca: Cornell University Press, 1967), pp. 167–206.

7. Saul N. Brody, *The Disease of the Soul: Leprosy in Medieval Literature* (Ithaca: Cornell University Press, 1974).
8. D. W. Robertson, Jr., *A Preface to Chaucer: Studies in Medieval Perspectives* (Princeton: Princeton University Press, 1963), plates 59, 60, 61, 62, 66.
9. His writing of lyrics is one of the ways in which he obtains a reputation for courtliness. In the course of the narrative there are numerous references to how his courtly audience received and celebrated his poetry. For instance, he relates how lyric XVIII pleased those who were in good spirits because of women —they rejoice in the praise of women, as true knights should (1357); the truly wise, but not the foolish, understood lyric XXXIII (1398); lyric XXXVIII came to be much sung during jousting (1425). The acceptance of Ulrich's courtly poetry by the courtly audience implies their acceptance of his courtliness.
10. See Bechstein, *Frauendienst,* pp. 316–317, nn. 1828, 1830; and Goldin, *The Mirror of Narcissus,* pp. 172–175.
11. *Recueil Général et Complet des Fabliaux des XIIIe et XIVe Siècles,* eds. Anatole de Montaiglon and Gaston Raynaud, Vol. II (Paris: Librairie des Bibliophiles, 1877), pp. 92–113. The translation is based on "William and the Falcon" in *Fabliaux: Ribald Tales from the Old French,* trans. Robert Hellman, Richard O'Gorman (New York: Thomas Y. Crowell, 1965), pp. 81–92.
12. See "Prestre et Alison," in *Recueil Général* II: 11 ff. The fabliau is discussed by Per Nykrog, *Les Fabliaux: Étude d'-histoire littéraire et de stylistique médiévale* (Copenhagen: Enjar Munksgaard, 1957), pp. 74 ff.
13. See Gordon M. Shedd, "Flamenca: A Medieval Satire on Courtly Love," *ChauR* 2 (1967): 43–65, an article to which this discussion is indebted. The edition quoted in the text is *The Romance of Flamenca: A Provençal Poem of the Thirteenth Century,* ed. Marion E. Porter, trans. Merton Jerome Hubert (Princeton: Princeton University Press, 1962). The translation given here is the author's.
14. Shedd, "Flamenca," p. 56, n. 11.
15. F. N. Robinson, ed., *The Works of Geoffrey Chaucer,* 2d ed. (Boston: Houghton-Mifflin, 1957), p. 533. All subsequent quotations of Chaucer are from this edition.
16. See above, Chapter I.
17. On these principles, see A. O. Lovejoy, *The Great Chain of Being* (Cambridge, Mass.: Harvard University Press, 1948); Alan M. F. Gunn, *The Mirror of Love* (Lubbock, Texas, 1952);

J. A. W. Bennett, *The Parlement of Foules* (New York: Oxford University Press, 1957); and John V. Fleming, *The "Roman de la Rose": A Study in Allegory and Iconography* (Princeton: Princeton University Press, 1969).

18. As Bennett points out (pp. 179–180), there are several similarities between Nature in the *Parlement of Foules* and Theseus, and none more central than that each acts "as a mouthpiece or conscious agent of divine purpose."

19. R. E. Kaske, "The Canticum Canticorum in the Miller's Tale," *SP* 59 (1962): 479–500.

20. E. T. Donaldson, "Idiom of Popular Poetry in the Miller's Tale," *English Institute Essays, 1950* (New York: Columbia University Press, 1951), pp. 116–140; Gardiner Stillwell, "The Language of Love in Chaucer's Miller's and Reeve's Tales and in the Old French Fabliaux," *JEGP* 54 (1955): 693–699.

21. What Chaucer says of Jason in *The Legend of Good Women* could also be said of either of them:

> O, often swore thow that thow woldest dye
> For love, whan thow ne feltest maladye
> Save foul delyt, which that thow callest love!
>
> [1378–1380]

Cf. the aube in the Reeve's Tale, discussed by R. E. Kaske, "An Aube in the Reeve's Tale," *ELH* 26 (1959): 295–310.

22. In the Miller's view, the only difference between the aristocrat and the lower-class man is the difference which class structure establishes. Their privileges may be different, but their needs are the same (*I am a lord at alle degrees,* says Absolon [3724]). High-minded aristocrats may live in Greece, but not in the Miller's England.

23. Paul Beichner, "Chaucer's Hende Nicholas," *MS* 14 (1952): 151–153.

24. It is suggestive that January, when confronted with the alternatives put before Chaucer in the *Parlement of Foules,* rejects the legitimate possibilities of living a chaste life or marrying in order to procreate (1446–1456). Being *likerous,* he can neither accept asceticism nor natural love. Since he chooses the lustful Venus, the lustful Venus accepts him (1722–1728).

25. Robertson, *A Preface to Chaucer,* pp. 275–276, 470–472.

26. Paul G. Ruggiers, *The Art of the Canterbury Tales* (Madison: University of Wisconsin, 1965), p. 237.

27. The general outlines of the changing social structure are drawn by Wallace K. Ferguson, *Europe in Transition: 1300–1520* (Boston: Houghton-Mifflin, 1962). Additional insights are supplied in such books as J. Huizinga, *The Waning of the Middle Ages: A Study of the Forms of Life, Thought and Art in France and the Netherlands in the XIVth and XVth Centuries* (New York: Doubleday, 1956); and Sylvia Thrupp, *The Merchant Class of Medieval London, 1300–1500* (Chicago: University of Chicago Press, 1948).

28. See Roger Sherman Loomis, "Arthurian Influence on Sport and Spectacle," in *Arthurian Literature in the Middle Ages: A Collaborative History,* ed. Roger Sherman Loomis (Oxford: Oxford University Press, 1959), pp. 553–559.

Bibliographic Note

The following studies deal with aspects of the subject considered in this chapter.

On Ulrich von Lichtenstein: Hans Arens, "Ulrichs von Lichtenstein Frauendienst," *Palaestra* (1939); Otto Hofler, "Ulrichs von Lichtenstein Venusfahrt und Artusfahrt," *Studien zur deutschen Philologie des Mittelalters,* Festschrift Friedrich Panzer, ed. Richard Kienast (Heidelberg, 1950); Karl Ludwig Schneider, "Die Selbstdarstellung des Dichters im Frauendienst Ulrichs von Lichtenstein: Bedeutung und Grenzen des Autobiographischen in der alteren deutschen Dichtung." *Festgabe für Ulrich Pretzel zum 65. Geburtstag dargebracht von Freunden und Schülern* (Berlin: Schmidt, 1963), pp. 216–222.

On *Flamenca:* Philip Damon, "Courtesy and Comedy in *Le Roman de Flamenca,*" *RPh* 17 (1964): 608–615; Guido Favati, "Studio su *Flamenca,*" *SMV* 8 (1960): 69–136; Herman Weigand, "*Flamenca:* A Post-Arthurian Romance of Courtly Love," *Euphorion* 58 (1964): 129–152.

On fabliaux: J. Bédier, *Les Fabliaux,* 5th ed. (Paris: Champion, 1925); Walter Morris Hart, "The Fabliau and Popular Literature," *PMLA* 23 (1908): 329–374, and "The Narrative Art of the Old French Fabliaux," in *Anniversary Papers by Colleagues and Pupils of George Lyman Kittredge* (Boston: Ginn, 1913), pp. 209–216; Alberto Varvaro, "I *fabliaux* e la societa," *SMV* 8 (1960): 275–299.

On Chaucer: Edwin B. Benjamin, "The Concept of Order in the Franklin's Tale," *PQ* 38 (1959): 119–124; D. S. Brewer, "Class Distinction in Chaucer," *Speculum* 43 (1968): 290–305; C. Hugh Holman, "Courtly Love in the Merchant's and the Franklin's Tales," *ELH* 18 (1951): 241–252; C. S. Lewis, *The Allegory of Love: A Study in Medieval Tradition* (London: Oxford University Press, 1953); Charles Moorman, "Courtly Love in Chaucer," *ELH* 27 (1960): 163–173; Charles Muscatine, *Chaucer and the French Tradition: A Study in Style and Meaning* (Berkeley and Los Angeles: University of California Press, 1957); Margaret Schlauch, "Chaucer's 'Merchant's Tale' and Courtly Love," *ELH* 4 (1937): 201–212; John M. Steadman, "Courtly Love as a Problem of Style," *Chaucer und seine Zeit: Symposion für Walter F. Schirmer,* ed. Arno Esch, Buchreihe der *Anglia,*

Zeitschrift für englische Philologie 14. (Tübingen: Max Niemeyer, 1968), pp. 1–33; Germaine Dempster, *Dramatic Irony in Chaucer,* Stanford University Publications in Language and Literature IV (Stanford, 1932); Edmund Reiss, "Dusting off the Cobwebs: A Look at Chaucer's Lyrics," *ChauR* 1 (1966): 55–65.

Also, Gervase Mathew, "Marriage and *Amour Courtois* in Late Fourteenth Century England," in *Essays Presented to Charles Williams* (Oxford: Oxford University Press, 1947); Hellmut Rosenfeld, "Die Entwicklung der Ständesatire im Mittelalter," *ZDP* 71 (1951): 196–207, and "Die Literatur des ausgehenden Mittelalter in soziologischer Sicht," *WW* 5 (1955): 330–341; Norman Susskind, "Love and Laughter in the Romans Courtois," *FR* 37 (1963–64): 651–657.

Index